A HISTORY
OF
HERESY

A HISTORY
OF
HERESY

DAVID CHRISTIE-MURRAY

Oxford   New York

OXFORD UNIVERSITY PRESS

1989

To Sheila—who married the greatest heretic of them all

Oxford University Press, Walton Street, Oxford OX2 6DP

Oxford New York Toronto
Petaling Jaya Singapore Hong Kong Tokyo
Delhi Bombay Calcutta Madras Karachi
Nairobi Dar es Salaam Cape Town
Melbourne Auckland

and associated companies in
Berlin Ibadan

Oxford is a trade mark of Oxford University Press

First published 1976 by New English Library
First issued as an Oxford University Press paperback 1989

British Library Cataloguing in Publication Data
Christie-Murray, David
A history of heresy.
1. Christian church, heresies, History
I. Title
273
ISBN 0–19–285210–8

Library of Congress Cataloging in Publication Data
Christie-Murray, David.
A history of heresy / David Christie-Murray.
p. cm.
Reprint. Originally published: London: New English Library, 1976.
Bibliography: p.
Includes index.
ISBN 0–19–285210–8: $9.00 (U.S.)
1. Heresies, Christian—History. 2. Sects—History. I. Title.
BT1315.2.C48 1989 273—dc20 89-3343 CIP

Printed in Great Britain by
The Guernsey Press Co. Ltd.
Guernsey, Channel Islands

Contents

Foreword

To write the history of Christian heresy adequately would be to compile a complete Church history. Moreover, it would take more than a single volume to deal with all the varieties of heresy that have appeared in two thousand years and to describe the measures that have been taken against them. This study does not pretend to be exhaustive and has been written to provide the general reader with an account of the principal strains of heterodox thought and the answers that the orthodox worked out in opposition to them. Theologians also may find it convenient to have a summary of this or that heresy and its history in more detail than they would find in a handbook and in less than they would discover in a definitive work; and although there is an alternative source of information, general Church histories, many written with admirable scholarship and clarity of style, it is not always easy to pick out the story of a particular strain of thought in the complexities of political and other activities.

The writing of any kind of history involves selection, and different writers vary in their opinion of the relative importance of different aspects of their subjects. The comparative significance of the early heresies is fairly easy to assess as they have been much described and they are sufficiently far away in time to be seen in perspective. The major heresies of the Reformation period are also easily discernible, but the proportion of space to be given to their ramifications in comparatively obscure countries such as Scotland and Ireland is difficult to calculate. They are also so inextricably mixed up with politics that again there is the temptation to write a whole history of the times in dealing adequately with them. As for modern heresies, they are so many, so varied and, some of them, so exotic, that those who study them may be forgiven for having favourites and resenting the superficial treatment they have necessarily received in a book of this kind. Let some critics be anticipated and perhaps disarmed by an acknowledgement of the desirability of more detailed accounts of some modern heresies than space has allowed.

In the few quotations from the Bible, translations have been used which seemed most appropriate for their context, mostly from the *Authorized Version*, sometimes from the *New English Bible* and once from the Book of Common Prayer. A certain acquaintance with religious phraseology and practice has also been assumed, though it is hoped that the equally irritating assumption of too much or too little has been avoided. Footnotes and references have been kept to a minimum.

CHAPTER I

The Doctrine of Heresy

Heresy, a cynic might say, is an opinion held by a minority of men which the majority declares unacceptable and is powerful enough to punish. He would not be far wrong; but the matter is not as simple as that, and an adequate definition needs narrower bounds. Though 'heresy' may be used of political and other beliefs, it is primarily a doctrine which is at variance with orthodox religious teaching. So Christian heresy means departure from Christian orthodoxy, and it is with the history of Christian heresy that this book is concerned. Believers in other religions are outside its scope; and, furthermore, adherents of such cults as witchcraft, when they exist within the context of Christendom, should not strictly speaking be thought of as heretics, but rather as members of minority faiths surviving from pre-Christian times.

While on the one hand it is easy to define Christian heresy as departure from orthodox Christian belief, on the other it is not so easy to define what orthodoxy itself is. A superficial glance at history might indeed seem to justify our cynic in his view that heresy is the disagreement of a minority with the contemporary majority view. God, it has been said, is on the side of the big battalions; orthodoxy, it could be added, is what they say about him. When the later Roman emperors adopted Christianity, they did so partly because they believed that it would be a unifying force in an empire under pressure. They were concerned that believers were united in the same doctrine and the Church undisrupted by warring factions holding different beliefs. Later still, the association of pope and emperor, within that Holy Roman Empire which formed the main territory of Christendom, imposed a unity of doctrine greater than that in most other world religions. As a result of this unity heretics could be singled out the more easily. So, from the first official recognition of Christianity by the Emperor Constantine in AD 313, politics and religious orthodoxy went hand in hand, and Christians had to compromise their faith because of the demands made on them by secular culture. After the Reformation politics reinforced local orthodoxies even more strongly; to be a Catholic in Elizabethan England was not only heretical but potentially treasonable; in the Cevennes of the seventeenth century a Huguenot was an armed rebel against Louis XIV as well as against the Roman Church; and in eighteenth-century Paris the doctrines of Jansen, declared heretical, were used by a faction within the Catholic Church as a political stick with which to beat the French government as well as the Jesuits.

Orthodoxy cannot therefore be synonymous with Christian truth, for some of the local and temporary orthodoxies cancel each other out – if some are true, then others must be false. But if there are orthodoxies which are faulty, there must be for believers one that remains true, if only (as Plato might say) 'in the mind of God', and there must be a norm of Christian belief 'on earth' which reflects this idea and be the standard by which a man may be judged a true believer or a heretic. Until such a norm is established, any deviations from it are not discernible, and a heretic will remain simply one who holds a minority belief in any community which considers itself Christian, like a Catholic in Salt Lake City. The fact that Catholics form roughly half of all Christians throughout the world will not make him any less a heretic in the capital of Mormonism.

From very early on, until at least the nineteenth century, the Christian churches were more interested in emphasizing their differences than their unity. Few and feeble attempts were made to reconcile them and to find a basis of common faith. The ecumenical movement which is the glory of the twentieth-century Church has, in attempting to formulate such a basis, proved how difficult it is to find and define it. For if doctrinal statements are the criterion, it follows that those linked with denominations, such as the Anglican Thirty-Nine Articles or the Presbyterian Westminster Confession, were useless to meet the standard laid down by Vincent, a monk of Lérins, about the end of the fourth century, that there was in the Church a 'faith which has been believed everywhere, always and by all'. Even the great creeds, the Apostles' and the Nicene, are not adequate to form a universally agreed confession. For the Apostles' Creed excludes the Orthodox Church and some Protestant communities, while the Nicene, though including the Orthodox (except for the *filioque* clause, discussed in Chapter 11), Roman Catholics, Anglicans and Episcopalians, Lutherans and, perhaps, the Reformed (Calvinists), excludes some Protestant bodies which give official acceptance to no creedal statement. And the difficulty in the present century, which will be examined at greater length below, is that many members of churches which officially accept one or both the creeds, privately either disbelieve a number of the articles in them or interpret them symbolically in a way their formulators did not intend. In this they disagree with members of their own denomination as well as with those of other communions.

Since no creedal statement exists that is common to all Christendom, the ecumenical movement has tried from time to time to form one. In 1927 the Ecumenical Conference at Lausanne used the formula, 'Notwithstanding the difference in doctrine among us, we are united in a common Christian Faith which is proclaimed in the Holy Scriptures and witnessed to and safeguarded in the Ecumenical Creed, commonly called the Nicene, and in the Apostles' Creed.' In 1937, the Faith and Order Conference, held in Edinburgh, stated:

> We are one in faith in Our Lord Jesus Christ, the incarnate Word of God. We are one in allegiance to Him as Head of the Church, and as King of kings and Lord of lords. We are one in acknowledging that this allegiance takes precedence of any other allegiance that may make claims upon us.
>
> This unity does not consist in the agreement of our minds or the consent of our wills. It is founded in Jesus Christ Himself, Who lived, died and rose again to bring us to the Father, and Who through the Holy Spirit dwells in His Church. We are one because we are all the objects of the love and grace of God, and called by Him to bear witness in all the world to His glorious Gospel.

However, in 1948 the World Council of Churches limited its basis of admission to the simple recognition of Jesus as 'God and Saviour', which, to a theologian, implies as much in its three words as the Edinburgh Conference states in the two paragraphs quoted. If this had been all the belief required of Christians down the ages, there would have been comparatively few heretics. Unfortunately more detailed belief came to be required, as was inevitable, and more is required by almost every denomination to this day. The history of orthodoxy is the tale of what came to be required as the ages passed and the history of heresy its shadow.

If creeds cannot embrace the whole of Christendom, can they have a common loyalty to the Bible? But there is not one Bible; there are three. For the Orthodox and Roman Churches make no difference between the Old Testament and the Apocrypha. The Church of England and Lutherans include the Apocrypha but place it on a lower level than the Old Testament; some Protestant churches reject it altogether. In addition, the Bible is used as an authority to support the views of sects such as Christian Science which many of the orthodox would regard as so un-Christian as to be non-Christian. Some churches regard the Bible as their sole authority. Some interpret it allegorically or in the light of tradition. Some take from it doctrine only, others derive their church order from it. Some, such as the Seventh Day Adventists, draw part of their ethic from the Old Testament, some accept only those Old Testament ethics which are supported by the New. There are a thousand interpretations of the one book, often justifying diametrically opposite views. The Christian teetotaller may find it hard to accept Paul's admonition to Timothy to take a little wine for his stomach's sake except on the unlikely supposition that 'perhaps he rubbed it in'. Both the Christian pacifist and the Christian soldier can reconcile their actions by Christ's statement that 'he who takes the sword shall perish by the sword', for the pacifist can claim that this is a clear warning to the believer to eschew the use of weapons, while the soldier can argue that there must be someone to wield the sword of righteousness by which the aggressor is to perish.

The sacraments are not more inclusive of all Christendom than the Bible. For, on the basis that only baptized believers are accepted as Christians, bodies such as Quakers and Salvationists – even though Christ-inspired – are excluded.

These differences in attitude to creeds, Bible and sacraments and all other facets of Christian belief are caused by a fundamental difference of approach to Christian truth. The one corresponds very roughly with the Catholic-Orthodox genius, and the other with the Protestant. To the Catholic, Orthodox, high church Episcopalian and many believers in other communions, Christian truth is a living, growing organism. Their position is that Christ planted the seed, and as a seed contains within itself all the elements of the tree that is to be, so his life and teaching contained all the truths that the Holy Catholic and Apostolic Church should develop in the fullness of time. Christianity needs continuously to adapt itself to new cultures, civilizations and circumstances. The ideas and organizations suitable for a first-century agrarian culture and the modes of thought and outlook of the Graeco-Roman-Palestinian world are inadequate to meet twentieth-century needs. The Christian gospel has continuously to be rethought in the light of advancing knowledge. This is not to deny the truths of the past. They were not only valid for their day, but for ours as well, and our truths bear the same relationship to them as the crown of a tree does to its trunk. Cut the tree down and you cannot expect its topmost branches to remain unsupported in the air. Modern psychology may throw more light on the relationship of the human and divine natures in the one Person of Christ, subject of the arid but necessary controversies of the first centuries of Christianity; yet the conclusions reached by the ecumenical councils, which threshed out the orthodox statements concerning him in the Nicene Creed, are still regarded by authority as true and binding upon every right-thinking Christian.

Among these upholders of a developing tradition there are wide divergences of opinion, opening the way for accusations of heresy. Catholics, for example, may regard Anglicans as 'a withered branch' on the Christian tree. Anglicans may retort that at some point in history the Catholic Church developed away from the truth and grew awry. Their own stem grows straight and upright from the primeval stock, while the Catholic is warped and out of true. But go back far enough and there is a point where the trunk exists that is common to both before the branches part. And there are those such as the Modernists who maintain that although there is an organic continuity with the past, it springs from the oak that grew from an acorn dropped by another oak which served its turn and, in the course of time, decayed and died. We need not accept any past conclusions as binding for all time. So psychology may do more than throw fresh light on the two natures in Christ – it may destroy Nicene Christology altogether, and Christians would have to be prepared to modify, even reject, earlier definitions when the time is ripe.

Undoubtedly upholders of this type of view would say that when the creeds were first accepted as the doctrinal statements of orthodox belief, they were intended to be understood literally. However, a large number of people who regard themselves as convinced Christians do not today accept as literal historical facts the Virgin Birth and the bodily resurrection of Christ. They do not believe in their own bodily resurrection nor in the Second Coming as an event in future time, preferring to allegorize or spiritualize advent hopes. If such honest believers were accused of heresy they might be distressed, though a competent theologian could argue convincingly that the beliefs they rejected were part of the norm of Christian faith and that, in departing from them, they were in fact heretics. They could reply that, if to be orthodox Christians they must accept these articles of faith literally, they must be counted as heretics. On the other hand they might claim that, if they accept Christ as uniquely revealing God to them and showing the way to him, they are elevated by this simple affirmation of faith among the 'true believers', regardless of their views on the Virgin Birth. Orthodoxy must itself move with the times. If the great majority of Christian people came to reject the Virgin Birth – as an increasing number do – then it will be 'orthodox' to do so.

It could be argued that Church history has proved this point. What is regarded as orthodox by one age is condemned as heretical by another, and vice versa. The teachings of Origen (185–250), for example, one of the great Christian thinkers, though startlingly original in many respects, were accepted as orthodox in his own time but became the source of bitter and violent controversy in the fourth, fifth and sixth centuries. Some of his doctrines were condemned as heretical by regional synods in Alexandria, Cyprus, Jerusalem and perhaps (this is debatable) by a general council in Constantinople in 553. This poses the question that if the ground of orthodoxy could shift fourteen hundred years ago, when knowledge moved so much more slowly than it does today, why should it not do so now, when almost every week brings new information about the universe around us?

The 'Protestant' approach to the truth of Christianity is to look for it in a 'primitive church', where the faith was pure, free of dogmatic accretions, simple and obvious. In that golden age, say its adherents, when our Lord was present in his physical body or when the conviction of his resurrection was recent and not to be denied and the presence of the Holy Spirit was to be felt, seen and heard in signs of overwhelming power, his followers accepted him for what he was by virtue of a personal relationship, making definition unnecessary. Thomas Didymus cried out 'My Lord and my God' because he saw and touched the wounds of the risen Christ, not because an ecumenical council had agreed on a form of words. This happy state disappeared within a few years. By the time Paul was writing, heresy and schism were beginning to appear in the churches, since when they have increasingly fouled the history of Christianity. For those who take this view of the Church, all developments of the original faith are departures from the norm established by Christ himself and his immediate followers and are therefore heretical. The duty of true believers is to shed the accretions of later ages and return to the simple faith of the first disciples. Church history is full of attempts by Christian sects to discover and return to this idealized and largely mythical 'primitive Christianity'.

Christians teach that the work of the Holy Spirit is that he should lead Christian worshippers into all truth. It soon became plain, as orthodox and heretic alike claimed his authority for their conflicting beliefs, that any revelation he would make would not be written in letters of fire across the sky or engraved on angel-delivered plates of gold. Truth would come piecemeal and painfully through the clash of men's minds in controversy and at a cost of much suffering and often lives. In the final issue it was the Church that came to regard itself as the custodian of gradually revealed truth, and often to its shame it tried to do what the Holy Spirit by his nature cannot do, force men by threats and *force majeure* to accept beliefs against their will.

In his day Christ was challenged, 'By what authority do you do these things?' The Church receives the same challenge, 'By what authority do you claim your doctrines to be true?' Different sections of it reply in different ways. Roman Catholics answer that God appointed the Church itself as the supreme authority, meaning by this that the whole Church down the ages is infallible in matters of doctrine, for it is the body to whom God in Christ through the agency of the Holy Spirit has revealed and is continuing to reveal all truth. Catholics would probably differ among themselves as to who constitute the membership of the whole Church, some confining it rigidly to their own communion, others extending it to include believers in other churches who, although in error, follow Christ to the best of their ability. For every individual member of the Church is fallible; but his errors are corrected by the Spirit-guided thinking of the whole Church spread over the centuries, so that, when the time is ripe for the Pope to make a pronouncement *ex cathedra* that a well-tested doctrine is true, the Catholic faithful accept it as an obligatory dogma. The authority of the Church is, under God, superior to every other. It was the Church that established the canon of Scripture and is its arbiter and interpreter; it is the Church to which the individual conscience must submit and by which the enthusiasm of charismatic leadership is disciplined and guided.

The Protestants replaced the doctrine of the infallible Church with that of the infallible Book. The Bible, the written Word of God, is the final court of appeal, by which the Church itself must be judged, and any of its doctrines which is not to be found in the Bible is not binding on the believer. For although it is true that the Church, after a period of trial and error, fixed the canon of Scripture, in reality the books chose themselves – it was their innate authority that compelled the Church to recognize them, as one can plainly see when comparing the canonical with the non-canonical writings. The authority of the Bible is greater than that of the Church, for, when we want to know what we should believe or how we should behave or where the living Word of God may be discerned in all his truth and beauty, it is to the written Word that we turn as, in the words of the Anglican Thirty-Nine Articles, containing 'all things necessary for salvation'. If we did not have the Church already, we could construct it from the Bible; if on the other hand we did not have the Bible, we would have nothing by which to test the pronouncements of the Church.

The radical wing of Protestantism, as represented by such bodies as the Society of Friends, finds the final authority in the God-guided inner light of the believer's individual conscience. They say that in the final issue it is this which must choose between the conflicting claims of different Christians and judge whether the Church be in error at any one time. They can point to periods when certain individuals stood alone against majority opinion, and were later proved to be right. Even the Bible has different levels of morality which must be judged by the individual conscience, and there are occasions when moral judgements have to be made and action taken for which neither Church nor Bible gives clear mandates.

Finally, there are bodies such as the Mormons and Christian Scientists which set the authority of charismatic leadership above that of Church, Bible or Inner Light, following the visions of their respective founders.

It has been rightly said that the Christian Church, while concerned with uniformity in religious practice, always made doctrine the central criterion of orthodoxy.[1] But a church possesses not only a body of doctrine. It has a constitution or church order. It worships in a particular way. It has an ethos, a characteristic attitude to life. And it gives allegiance to a system of ethics which may differ in some details from those of other churches.

Heresy, although strictly speaking a departure from orthodox doctrine, arose easily when reformers rebelled against practice, or against the church order and constitution accepted in their locality and age, or the type of worship commonly followed, especially sacramental worship. Rebels could express their heterodoxy in a new outlook on life which outraged the attitude of normal Christians in their time, or could combine their creeds with ethics which shocked and repelled the upholders of current morality. Since practice, constitution, ethos and ethics came to be closely allied with doctrine, it was easy for a man who opposed any of them to be classed as a heretic. Luther, in attacking the sale of indulgences, challenged the doctrine which led to the practice, that relief from Purgatory could be bought. It was a short step to the denial of the existence of Purgatory itself, to which the reformers could find no reference in Scripture. The constitution of the Roman Catholic Church placed the Pope at its head from very early times, and Christians who did not accept this were considered schismatics, even if orthodox in every other way, until 1870. But, when in that year the infallibility of the Pope was declared an essential dogma of the Catholic faith, those who did not accept it were classed as heretics as well as schismatics.

Protestants who reject some ritual aids or ceremonies in their worship oppose the doctrine that lies behind them – for example, when low church Anglicans celebrate Holy Communion standing at the north side of the Holy Table (no altar is mentioned in the Book of Common Prayer). They do so to avoid the suggestion inherent in the more usual 'eastward position' that the officiating priest is repeating the sacrifice of the mass and causing the real

[1] Bryan Wilson, *Religious Sects: A Sociological Study* (Weidenfeld & Nicolson, World University Library, 1970), p 15.

presence of Christ to manifest itself in and by his consecration of the elements. The seven sacraments of the Roman Church, the two of the Anglican and Episcopalian, and the absence of them among the Society of Friends, must make members of one of these communions heretical in the eyes of the others, because the sacraments are not only part of worship but expressions of doctrines which believers would regard as fundamental to their faith. The early Quakers probably angered the orthodox as much by their new ethos of refusing to recognize titles and keeping their hats on in the presence of magistrates as by their heterodox worship and doctrine. The early Mormons were regarded as heretical partly because of their polygamy, which conflicted with the 'doctrine' of Christian monogamous behaviour, and the members of the Oneida Community were condemned for their alleged practice of free love. The dividing lines between doctrine on the one hand, and constitution, practice, ethos and ethics on the other, are very slender.

As stated earlier, until a norm of Christian belief is established a heretic will remain one who holds a minority Christian belief in a Christian community. By the same token, the orthodox will remain those who hold the majority view. It is clear that orthodoxy and heterodoxy will differ according to whether one takes a local or a world view. But the truth of Orthodoxy as opposed to orthodoxies has little to do with numbers. Christianity began as a tiny Jewish sect, itself a heresy in the eyes of Pharisee and Sadducee. Yet to the modern Christian, the minuscule sect was right and world-wide Jewry wrong. To every founder of a Christian heretical sect, no matter how insignificant, the same hope must appear, that time will prove him right and the established churches to be in error. In the last century new sects, assisted by the media, have perhaps grown relatively as fast as the Christian Church in the first hundred years of its existence, and today there are more than a million Seventh Day Adventists, over two million Jehovah's witnesses and perhaps as many as eight million Pentecostalists. Is orthodoxy to be found among them and, if so, in which one?

The problem is not made easier because of the recognition by the established churches of certain doctrines that were once regarded as heterodox. There is a curious dichotomy in human thought here. Contemporary orthodoxy is admired as an expression of true belief, and contemporary heresy condemned, often with some revulsion. But the orthodox look back with admiration to the heroes and martyrs of the faith whose self-sacrifice in opposing the majority opinion of their times won for their successors the right to believe 'the Truth'. An original spiritual thinker is, it is said, like a great artist or musician, one who is ahead of his time, and therefore generally ostracized by the contemporary spiritual bourgeoisie.

The great prophets of Israel, to whom so much ethical and spiritual advance is due, almost all met persecution and martyrdom, as did the founder of Christianity himself, and this pattern has repeated itself down the ages.

Originality, sincerity and conviction do not in themselves make an opinion correct, and there have been false prophets in the past as well as true. The claim that 'the blood of the martyrs is the seed of the Church' does not alter the fact that martyrs have died for mutually exclusive 'truths' and some for unequivocal heresies.

It is worth trying to examine the motives of some of these men, who were often more humble, more admirable in their personal lives and more loving than their orthodox opponents and yet were perhaps justifiably condemned as heretics.

1. Heresy is often a conservative reaction, brought about by an attempt to turn back the clock to an imagined early ideal. For instance, Montanism in the second century was a revolt against the increasing organization of the Church. It took its name from Montanus, who considered Christianity to be falling away from its first fervour and spontaneity, and this he tried to recapture. However, if it is to fit itself for contemporary life and the ages to come, the Church must advance.

2. The Church has always to try to hold in balance tendencies which oppose each other. One pair of these is the prophetic and the priestly. In all religions there are enthusiasts, believers who stress the fervent, emotive side of their faith. At the other extreme are those who uphold the importance of what they regard as the 'right' doctrine, who believe that the worship of God must be carried out 'decently and in order' (1 Corinthians 14:40). Christianity began with an outburst of charismatic activity that, in the course of time, settled into an ordered church in which priestly authority replaced the primary prophetic enthusiasm. But ordered worship, however beautiful, can become dull through repetition, and the history of Christianity is sprinkled with reactions against churches which failed to feed the emotions of their worshippers. The emotional may be emphasized at the expense of true doctrine, and the result be the setting up of a new, heterodox church. This in time itself becomes respectable and staid, often to be reacted against in turn by a new movement within it, trying to recall it to *its* primeval charismatic fervour. And this new movement may become another heretical church or at least a schismatic one.

3. A second pair of opposing tendencies is the subjective and objective emphases in worship, both of which have several facets. It has been said, for example, that the Roman Church needed religion for practical living (objective) whereas the Greek Orthodox needed it to reveal the nature of God (subjective). In the west this could

lead and sometimes it has led to an over-emphasis on 'the social gospel', and in the east to an over-emphasis on mysticism, both of which, in their extreme forms, could lead to heresy; for the former stresses human effort and belittles the grace of God, and the latter neglects practical care of humankind in striving after a mystical relationship with the Supreme Being.

Subjectivity also tends to emphasize the importance of the conscience of the individual vis-à-vis the collective authority of the Church. He becomes a Luther who says, 'Here stand I – I can no other'. It is easy to see how such a man can become a heretic. What is not so easy is to recognize heresy in a certain type of objectivity, which is far commoner among religious people: the limitation of personal development, and often of responsibility, by the uncritical acceptance of everything authority teaches without the courage to face the difficulties that any sensitive or thinking man can see exist. The parrot cries, 'The Church teaches', 'The Bible teaches', can be every whit as heretical as 'Here stand I', though not recognized as such because the believer appears to be a child of his church more loyal than the average.

4. Heresy can be the over-emphasis of a neglected truth or an over-reaction to a truth too strongly stated. Thus, most of the Christological heresies of the first centuries were attempts to stress the humanity or divinity of Christ's nature against opponents who too strongly emphasized the opposite. In later times it could be said that Christian Science met with initial success because the Church had largely forgotten its healing mission; or that Pentecostalism gains its strength from the lack of positive teaching from orthodox pulpits about the work of the Holy Spirit.

5. A third pair of opposing tendencies is summed up in the phrase 'the ministry of the Word and sacraments'. Orthodox Christianity recognizes that these complement, not rival, each other, and that there needs to be a proper balance of the two elements in the unity of its ministry. But the mass-repetition (literally) of masses by chantry priests in the Middle Ages, and the emphasis on preaching at the expense of the sacraments by some Protestant sects, together with the rejection of both by yet others, could all be regarded as the over-emphasis which is heretical in tendency, if not in fact.

By applying standards crystallized out from the above five categories of Christian beliefs, it is easy enough to find heretics. Even the most orthodox believer has only to look in his mirror; for in some detail, in some false emphasis, he will fall short of that orthodoxy which is 'in the mind of God'. And it is correspondingly difficult to define what even the earthly norm of orthodoxy should be. The simple recognition of Jesus as God and Saviour quoted above may be a start, together with the rejection of any faith which rejects

or is inconsistent with the divinity of Christ. Organically connected
with the divinity of Christ is the doctrine of the Trinity. Even these
simple bases exclude the many sitting in orthodox pews who privately
believe that Jesus was merely a man, though a very special one,
who more than any other has shown us what God is like. And are
Unitarians who reject the doctrine of the Trinity but who sometimes
magnificently follow the Christian ethic and ideal not Christians?

All that can be stated for certain is that as the ages passed
there emerged a body of belief which came to be generally
accepted as orthodox. There have always been those who, privately
or openly, have differed from it in one article or another and yet
have regarded themselves as being true followers of Christ and his
Way. And so we come full circle. For the best that can be done
is to trace the building up of this norm of belief and to define departure
from it as heresy. To define a sect or an individual as heretical will
be simply to recognize that they do not give allegiance to some
part of the accepted norm of belief; it will be a statement of fact and
not a pejorative judgement. How far orthodoxy is a true reflection of
that Orthodoxy which is in the mind of God, perhaps only he can
tell. For theologians are finite men trying to bind the Infinite
Indefinable within the bonds of words; and that cannot be done.

CHAPTER 2

The Judaizers

Christianity was originally a heterodox minority within Judaism. Its first adherents, including its founder, were loyal Jews, attending the synagogues, visiting the Temple for the great feasts, sharing the Messianic hope and faithful to the Law of Moses, though Jesus, in claiming to fulfil that Law, penetrated to its spirit rather than obeyed contemporary interpretations of its letter. The heterodoxy lay in the proclamation of the apostles, Jews to a man, that a convicted criminal had been raised by God from the dead and was the Messiah for whom Israel had been waiting. The doctrine was unorthodox rather than heretical; it did not strike at the roots of Judaism, and the opposition to its proclaimers was not as total as a cursory reading of Acts might suggest.

For in the first Christian community there were two distinct bodies, the Hebrew-speaking Judaeo-Christians and the Hellenists or Greek-speaking group. The latter probably contained a number of proselytes. Acts, written by a Greek for Greeks and hostile to Judaeo-Christianity, does not show the close connection recognized by modern scholars that existed between Judaism and very primitive Aramaic-speaking Christianity.[1]

For although the high priests, Sadducees and Temple militia were hostile to all the first Christians, there was no reason for the Pharisees, who held the Messianic hope, 'to condemn *a priori* a movement stemming from Jesus',[2] nor to oppose the 'Hebrews' among his followers. In fact they may have approved of them, as the Jerusalem man in the street seems to have done, for their fervency and zeal for the Law. Their attitude to the Hellenists may have been different, as appears from Saul's support of the stoners of Stephen. But the Church in Jerusalem, headed by James, referred to

[1] See, for example, Jean Danielou and Henri Marrou, *The Christian Centuries*, Vol 1: *The First Six Hundred Years* (Darton, Longman & Todd, 1964), p 3.
[2] Ibid, p 7.

in the Scriptures as the Lord's brother, played an important part in
the development of Christianity until the Fall of Jerusalem in AD 70,
and its members did not cease to regard themselves as loyal Jews even
if they were alone in witnessing to the fulfilment of the Messianic
hope. What is more, they regarded themselves as the headquarters
of their new movement; what was happening in Asia Minor was
peripheral activity on the outskirts of their world, and the reader of
Acts needs to realize this to avoid receiving a wrongly balanced
picture of the early Church.

For more than half of Acts deals with the activities of Paul, and of
the Epistles thirteen are his and the remaining eight are divided
among five authors (in the *New English Bible* this proportion is
represented by 188 pages of Pauline writing to 35 of the rest). Through
the New Testament Paul has had more influence on Christian
development and thought than any other thinker of the first century
except Jesus Christ himself. Yet, when the crisis came, it was to the
Church at Jerusalem that Paul had to appeal for confirmation of
his policy, and it was Jerusalem's writ, through James, that ran
through the Christian world.

Paul's originality, in the sense both of a practice that is new and
the more fundamental one of going to the *origo* or root of the
matter, lay in his treatment of Gentile converts to Christianity.
Judaism recognized two classes of Gentile converts to its own creed.
There were the God-fearers, who abandoned idolatry and the worship
of other gods, observed the Sabbath and the Jewish food regulations,
attended synagogues and followed the Jewish ethic. There were also
the proselytes who, by submitting themselves to circumcision, baptism
by immersion and the obligation to offer sacrifices in the Temple at
Jerusalem, became completely Jewish by religion. It would have
been natural for Paul, a Pharisee of the Pharisees as he acknowledged
himself to be, to accept these two classes of convert and adapt
their terms of membership of the Christian Church to the conditions
required of God-fearer and proselyte. His practice was very different.
It was to preach first to the Jews in every city he visited, then,
when they rejected him, to turn to the Gentiles. It was part of his
genius that he realized that the Spirit of God dwelling within a man
was the inspiration of the good life, not adherence to a code of law,
however noble; and that Jesus had come to set men free by making
it possible for them to receive this Spirit, not to bind them nor to
lay irrelevant burdens upon them. Paul admitted Gentiles, therefore,
without obliging them to be circumcised or to obey the Law of
Moses.

Such preaching and practice appalled Jewish Christians, especially
many of those from orthodox Jerusalem. They challenged Paul in
Syrian Antioch, preaching that those Gentile converts to Christ who

had not been circumcised could not be saved unless they submitted themselves to the rite and the full rigours of the Mosaic law. The controversy arising from this was bitter, and it was resolved to submit the question to the parent church at Jerusalem.

The Council of Jerusalem was held in AD 49. As remarkable as Paul's insight into the role of the Spirit in the life of the believer was its final ruling, which was to be of crucial significance in the history of the Church. It would have been natural for the Jerusalem Christians, loyal Jews that they were, to repudiate Paul who seemed to be admitting to their religion men who were neither proselytes nor God-fearers. For they still thought of themselves not as founders of a new religion but as Jews who, in following Jesus the Messiah, were fulfilling the hope of Judaism itself. But after a long debate in which there were almost certainly more speakers on the side of the orthodox Jewish view than against it, the apostle Peter swayed the meeting in favour of Paul by recalling how he himself had been chosen by God to evangelize certain Gentiles. Though not mentioning Cornelius by name, he reminded the council that the Holy Spirit had been granted to the centurion and his family and friends as spontaneously and as fully as to the apostles at Pentecost, concluding: 'It is by the grace of the Lord Jesus that we are saved, and so are they.' (Acts 15:11.) Barnabas and Paul clinched the matter by recounting the signs and miracles worked by God through them among the Gentiles; and James, head of the Jerusalem community and, as the brother of Jesus, probably regarded as spokesman for the whole Christian Church at that time, gave his decision. All that was to be required of Gentile converts was that they should abstain from things polluted by contact with idols, from fornication, from anything strangled and from blood. Scholars disagree as to exactly what these prohibitions entailed, and there are different versions in different manuscripts. The aim seems to have been to forbid practices which would prevent Jewish and Gentile Christians from eating together – in some cities they may even have formed two distinct communities – and to demand a standard of ethical conduct worthy of followers of the Messiah; for the Jews of that age strongly disapproved of the licence in contemporary pagan society. Yet what was far more important than the prohibitions was the lack of demand for circumcision and obedience to the Law. In fact, with hindsight, it can be seen as the cutting of the umbilical cord connecting Christianity and Judaism, for once Gentile converts were admitted on terms which did not require them to adopt practices and a code which would have seemed to most of them irksome and irrelevant, it was possible, even probable, that they would outweigh the Jewish Christians by sheer numbers.

Thus Paul's insight became the norm of Christian doctrine and practice with regard to the Jewish Law, and Christianity itself was liberated to develop according to its individual genius. It ceased to be a sect within Judaism and became a religion in its own right. But Jewish Christians, probably a majority of them, did not accept the ruling of the Council of Jerusalem without a struggle, which continued until the Fall of Jerusalem to the Romans in AD 70. This brought the destruction of what was left of the Church there, together with the annihilation of the Jews as a nation and obliteration of their influence among Christians. Paul, meanwhile, continued to face Judaizing opponents wherever his missionary endeavours took him, and for generations after his death, until the fourth or even fifth century after the coming of Christ, the Judaeo-Christian strain survived as heretical minorities in an increasingly Gentile-orientated Church.

It can be seen, from the standpoint of history, why Christianity could not continue within Judaism. The daughter religion, though bearing strong family likenesses to the mother and unmistakably her heiress, possessed a different nature and had to strike out independently. As Paul said, laws and regulations are a tutor whose job it is to lead ethically immature men to moral adulthood. But adherence to law does not make a man inwardly moral. True goodness comes when a man yearns to become the best he can be, not because external laws force him to be righteous by threat of punishment or fear of nonconformity. 'Blessed are they that hunger and thirst after righteousness,' Jesus had said; and Paul saw that such hunger was prompted not by the Law but by the indwelling Holy Spirit of God. Judaism had a distinctive character, a legal one from which escape was not possible, for all the genius of its prophets, some of whom themselves saw that the only true road to morality was for a man to long for it with his whole heart. Jeremiah had written, 'This is the covenant which I will make with Israel after those days, says the Lord; I will set my law within them and write it in their hearts; I will become their God and they shall become my people. No longer need they teach one another to know the Lord; all of them, high and low alike, shall know me, says the Lord' (Jeremiah 31:33-4).

Jeremiah wrote this at a time of national flux and disaster, when it might have been possible for Judaism to develop along the prophetic rather than the legal path, but the history of the following centuries decreed otherwise. In the Judaism into which Jesus was born, the Law, with all its minutiae of commentary and interpretation, bound the loyal Jew like a fly cocooned in a spider's web. The Christian doctrine of the freedom of the Spirit was the antithesis of this, as Paul recognized when he wrote to the Galatians who had been seduced from their allegiance to his gospel by Judaizing Christians,

'Christ set us free, to be free men. Stand firm, then, and refuse to be tied to the yoke of slavery again' (Galatians 5:1).

Not only was it essential for the new religion that Gentile Christians be freed from Jewish links; there was also a danger that the tide of Jewish nationalism, flowing ever more strongly as the first century passed, might sweep Judaeo-Christians back into their old faith. The influences upon them were complicated by the politics of the time. In AD 57 a wind of revolt against Rome was rising in the Jewish world, and even though Judaeo-Christians refused to commit themselves as a body to the anti-Roman movement, the pressures of nationalist appeal and pressure to be faithful to the old ways must have been extreme. There was also tension on this account between the Judaeo-Christians and the foreigners who had turned to Christ. Gentile converts, it could be argued, had sprung from a movement within Judaism. For them to repudiate circumcision and the Law was not only religiously wrong to a conservative Jewish Christian, but an act of political treason, a betrayal of the Jewish community of which the Gentile had become part by giving allegiance to the Messiah.

Perhaps in time the opponents of Paul would have reversed the Jerusalem decree, but they were overtaken by events. In AD 66 the Jewish war began. The Christian community in Jerusalem withdrew to Pella, across the Jordan, and the tie with the Holy City, the spiritual capital of world Jewry as well as the temporal capital of the Jewish state, was snapped. The fall of the city four years later shattered any influence the Judaizers might still have had, though they persisted in small minorities for another four hundred years.

To accuse the Judaizers of being the first heretics, when it was they who were the loyal sons of their faith, seems scarcely just. Nor, since there were differing parties among them, was the ground of their heresy always the same. On the extreme right were the conservatives who held nearly the whole Christian faith, combining it with a rigid adherence to the Law of Moses. Their heresy was the failure to recognize that 'the fruit of the Spirit' had replaced the sanctions of the Law. On the left were the Ebionites, sometimes classed as Gnostics, who repudiated Paul as an apostate from the Law and rejected all the Gospels except a mutilated Hebrew edition of St Matthew. The majority of them also rejected the Virgin Birth and the divine nature of Jesus. They took the view that he was a man, like the great prophets of the past, the son of Joseph and Mary: At his baptism, 'Christ' descended upon him in the form of a dove and, because it was unthinkable that Messiah could suffer, departed from him before his crucifixion. The Ebionites, of whom there were several varieties, kept the Sabbath but, mixing fragments of Christian belief with scraps of Essene teaching,[3] rejected marriage, wine and the use of oil to anoint the body, which they despised, believing matter to be basically evil (a Gnostic doctrine). Some of their eccentricities were not declared heretical until later.

Between the two wings were many shades of opinion. A sect called the Nazarenes, for example, believed that Jesus was the Messiah, the Son of God, whose teachings were superior to those of Moses and the prophets. They also held the view, not unreasonable in the context of the times, that Christians of Jewish descent should be circumcised, observe the Sabbath and obey the laws governing foods, without necessarily demanding the same behaviour from Gentile converts.

With the disappearance of Judaea and the dispersion of her people, never to regain a homeland until the twentieth century, the future of Christianity passed into the hands of its Gentile adherents. Yet the legacy inherited from the parent religion was enormous. The development of Trinitarian theology did not detract from a monotheism which orthodox Christians held as strictly as any Jew. The Old Testament covenant relationship between Yahweh, God of the whole earth, and his Chosen People, was transferred to the Christian God and his Church. The sweep of history from Creation to the final victory of God, visualized by the prophets and in the Jewish apocalyptic writings, and the belief of the Hebrews that theirs was the only true religion and the one which would eventually be accepted by the whole world, were concepts taken over by and included in the Christian world-view. The Law and the Prophets became Christian holy books, the foundation of the Church's moral code, even though much in the way of ritual, food regulations, sacrifice and observance of days was no longer relevant or necessary. The Jewish Messianic hope had been fulfilled in Jesus. The synagogue, with its regular forms of worship, open to all comers, fathered the local Christian parish church, the liturgy of which bears many resemblances to that of its parent. From the Pharisees Christians inherited a sense of personal and corporate religion, doctrines of sin and repentance, a sense of the grace and forgiveness of God, belief in a future life with rewards and punishments, and the combination of a written and therefore certain and basically unchanging Law, with a growing tradition interpreting it to meet the different circumstances of succeeding ages.

With such an inheritance it may seem difficult to grasp why any Jewish Christian should ever be called a heretic. The heresy was a tendency rather than a specific doctrine. It has appeared since in every

---

[3] The Essenes were a Jewish sect who practised celibacy, worked hard, preferring agriculture to other occupations, denied themselves pleasure, were austere in food and clothing, held their possessions in common, eschewed slavery, hated war, prized honesty, took no oaths and helped the poor.

age of the Church and can be found issuing from the pulpits and sitting in the pews of many an orthodox denomination today. Wherever a Christian believes that he can earn salvation by church attendance, adherence to a moral code, 'Sabbath' observance, in short, keeping what he thinks is the Christian version of 'the Law', he is spiritually a Judaizer, especially if he maintains that it is possible for other believers to attain salvation only by following the same disciplines as he thinks essential. The left and right extremes of Puritanism and sacerdotalism are riddled with this particular heretical tendency, and from it arises much of the intolerance which has bedevilled the relations between different Christian churches down the ages.

Paul and his spiritual descendants showed that the truly Christian path was freedom from legalism, beyond which spiritually mature and developed believers should be able to grow. But Paul gave an equally strong warning that liberty must not degenerate into licence. The fact is that there are two kinds of legalism, which might be described as prevenient and resultant. The former is that which is given as tutor, guide and prop to an immature believer or body of believers; it can be dangerous in that, instead of opening the way to God, it can become an end in itself and an idol. Where a religious man follows a code of behaviour or gives allegiance to a creed because it will win him salvation and heaven, or because his failure to observe it will be punished in this world or the next with *delirium tremens*, venereal disease or hellfire, or simply for appearance' sake, he is on the road to heresy. Resultant legalism occurs, on the other hand, if a man is so in love with God and his neighbour that he joyfully embraces and accepts a discipline of worship and behaviour to express his adoration and philanthropy, whether his own or given him by his church. This is true religion. Augustine wrote, 'Love God and do what you like', for it follows that the loving of God will transmute 'what you like' into what he likes.

Heresies do not die but appear in new guises. So, in the twentieth century, the old Judaism has appeared in the shape of Seventh Day Adventism, which requires of its followers to observe Saturday rather than Sunday as the weekly holy day, arguing that keeping the Sabbath is one of the Ten Commandments and therefore binding upon believers. Adventists also follow at least some of the food regulations of the Old Testament, such as the prohibition to eat pig-meat in any form.

Here must be repeated and stressed the caveat mentioned in the first chapter. The use of the word 'heresy' in this book is not to be taken pejoratively but as a statement of fact, given the premises so far outlined. Through the ages of Christendom, a body of belief will be seen to emerge which is generally recognized and labelled as 'orthodoxy'. To differ from it will be heterodox, and to diverge from it beyond a certain point – not always easy to define – will be heresy. To call this belief orthodox, that heterodox and the other heretical will be to state facts, not to apportion blame. In stating that Seventh Day Adventism is a revival of the old Judaizing tendency, and in drawing similar parallels in later chapters, the intention is simply to show that tendencies and patterns of thought repeat themselves. By his keeping of Saturday rather than Sunday as a holy day, and by his refusal to eat bacon, a Seventh Day Adventist is heterodox, in that he differs from the great mass of Christians. He has a perfect right to adopt these practices for himself and his co-religionists if they arise from his personal vision of the will of God whom he loves and whose commands he believes these to be. However, were he to insist that salvation could only be won by obedience to these sections of the old Jewish Law, he would be classed as a heretic and a modern Judaizer. For this would indeed be to replace the living Spirit by a dead letter.

CHAPTER 3

Gnosticism

Gnosticism has already been mentioned in connection with the radical Judaeo-Christian sect, the Ebionites. The name (from the Greek *gnosis* = knowledge – since Gnostics claimed to have a secret knowledge which was the key to salvation) is given to a group of systems taking colour, chameleon-like, from their intellectual surroundings. Their beginnings preceded Christianity by many years. These systems were philosophical in that the problem which concerned all Gnostics was the reconciliation of the existence of evil with God who is good; religious because they offered salvation.

The basic premises common to the many varieties of Gnostic belief were that since God is good and the material world is evil, he cannot have created it. A digest of the systems would read something like this: God, pre-existent, First Father or Principle, eternal Aeon, as Love abhors dwelling alone. He therefore created the Pleroma (fullness), containing a number of spiritual beings – in some systems paired in sexes – numbering up to thirty. These derived their descent from the One but deteriorated as they approached the boundary of the Pleroma. The last of them, sometimes called Sophia (Wisdom) gave way to lust and bore the Demiurge (Craftsman, worker for the people), who either created the material world himself or was the father of the god who created it.

Beyond the Pleroma was matter, inert, powerless, but coeternal. This was fashioned by the Demiurge or the god who was his son, sometimes equated with Jehovah, the maleficent god of the Old Testament, after the model of the ideal world which existed in the mind of the supreme God. He either could not or did not prevent this, and in some systems was ignorant of the Demiurge's work. Later Gnostics borrowed from the Christian scheme, calling their aeons by such names as Logos, Monogenes, Zoe and Ecclesia. Christ and the Holy Ghost were two of the last aeons put forth, Jesus being one

in whom something of all the others was to be found. Christ came
to bring gnosis. The Demiurge created the material part of man, but
Sophia, man's mother (or grandmother) infused her spiritual essence
into him unknown to the Demiurge, hence his 'spark of the divine'.
Either all men had this spark or some only; most Gnostic systems
believed that many men had nothing of spirit in them and would be
annihilated. Where the divine spark existed it was to be found in the
mind, of which the body was the earthly prison, and salvation
would come through a combination of gnosis, faith and works.

The planets exercised a maleficent influence on man. Above their
spheres within spheres God dwelt beyond fate and death and evil gods.
Man had to get to know the gates he would have to pass from
sphere to sphere, the god or demon that would confront him at
each and the proper password to be given at every frontier. To
know and name a demon was to deprive him of his power. This
knowledge was gnosis, revealed and universal, incorporating
whatever there is of truth in all religions.

Salvation was not by mere faith and love but by revealed
speculative knowledge, esoteric intuition or by magical rites,
instruction and initiation. The heart of Gnosticism was mystery,
freeing spirit from matter, presenting truth in the form of mysteries,
emancipating worshippers stage by stage and bringing them into the
realm of pure spirit. In Christian Gnosticism knowledge was
supposed to come from oral teaching of Jesus, which was never
committed to writing.

There were three stages of Gnostic development. The pre-Christian
drew its inspiration from Greek, Jewish and eastern sources. In the
second stage, a still mainly heathen Gnosticism used Christian ideas
to fill up gaps – Jesus, for example, appearing as the agent of
man's redemption. The third stage presented Christianity modified
by Gnosticism to make it acceptable to religious-minded, intellectual
pagans, and in this form was heretical and a real danger to
orthodox Christian belief.

In spite of its closeness to Gnostic speculation some scholars
deny that a body of work called the Hermetica, alleged revelations of
Hermes Trismegistus, originally the Egyptian god Thoth, had any
influence on Gnosticism. Others claim it as a principal source.
Whatever the truth, the two share a marked similarity of ideas,
ideas which must have been in evidence just before and after the
beginning of the Christian era, and the Hermetica and Gnosticism
had a common ancestor in Platonism. The literature developed
between 100 BC and AD 200 and taught the existence of a Primal
Being who was Mind, Life and Light. Mind created a second
demiurgic Mind who in turn created the universe, including the
seven planets. These were called Governors, for their cycles ruled

the material world through Destiny (astrological ideas are prominent here). Primal Mind also created an archetypal Man in his own image. Man, filled himself with a desire to create, descended through the celestial spheres and begat upon Nature humankind, who derived their mortal bodies from their mother, and their immortal souls from their father.

One of the texts of the Corpus Hermeticum, a still extant collection of hermetical writings, the Poimandres, shows how the human soul can be saved from enslavement to the planets and ascend through the seven spheres to the highest heaven whence his father came. Gnosis is the key, knowledge of the gates of the spheres, the passwords needed to pass them and the names of the demons guarding them, as in 'orthodox' Gnosticism.

From Greek philosophy the Gnostics borrowed the Platonic doctrine of ideas which taught that everything in this lower, material world was a copy, more or less imperfect, of a perfect idea, celestial and immaterial, in the mind of God. There is thus an idea or ideal of 'doghood' to which every dog of flesh and blood which has ever existed and is ever to exist, from chihuahua to St Bernard and Pekingese to husky, is an imperfect approximation. All the qualities of all physical dogs do not make up the idea of 'doghood' any more than the exercise sometimes undertaken by students of statistics, of superimposing fifty silhouettes of co-eds upon each other, makes up the ideal or even a recognizable woman. But a dog – or a girl – can be judged by the closeness with which they approach the ideals (though unknown by finite man) in the mind of God with whom alone all ultimate Reality dwells. From Plato the Gnostics may also have borrowed their conception of aeons, which have some of the features of his 'ideas', and some of the qualities of the intellectual beings to whom, Plato surmised, God had delegated the task of making the material world. The Greek philosopher certainly used the title 'Demiurge' for the creator of the world in his *Timaeus*. Other schools of Greek thought, dualistic in their ideas such as Orphism, and philosophies which asserted that matter was eternal, also influenced Gnosticism, which believed matter to be coeternal with God.

The influence of Oriental mysticism came partly from Jewish sources. The Cabbala, which has had an inordinate effect on European occultism down the ages, strongly influenced Gnostic philosophy. Its mystical jargon and esoteric teachings, founded on allegorical interpretations of scripture uncommitted to writing but orally passed down by adepts who communicated knowledge to initiates, appealed strongly to the Gnostic cast of mind. The cabbalistic system differed from the Greek in teaching that matter was not eternal. The universe was spiritual and God was pure Spirit.

The first man emanated from God who made nine other Sephiroth (emanations) from which the material universe was formed.

Another possible source of Gnostic philosophy lay in some aspects of Judaism itself. The pre-Christian Jewish sect of the Magharians, rebellious and heterodox, distinguished between God and an angel who created the world. In this way they accounted for the anthropomorphic descriptions of God in the Old Testament. Certain Coptic books discovered at Nag Hammadi in 1946 also show the existence of Gnostic strains in Judaism. Other eastern sources are some astrological doctrines of Babylonian Magi, Syrian religious ideas, and Persian dualism arising from Zoroastrianism, which taught the existence of two independent coeternal principles of good and evil. This last, by introducing a sophisticated angelology into Judaism, provided beings who were the equivalent of the Gnostic aeons.

Not all scholars agree, however, that Gnosticism was a derivative philosophy, although it clearly borrowed elements from many sources. It was, they say, a new movement, rebelling against what seemed to its adherents to be an absurd and wicked world. For Gnostics were often sensitive, intelligent and religious men whose beliefs arose from personal experience. Some authorities do not regard them as heretics at all in the Christian era but as forming a new religion with special views about God, the world and men. God is a suffering God; the world is in error (an expression reminiscent of Christian Science); man is a stranger here, for Heaven is his home; and his inward self is of the same substance as God.

Gnosticism, though beginning before Christianity, had early connections with it. Dositheus, said to have been a disciple of John Baptist and therefore a contemporary of Jesus, was a Gnostic. He inspired Simon Magus, regarded by some Samaritans as 'that power of God which is called "The Great Power"' (Acts 8: 10) – that is, as the chief emanation from the Deity and thus entitled to divine worship. It can be seen that the unorthodox Judaism of the Samaritans could lead easily to heresy both while they remained Jews and among those of them who became Christian. Simon is shown in Acts as a Christian believer, baptized by Philip and reacting humbly when reproved by Peter for trying to buy the gift of the Holy Spirit with money. But he reneged, for though not necessarily a full-blown Gnostic himself, the patristic writers regarded him as the father of heresy, the begetter of several Gnostic systems and the first to combine Gnostic elements with Christianity. He was the reputed author of a Gnostic work called *The Great Revelation*, of which fragments remain. Not only was he a Samaritan Messiah, but, according to Justyn Martyr, writing about a century later, he went further, claiming to be the first or supreme God. One of the sects he founded, known as the Simonians, supported him in this, maintaining that he had come to save the world from the angels who were misruling it. Irenaeus wrote of him: 'This man, then, was glorified by many as if he were a god; and he taught that he himself had appeared among the Jews as the Son but descended in Samaria as the Father while he came to other nations as the Holy Ghost. He represented himself, in a word, as being the loftiest of all powers, that is, the Being who is Father over all.' He also claimed to be an emanation from the Deity, and that a certain Helena, whom he had redeemed from slavery at Tyre, was an emanation from him, the first conception of his mind, the mother of all through whom, in the beginning, he conceived the idea of forming angels and archangels and the powers by whom this world was formed. 'This conception leaping forth from him and comprehending the will of her father, descended to the lower regions (of space) and generated angels and powers by whom also he declared this world was formed.'

One of Simon's disciples was Menander. He practised magic, for Gnosticism was theurgical as well as theological. He preached at Antioch that those who followed him would not die, and is chiefly important as being a link in the Gnostic succession, for his disciples, Basilides and Saturninus, both developed their own versions of the creed. The former made a great synthesis of Simon Magus doctrines, full of apocalyptic ideas. He taught that there were 365 heavens, each corresponding to an angelic order, and that Jesus was not crucified but that Simon of Cyrene, who was compelled to carry the cross, was transfigured into the likeness of Christ and was crucified instead. Jesus was given the appearance of Simon and, standing by, laughed at the mistaken Romans and Jews. This version of Gnosticism was a variety of Docetism (from the Greek *dokeo* = I seem) which, arising from the Gnostic dislike of matter and suffering as associated with God, taught that Jesus's body was not a real one. A very early heresy, Jerome wrote that it came into vogue 'while the Apostles were still surviving, while Christ's blood was still fresh in Judaea, the Lord's body was asserted to be but a phantom'; and in John comes the assertion that 'every spirit which acknowledges that Jesus Christ has come in the flesh is from God, and every spirit which does not thus acknowledge Jesus is not from God' (1 John 4: 2). The Docetists taught that the Redeemer came to deliver the divine spark of goodness in man, but since matter is evil, he had to assume a phantom body which appeared like a normal earthly one but was of heavenly, immaterial origin.

Saturninus, also active in Antioch, between AD 100 and 150 preached that the God of the Jews made six planetary angels, these beings together opposing the hidden God. The angels created man as a creature crawling upon earth till the hidden God gave him some of the light. Saturninus was the first Gnostic to distinguish two kinds of men, those who had the light and those who did not, teaching that what was created by the angels was fundamentally different from that given by God.

The Gnostic succession has been followed from Simon Magus to Saturninus. Two other possible strains are mentioned in the New Testament. The Apollos, who is mentioned by Paul as inspiring one of the factions in the Corinthian Church (see the early chapters of I Corinthians), seems to have taught that Christ was Wisdom (Sophia) who figured in certain Gnostic schemes. Wisdom had come into the world and been ignored by its rulers, and Paul is interpreted by some readers of the first Corinthian letter to have reproved him for making a gnosis out of Christianity. The Nicolaitans mentioned in Revelation (2:6, 15) as hated by God may not be the same as the sect condemned by the patristic writers a hundred years later. If they were, their heresy was the common Gnostic condemnation of the Creator God of the Old Testament. A considerable impetus to Gnosticism in Messianic Judaeo-Christian groups in Asia was given by the Fall of Jerusalem in AD 70.

The first to formulate 'Christian' Gnosticism is said to have been Cerinthus. Contemptuous of the Judaeo-Christians who clung to circumcision and the Sabbath, he taught that the world was not created by God but by a power remotely distant from him. Jesus was the son of Joseph and Mary. 'Christ' descended on him at his baptism in the form of a dove and deserted him before the crucifixion, leaving the man Jesus to suffer. Cerinthus looked forward to a millennium when Messiah would rule for a thousand years in peace.

A disciple of Cerinthus was Carpocrates who taught at Alexandria. He differed slightly from his master in that he preached that the world had been created by angels, but his Christology was almost identical with that of Cerinthus except that believers, he said, were able to partake of the same power, which made them Christ's equals. Armed with this, they could scorn the archons who had made the world, and work the same miracles as Jesus. Carpocrates did not accept Cerinthus' millennial dreams. Man could be free of the archons only after having been the slave of the vices over which they presided, otherwise they were doomed to reincarnation in order to pay their debts. This amoralism seems to stem from Gnostic rebellion against the Jewish God and the Law and, allied with the contempt for angels and violent rejection of creation, obeys the principles of classic Gnosticism.

Cerinthus and Carpocrates were small fry compared with the arch-Gnostic heretics Marcion (100–60) and Valentinus, of unknown dates though he lived in the second century AD. Marcion, born at Sinope on the Black Sea, the son of a bishop, and after a possible start in life as a sailor probably a bishop himself, came to Rome some time after 138. He was a wealthy man and generous to the Church, but this did not prevent his expulsion by the presbyters for heresy. His followers formed themselves into a separate body known as Marcionites, thus adding the sin of schism to that of heresy, and claimed to preach a purer Christianity than the orthodox. They have been called the first Dissenters.

Marcion's own writings perished (indeed, nearly all our knowledge of Gnostic teachings comes from orthodox apologists such as Justin Martyr, Irenaeus, Hippolytus and Epiphanius), and his ideas are found only in those of his opponents, such as Tertullian's *Against Marcion*. He does not seem to have been even an orthodox Gnostic, if the many varieties of the heresy can allow of the existence of such a being, for he did not profess to have a need of gnosis. He preached that salvation was gained by simple faith in the Gospel. There existed a supreme God of pure benevolence not found in the Old Testament, in which a different, Just God was portrayed. He was the creating Demiurge, with properties of anger, jealousy and desire to punish. The New Testament God was a Kind God who, pitying mankind, sent his son to rescue humanity. Those loyal to the Demiurge were inspired by him to crucify Christ, but this action brought about the defeat of their god, for the Kind God demanded satisfaction from the Just God who acknowledged that he had sinned in killing Jesus in ignorance. He would pay for his error by giving the Kind God the souls of all who should believe in him. As a result of the payment made on the cross by Jesus, men were saved by grace. Christ also rescued from the underworld those who had died previously and had not in their lives obeyed the Demiurge. All God required of men was faith in his love, for he has freed men from the legalistic requirements of the Just God and his creature, Judaism.

All matter was evil, and not only man's body but his spirit were evil too, though Marcion recognized that there was an antithesis between spirit and flesh. He denied the reality of Christ's body and his physical resurrection. He rejected all the Gospels except Luke's, which he edited radically to suit his own views, changing 'I am come not to destroy but to fulfil the law', for example, into its opposite, 'I am come not to fulfil but to destroy the law'. He made the first collection of Paul's epistles, omitting the two letters to Timothy and Titus, and must be regarded as founding the New Testament canon, anticipating Irenaeus by some years. He refused to allow marriage after baptism, dividing his disciples into an élite of baptized or 'perfect', who led lives of extreme asceticism, and unbaptized, living ordinary lives. The latter supported the Perfect and were baptized at the end of their lives. In spite of its discouragement of marriage and children, with the result that Marcionism could be maintained only by recruitment, it continued as an organized sect into the fifth century, claimed by its adherents to be a return to the purity and ideals of the primitive Gospel. It had a particular appeal to eastern parts of the Roman Empire.

If the amount of hostile writing he inspired among the orthodox authorities is a criterion of importance, Valentinus was the greatest of them all. Irenaeus, Tertullian and Clement of Alexandria all wrote against his teachings which were given, like those of some other famous Gnostics, at Alexandria. In his system Depth and Silence were both pre-existent in invisible ineffable heights. Together they generated the Pleroma consisting of thirty aeons (patterns of thought, archetypes). The youngest of these was Sophia (Wisdom) who possessed free will. She chose to give way to 'passion'–an emotion which she thought was love. This had arisen among the higher aeons and was passed to Sophia as if by contagion, like an illness which starts in some parts of the body and breaks out in others. What she experienced was in fact hubris (pride), which lusted to understand the unfathomable depth of God. But the philosophical reason cannot understand the mysteries of God, and Sophia's fall resulted, but as the outcome of a necessary process within God himself.

In the empty space devoid of knowledge created by her sin, Sophia gave birth to Jesus in remembrance of the higher world, but with a kind of shadow over him. Jesus rid himself of this and found his way back to the spiritual domain. Left alone outside, Sophia was subject to every sort of emotion–fear, despair, ignorance–from which the elements of the world and the world-soul of the Demiurge were to be derived.

At her request Jesus asked the aeons to help Sophia, and after the Holy Spirit had revealed God's gnosis to them, together they formed the Saviour, Christ, the perfect expression of the spiritual world. He was sent with his angels to Sophia, the world-spirit in exile, and delivered her from her passions, which became the world.

There are three strata of reality in the universe: the sublunar material world, dominated by the Devil; the celestial psychic world ruled by the Demiurge, who is the same as Yahweh and tends to be hostile; and the world beyond the planets, where Sophia and the spiritual beings dwell. Man has three divisions corresponding to these: his material body; his soul, the seat of ethical awareness and the power of reason; and his spirit, which dreams unconsciously within him and is the divine spark, of the same substance as Sophia and even God.

Not all men are spiritual. The lowest, the pagans, are materialists. Others called psychics have a soul and believe in the Demiurge, but are unaware of the spiritual world above–these include the Jews and the ordinary Christian churchgoers. Those who are spiritual are open to the promptings of their guardian angel who accompanies them throughout their lives, reveals gnosis to them, forms a couple with them and is not allowed into eternal bliss without them. The divine spark in man needs to be fanned by the divine counterpart of the self in order to be finally reintegrated.

History is a necessary progress from materialism and paganism by way of religion and ethics to spiritual freedom gained by gnosis. The world-spirit in exile must go through the inferno of matter and the purgatory of morals to arrive at the spiritual Paradise. The spirit in man is united with the soul so that it may be formed and educated in practical life, for it needs psychic and sense training.

Christ, who brings the revelation of gnosis (self-consciousness), clothed himself with Jesus at baptism and saves all spiritual mankind through his resurrection, but had only a spiritual body. Men can now become aware of their spiritual selves through him and return to their heavenly origin. When every spiritual being has received gnosis and become aware of the divinity within himself, the world-process will end. Christ and Sophia, after waiting at the entrance of the Pleroma for spiritual Man, will enter the bridal chamber to achieve their union, followed by the Gnostics and their higher selves, their guardian angels. They are also bride and groom who in the Pleroma will perform 'a spiritual and eternal mystery of sacred marriage' which is the complete union of the 'I' and the 'Self'.

Other Gnostic sects were the Elkesai, the Barbelognostics and the Sethians. The first, like the nineteenth-century founder of the Latter-day Saints to whom the Book of Mormon was communicated, received their revelation of God in a book delivered to them by an angel. The Barbelognostics, who were attacked by Irenaeus in his *Against Heresies*, drew their inspiration from *The Apocrypha of John*, a work recently discovered, belonging to the first and second centuries. This contains all the elements of Gnosticism but is a non-Christian system and should not have been attacked by Irenaeus as a heresy but as a pagan sect. The Sethians taught that after God the Father there came as aeons of the Pleroma the Son and Holy Spirit followed by Christ and the Church. They produced Sophia, who from her union with the lower waters gave birth to seven sons, Ildabaot, Iao, Sabaoth, Adonai, Elohim, Astaphain and Horaios (the seven Old Testament names of Jehovah), who made man in their own image. Christ descended through the seven heavens, to the astonishment of the powers, adopting the shape of the angel of each as he descended.

The occidental form of Gnosticism declared God to be one, not two, disagreeing with Valentinus' Depth and Silence. The Demiurge was not hostile but ignorant and friendly. Ptolemaeus, one of their leaders, taught that Christ had a soul and psychic body, a doctrine that implied that both 'psychic' and 'spiritual' man could be saved.

This system was a compromise with Church doctrine, but even a friendly Demiurge is not the God and Father of Christ, Christ is not a real man, and the spiritual immortality of the Gnostic is not the same as the doctrine of the Church, which taught a bodily resurrection and a final ending of the material universe, or at least its replacement by 'a new heaven and a new earth'.

Even after its disappearance as organized sects during the fifth century, Christian Gnosticism has continued as a strain of thought in much speculation since. Origen believed that the Fall was due to decisions made by spirits who lived in the spiritual world before the earth was created and who exercised the free will they had been given by God. He used this belief in free will to attack the Gnostic belief that only a few men, the 'spiritual', would be saved. Origen's theological system was the end of the process of any attempt at Christianizing Gnosticism.

Though Plotinus (c. 203–62), the founder of Neoplatonism, wrote a famous treatise against Gnosticism, he was himself affected by it, and the philosophy thus influenced two main streams of western thought, Christian theology and Neoplatonic theory. Gnostic sects had little influence after the second century. But Marcion, and an ex-Christian Syrian Gnostic called Bardaisan, inspired Mani, the founder of Manicheism, who first preached at Ctesiphon, the capital of the Persian kingdom, in 242. Since this new religion was not Christian and therefore not a heresy, it is not the concern of this book. It is, however, important in that it contained many of the Gnostic doctrines derived from Christian heresy; and it became so strong that in the fourth century there was a possibility that it might have superseded Christianity. St Augustine of Hippo was a Manichee for twelve years and is thought by some to have brought Manichean influence into the Christian Church. Through the Manichee sect called the Paulicians, exiled by Justinian and settling in Bulgaria, the creed came to Europe and became the father of a number of Christian Gnostic heresies. Basil, a twelfth-century monk, founded the Bogomili, or Friends of God, with tenets akin to those of the Manicheans and Gnostics. They flourished throughout the Balkans in spite of Basil's death at the stake in 1118, and survived until the Turkish conquest in the sixteenth century.

The Paulicians were also possibly the spiritual ancestors of the Albigenses or Cathari who flourished mainly in Lombardy and the south of France in the twelfth century. They taught that matter and the life of the senses associated with it were utterly evil and were the creation of a maleficent god. Christ came to save men's souls, not their bodies, and his body, crucifixion, resurrection and ascension were apparent, not real. Marriage and procreation were wrong, abortion being used to counter mistakes. Suicide was sometimes commended and even assisted, if the believer's nerve failed him at the moment of self-destruction. Like some other Gnostic sects, such as the Manicheans, the Cathari (Pure Ones) divided themselves into an inner circle of the Perfect or Catharistae (Most Pure) and an outer of Hearers or Adherents. The Catharistae abstained from marriage, trade and bloodshed, eating flesh, cheese and eggs, and lived extremely ascetically. The Hearers were allowed meat, though not themselves permitted to kill, and marriage, but not children. Otherwise they were free to live as they liked, and were consequently attacked by their opponents for their licence, although they were required to be purified and perfected on their deathbeds.

Echoes of Gnosticism are to be heard in a number of sects down to the theosophical movement of the last hundred years, and the Gnostic spirit is to be found in some very orthodox pews. The Gnostics tried to solve the problem of evil by interposing a number of graded beings between the supreme God and the creator of the material world. Christians have ascribed the fall of man and the introduction of evil into the universe to the action of the Devil, created by God as Lucifer, Son of the Morning, who fell into rebellion against the Most High through pride. But if God is ultimately responsible for all that is, there is not much difference between there being a dozen emanations between him and the evil in creation, or just one. Gnosticism was dualist. Much of the thinking of the ordinary Christian unversed in theological subtleties is dualist, in that he believes in the existence of a personal force of evil which is only a fraction less powerful than God. He has an idea which could be expressed symbolically as an image of God as a white horse running a race with the Devil as a black one: they run neck and neck for the whole course of time, the white horse just pipping the black one at the finishing post by a short head as the last trump sounds for the beginning of eternity. Even then, evil will not vanish – Satan will simply be bound. But Christianity is monist, not dualist.

Much Puritanism in Catholic, Protestant and Orthodox history has been founded on the belief that matter, the physical, the body and its appetites, are fundamentally evil. Such a belief is Gnostic, contrary to the faith which is a basic tenet of both Judaism and Christianity that when God created his *physical* universe, he looked upon his work and saw 'it was very good'. It was after he had finished that evil was introduced. Gnostics saw salvation as a recovery of a spark of the spiritual from the ashes of the physical, which would eventually be destroyed. Orthodox Christianity believed in the creation of a new heaven and a new earth by God who would redeem his whole creation, although in the light of new knowledge about the universe theologians are wise to be reticent and hold a reverent agnosticism as to exactly what this belief may mean. Gnosticism claimed a knowledge of inner truth which its followers alone held. Christian sects all down the ages have claimed that they only had the revelation, exclusive if not esoteric, of a 'full Gospel' which contained a hundredfold of truth to the ordinary Christian's thirty or fortyfold.

For the contemporary orthodox who had to face the immediate challenge of Gnosticism the dangers were many. The denial of the real body of Christ and consequently of his genuine manhood meant that he was different from the human race. He was no 'second Adam' who 'to the fight and to the rescue came', proving, because 'he was tempted in all points like as we are', that man could live the victorious life in the strength of God by becoming man himself and living it. The denial of the real resurrection of Christ meant the loss of the guarantee of final victory over death. The Gnostic contempt for the moral law, as of no relevance or importance to the truly spiritual, led either to extreme asceticism or extreme licence, for, since the body was evil, it did not matter if it was mortified or indulged. Christians might sympathize with the asceticism, which some of them practised themselves; but even this was a calling only for some, and common sense, recognizing the world as it is, saw that society needed a moral code if it was to continue to exist at all, and that for the ordinary man self-discipline and moderation in all things are kindred qualities. Worst of all, Gnosticism's inferior Demiurge meant the belittling of the role of God as Creator and removed him to a realm in which he dwelt apart from and unconcerned with men, a conception to appear again among the eighteenth-century Deists. But Christianity's glory was that it saw him as a loving Father with a personal concern for his creation and every living being in it. 'He that hath seen me hath seen the Father,' said Christ, bringing God into the room where he was speaking. The Gnostics put him beyond the galaxies.

CHAPTER 4

Montanism

Phrygia in Asia Minor, where Montanism developed, had been a centre of the orgiastic rites of Cybele and Dionysius and in more recent times featured a 'dancing Dervish' type of activity. It has been suggested that Christian heterodoxy derived from the Dionysian revels. But it is as unlikely that it was the descendant of the Greek paganism, as that it was the ancestor of the Mohammedan ecstasy – although it is interesting that the same type of worship is found in different religions succeeding one another in the same region. The most that can be said is that similar tendencies continue to show themselves down the ages, and Montanism can in any case be seen to be a logical development of certain strains which existed in the Christianity of Asia Minor.

Montanists, sometimes called Phrygians, took their name from Montanus, who started his movement about AD 156 at the city of Hierapolis. The movement was conservative, claiming to return, as so many sectaries since have done, to what were considered to be the practices and beliefs of the primitive Church, and also asserting that a new or at least renewed dispensation of the Spirit had arrived. At his baptism the Holy Spirit spoke through Montanus in tongues, thus reviving the charismatic emotionalism and practices of such churches as that of New Testament Corinth and reacting against the coldness and formalism which were allegedly creeping into contemporary Christianity. Reacting also against the Church's laxity, Montanus introduced extreme asceticism. Celibacy was demanded of all Christians, marriage being discountenanced and second marriages absolutely forbidden. Rigorous fasting, far more demanding than that of the ordinary Church, was enjoined. For example, a pre-Easter fast of two weeks as opposed to the normal one was required, and many new fasts were added, together with a novel type of abstinence called zerophagy, the eating of dry foods only.

A practice of severe penance was revived, and absolution for any mortal sin after baptism refused. Martyrdom was invited and Christians who took steps to avoid it were condemned. It was the ambition of Montanism to be the party of martyrs.

The sect preached certain themes which are to be found repeatedly in similar puritanical and charismatic movements down the centuries. The end of the world was imminent. Christ was to return in the immediate future, his advent to be associated with the resurrection and the Last Judgement. He would reign for a thousand years[1] in the New Jerusalem, which was to descend upon Phrygia (unlike the nineteenth-century Jezreelites of England who were to *ascend* from Gillingham in an edifice specially built for the purpose, which now serves the more mundane purpose of a terminus point for buses, not a launching-pad for saints). After that would come the end of history and the final accomplishment of God's will.

Montanus had as his principal lieutenants two prophetesses, Priscilla and Maximilla, and other women were included among the officials of his sect. Maximilla's tendency to prophesy disasters which did not happen would have proved embarrassing if failure in prophecy could be shown ever to have embarrassed a sect. To another sister Christ appeared in the form of a woman, thus anticipating by some sixteen hundred years that lady leader of the Shakers who prophesied that he would return at the Second Coming in female guise. Another Montanist woman saw a soul in bodily shape, 'not a vivid and empty illusion, but such as could be grasped by the hand, soft, transparent, and of an ethereal colour and in form resembling a human being', a description which suggests an ectoplasmic manifestation. The experience and phenomenon, if not imaginary, is of a kind claimed by some Spiritualists and suggests that Montanists accepted the idea of the corporeity of the soul.

A minor unorthodoxy of the Montanists was that they were, with certain other Christians who did not belong to their sect, Quartodecimans; that is, they held that Easter should be celebrated on the fourteenth day of the moon in the month of Nisan. The orthodox observed it on the Sunday after the fourteenth lunar day.

The history of Montanism can be briefly told. From its beginning in about 156 it seems to have caused little stir for about fifteen years, but from 171 onwards it was opposed by Apollinarius, Bishop of Hierapolis. Montanists were to be found in North Africa, especially at Carthage, Rome and Gaul. In 177 Irenaeus, who was later to write against the sect in his *Against Heresies*, and was then a priest at Lyons, accompanied the confessors who discussed Montanism with Eleutherius, Bishop of Rome. Although Montanus

[1] A belief known as Millennarianism, or Chiliasm, and held by some Jews as part of their Messianic hope as well as by a number of Christian sects.

preached no doctrine heretical in itself – his heresy lay, as it so often does, in a lack of balance deriving from over-emphasis of some parts of faith and practice at the expense of others – nor was accused by his enemies of doing so, he received a general condemnation from the first synod of bishops, probably of bishops only, held in Asia Minor, and his followers were expelled from the Church and debarred from communion.

However, neither the opposition of other Christians nor the persecution of the Montanists for their Messianic views by the Emperor Severus from the beginning of his reign in 193 checked the spread of the movement. During the last decade of the second century its growth led to new refutations, chiefly from Apollinarius, and its strength grew at Rome during the episcopate of Victor (189–99), although the Roman Christians for the most part continued to reject it. Two Roman schools of Montanism, under Eschines and Proclus, spread the sect's doctrines. Proclus, who taught from 199 to 217, was admired for his literary talent by the most famous Montanist, Tertullian.

Tertullian, born about 160, converted to Christianity in 195 and to Montanism in about 207, was one of the foremost Christian thinkers of his age. He was a practising lawyer with a far-ranging mind, well read in philosophy, history and Greek, with marked gifts as a controversialist. He was one of the first to state explicitly that the Holy Spirit was God equally with the other two Persons of the Trinity. Thinkers eminent in their own disciplines are sometimes, surprisingly, members of unorthodox minority sects, yet although Tertullian was clearly inclined to fanaticism, he had too good a mind to be attracted by mere extravagance. In the climate of the times there was clearly some need which was met by the stringent demands that Montanism made of its followers.

Tertullian's adherence to the sect strengthened it, but its success was due not to the influence of one man but to its organization. From its headquarters in Phrygia it sent out itinerant preachers, supported by the gifts of the faithful, and, as is shown by the success of Jehovah's witnesses today, where there is intensive propaganda by door-to-door visitors, conversions follow. The movement continued into the fourth century when Justinian took vigorous measures to suppress it, and survived until the fifth when it died from natural causes. Many of its tenets have, nevertheless, been revived in different sects down the ages to the present century.

The fault of Montanism in the eyes of the orthodox was that it exalted itself above the official hierarchy of the Church. It was accused of worse than that by its opponents, who almost certainly overstated their case, as is common in polemics. Montanus taught, they claimed, that the Holy Spirit in descending upon him and his followers, did so in a higher fashion than Pentecost, raising them not only above the Apostles but even above Christ himself. Montanist contempt for Christian officialdom is probable, for those puritan movements which have sprung up repeatedly down the centuries, and which have prided themselves on holding a pure, primitive 'full Gospel' Christianity, have *ipso facto* regarded their beliefs and fervour as superior to the cold and corrupted sacerdotalism of the established churches of their day. It is probably true that individual fanatical Montanists made extravagant claims for the Holy Spirit's work through them – after all, had not Christ himself said, 'He who has faith in me . . . will do greater things still [than I]' (St John's Gospel 14:12). But the movement is scarcely likely to have spread and survived for over two hundred years if it was as immoderate as its opponents claim. Nor was it alone in some of its beliefs. The immediate return of Christ seemed supported by ample authority in the New Testament. A bishop of Pontus, almost contemporary with Montanus, said that the Second Coming would happen within two years, convincing his followers to such an extent that they ceased to cultivate their fields and gave away their houses and goods, while another in Syria led his flock into the wilderness to meet Christ there.

Orthodox Christians of Montanus' day accepted the administrative regularity which was growing up under their bishops. There was also a feeling that inspiration through prophets had ceased with the apostolic age. They had had their part to play in the infancy of the Church, but now it had matured beyond them to a state more responsible if less exciting. Montanism was dangerous for the following reasons: in its over-emphasis on Adventism, which sapped missionary enterprise and far-sighted planning for the extension of Christ's kingdom; its charismatic gifts, which made the faithful neurotically excited and discontented with the quiet virtues of everyday Christian living; its lust for martyrdom which, carried to its logical conclusion, would have destroyed the Church; and in its insistence on universal Christian celibacy which would equally have wiped it out. The hindsight of history shows that Montanism was too much separated from the main development of the Church to be acceptable to the orthodox because it tried to keep alive an archaism which was outdated.

Adventism survived in other sects, as will be seen, and is very much alive today in a number of evangelical communions and bodies such as the Seventh Day Adventists and the Foursquare Gospel, one of whose four main emphases is a belief in Jesus as 'Coming King'. There is probably a greater interest in charismatic gifts today than there has ever been, glossolalia and spiritual healing being practised not only in the world-wide Pentecostalist churches but in many of the older established denominations. Emphasis on the guidance of the

Inner Light of the Spirit is to be found among the Plymouth Brethren and the Friends. Puritanism in the two senses of a more rigorous morality (no drinking, no smoking, no 'worldly' amusements, strict sexual standards, in some cases refusal to belong to 'worldly' associations such as political parties and trade unions) and acceptance of a more primitive, purer, 'full Gospel' which 'gets back to the Bible' and what is thought to be the original unadulterated teaching of Christ, allegedly corrupted in the main line denominations by sacerdotalism, is a recurring theme in Christian sectarianism. Only universal Christian celibacy and the ambition for martyrdom of the Montanists have completely disappeared. Their puritanical spirit has always remained alive.

Both orthodox organization and heterodox enthusiasm are necessary for the continued vitality of any creed. If Christianity were to develop into a completely unchallenged pattern of theology and organization, it would die of inanition. Orthodoxy needs to be disturbed if it is to live. However, if 'enthusiasm', in the eighteenth-century sense of the word, had its complete way, Christianity would fragmentate into chaos and spiritual anarchy, every believer a law unto himself. Heterodoxy needs to make its contribution, if only as an irritant, and then to sink into orthodoxy, ready for the next challenge. Sometimes it needs, as happened with Montanism, to raise a counter-heresy against it, to be examined and rejected by the faithful.[2] For believers in any creed both elements are essential if it is to live and develop.

---

[2] St John's Gospel was so much the favourite of the Montanists that some of their extreme opponents refused to give Christ the title of Word or Logos and became known as Alogi – a heresy so petty in both senses of the word that it is not so much as mentioned by many Church historians.

CHAPTER 5

Monarchianism

Youthful Christianity, daughter religion of strictly monotheistic Judaism, was early faced with the problem of three Persons in one God. The conception of the Trinity was not worked out in committee by a council of greybeards trying to make the new religion as difficult as possible by enunciating a series of statements such as are to be found in the so-called Athanasian creed, which seem at first sight not so much paradoxes as downright contradictions. It arose out of the Church's experiences of Christ and of the Holy Spirit, and the problems which believers had to face of the relationship of these two beings to God. Convinced that God was One, they had to reconcile to their conception of him the distinct functions of the creatorship of the Father, the redeeming and saving power of the Son, and the advocacy, intercession, comforting and revealing characteristics of the Spirit, which made the third Person much more than a mere emanation.

The first problems to present themselves were Christological rather than Trinitarian. They concerned the mystery of the Person of Christ. The records of his life showed that he was completely man, a being who had existed like any other during a span of years, an entity of flesh and blood who experienced joy and sorrow and all the other human emotions, and who was 'tempted in all points like as we are' (Hebrews 4:15). But his resurrection made him something more, and after it his disciples would all have echoed with sincerity Thomas's 'My Lord and my God', while Paul repeatedly spoke of him in language which could rightly be used only of the Deity. Jesus of Nazareth was fully and uniquely God, not a human being upon whom some power of God had been temporarily grafted nor, as is sometimes said, a son of God (even though *par excellence*) in the sense that all men are sons of God. A number of heresies arose out of Christian attempts to define the indefinable and to reconcile the relationship of the Godhead and Manhood in the Person of Christ.

Strict monotheists, as the orthodox early Judaeo-Christians were, faced with the challenge of the Person of Jesus Christ, had two choices. Either he was a man specially chosen by God (and there was an *a priori* argument in favour of this, in that the expected Messiah was in Jewish tradition to be a human king of David's line), in which case the Apostles, including Paul, had made exaggerated claims about him; or, as seemed confirmed by his resurrection and their experience of his salvation which they were convinced was an objective reality, not a subjective illusion, he was God, in spite of the difficulties that such a view entailed. Early heterodox individuals and sects, such as Cerinthus, Carpocrates and the Ebionites, took the former view, as did the Monarchians who are the subject of this chapter, though they sometimes disguised or modified the idea. The orthodox, faced with the wonder of the fact of Christ, did not, until forced by heresy to do so, attempt to define him so much as to give him titles taken from New Testament writings and full of significance. He was Kyrios, Lord (the Greek word used for the Hebrew Adonai, God himself). He was the Wisdom of God. He was the Son of God, but evidently not with the analogy of human fatherhood and sonship in mind, for he pre-existed his incarnation 'in the form of God' and as 'the express image of his [God's] person'. He was the Logos or Word of God, existing in the beginning 'with God' and 'was God'. Whatever the origin in philosophical thought of the conception of the Logos (and there are several possible), and although there are inconsistencies in his ideas, John stresses that the Word and God are the same and that the Word became flesh in Jesus of Nazareth. In his relationship to men Christ was Saviour, reconciling them to God by cleansing them from sin and opening the way for them to everlasting life; both eternal Priest unceasingly offering himself, the eternal sacrifice; King; Alpha, the Beginning (God created all things through him) and Omega, the end (God will sum up all things in him, whether in heaven or on earth).

Irenaeus, Bishop of Lyons from 177 and a spiritual grandson of the Apostles in that he had been taught by Polycarp, Bishop of Smyrna, who had been familiar with John and others who had known Jesus, has been called the first systematic theologian. He made an early statement of the orthodox Christological position. The Logos, he taught, was the Son of God, the Mind of God, God the Father himself incarnate in Jesus Christ. But Jesus was fully man too, who at every step of his life perfectly fulfilled what God had intended man to be and, as man's representative, won for him the right to be recognized by God as having met the divine demands. Yet in Jesus God himself suffered for men.

Irenaeus successfully walked the spiritual tightrope between tritheism and unitarianism, but a very slight over-emphasis on one side led to the heresy known, among other names, as Monarchianism (Irenaeus had himself written a tract against the Gnostics which he entitled *On the Monarchy* [sole rule] *of God*). The heresy took two main forms, Dynamic and Modalistic. The former conceived of Jesus as an ordinary man, born of the Virgin Mary, in whom there existed an impersonal power (Greek, *dynamis* = power) issuing from God. Since Jesus did not, according to this belief, derive any personality from God, it preserved the unity of God. Some Dynamic Monarchians were called Adoptionists because they taught that the *dynamis* descended upon Christ at his baptism or after his resurrection.

Modalists, sometimes called Patripassians because they maintained that God the Father suffered on the cross, and sometimes Sabellians or Noetists, held that the three Persons of the Trinity were three modes, conditions, titles or aspects of God, not Persons. They used the word *prosopon*, translated by the Latin *persona*, in its literal meaning of an actor's mask, with which performers in the contemporary theatre indicated and changed their characters. God could manifest himself as Christ or as the Holy Spirit and, when the part was played, the character would disappear until or unless required again.

As the years of controversy went by Modalism expressed itself more subtly. God in his own nature was one Person only. In his work as Creator he took the name of the Word who is God manifested in creation. The Trinity is not the three Persons of what came to be the orthodox Trinitarian belief, but relations of God to mankind. Thus, he revealed himself as Father when he acted as Creator in the beginning. As the incarnate Redeemer of the New Testament he reveals himself as the Son. He reveals himself as the Holy Spirit in his work as Paraclete (intercessor or advocate), Guide of the Church, Comforter and Sanctifier of souls. The work of the Creator and of the Son was regarded as having been completed, and when the mission of the Spirit is ended (presumably when all the faithful have been harvested at the end of time), God will put away his three actor's masks for good and resume the single, simple, undifferentiated being that he fundamentally is.

Dynamic Monarchianism was first in the field in the person of Theodotus or Theodorus, a Byzantine tanner, who said that Christ was a mere man. Although excommunicated by Victor, Bishop of Rome, about 198, his doctrine was developed by a disciple, Artemon, whose variety of Adoptionism was said to have influenced Paul of Samosata. He was followed by another Theodorus, a Roman banker, the two Theodoruses being intellectuals and called by some authorities the first rationalists. Though their guns were later spiked, this early exchange of shots between the Monarchians and orthodox proved but a skirmish; considerable battles were yet to be joined.

Praxeas of Asia Minor and Noetus, Bishop of Smyrna, were alleged by their contemporaries to be Dynamic Monarchians, and the latter gave one name, Noeticism, to the heresy. As so often, their teachings have mainly to be deduced from the writings of their opponents. They believed that God the Father, the Supreme Being who created the universe, himself took flesh of Mary, becoming the Son, Jesus. In Christ the Son was the Manhood, the Father the Godhead. The Father, crucified and killed, raised himself from death. Some Modalists moved from so stark a position to a modification – the Son in the flesh suffered and the Father and Spirit 'compassionated' with him.

It was Tertullian the Montanist who attributed Monarchianism to Praxeas, and he is suspected of having done this to discredit one who was an opponent of Montanism and had been sent to Rome to expose its shortcomings. Noetus, more certainly heterodox, was excluded from the church at Smyrna, but his disciple Epigonus was received more sympathetically on coming to Rome by her bishops, Victor and Zephyrinus, because he, too, was determinedly hostile to Montanism. His views, more philosophically expressed than the popular Monarchianism of Noetus, in stressing the Divine subsistence, denied the Son his proper place in the Godhead, and were handed on to Cleomenes, who in turn taught Sabellius, a Cyrenaen from Pentapolis. Sabellius, a Modalist, was so prominent in the history of the heresy, that he gave it one of its names, Sabellianism. He taught that the three Persons are three modes of God in the same sense that the sun is bright, hot and round.

Sabellianism came to Rome in which, as the capital of the Empire, every intellectual ferment seemed eventually to bubble, and appears to have been expressed subtly enough to deceive Pope Zephyrinus (198–217) and, at least temporarily, his successor, Callistus (217–22). Neither bishop was a theologian and both welcomed support from the Monarchians in their battles against other heresies. They were both warned of their error by a Roman theologian, Hippolytus, who accused Zephyrinus of having been bribed to favour Cleomenes' teaching and to have been himself a Monarchian, and Callistus of being a Modalist. Hippolytus' doctrine was that the one God had 'uttered' the Logos from himself, the same Logos who was in him invisibly, and had conferred on him his own substance with a view to creation. So the Logos had a subsistence distinct from the Father's but acquired by a free act of God. Origen, the great Greek father, held a similar doctrine, insisting on the inferiority of the Logos to the Father, later considered as much a heresy as Sabellianism itself.

Although the charges against the two popes rest on the assertions of Hippolytus, who was of that witch-finding temper which sees heretics under every bed, and of Tertullian, who had his Montanist axe to grind, Callistus does seem to have professed a modified Modalism. He stated that the Father and Son were the same and that the Spirit which became incarnate in the Virgin is one and the same as the Father. He denied that the Father suffered, but asserted that he suffered along with the Son. Callistus differed sufficiently from Sabellius, however, eventually to excommunicate him, and was promptly accused by Hippolytus of having done so as a trick. Hippolytus was not alone in making accusations – Callistus counter-charged him with believing in two gods. Orthodox Trinitarians were sometimes accused by their opponents of believing in three.

In spite of their excommunication, the Roman Monarchians survived and tried to set up their own church and bishop. Sabellius himself, whose views grew increasingly heterodox, returned to his own country and founded a school there. By 257, after his death, his doctrines were flourishing in Cyrenaica and dividing the Christians there, some bishops becoming Sabellian. They and the orthodox both applied to Dionysius, Bishop of Alexandria and a disciple of Origen, and he wrote letters in reply explaining in detail the distinction between the Father and the Son which had been confused by the Sabellians. The Sabellians of Cyrenaica then appealed to another Dionysius, Bishop of Rome, a clever move because the Roman bishops had an inclination towards Monarchianism. They criticized Dionysius of Alexandria on the grounds that he estranged the Son from the Father, asserting that the former did not exist before being engendered. There was, therefore, in his alleged view, a time when the Son had not existed. He was not eternal, but only a creature produced by God.

The Bishop of Alexandria denied that he had taught that Christ was not consubstantial with God. Dionysius of Rome convoked a synod which once more condemned Sabellianism. He wrote letters to the Cyrenaens instructing them as to how to refute the heresy, and a personal epistle to his namesake, who replied to it in a 'Refutation and Apology'. In this he said that he held basically the same position as Rome, but reserved the right to use his own vocabulary and express his own viewpoint. The two bishops agreed in their condemnation of certain Monarchian and Subordinationist errors (Subordinationism is any doctrine which subordinates one Person of the Trinity to the others, usually the Son to the Father), but the differences in Trinitarian theology between Rome and Alexandria were more pronounced than their agreement.

Modalistic Monarchianism had no sooner been declared heretical in its form of Sabellianism than the most notorious advocate of the

Dynamic form of the heterodoxy appeared in the shape of Paul of Samosata, Bishop of Antioch, 260–72. He was a typical easterner, unpopular in Hellenistic circles, which disliked his manner of life, his innovations and his theology. He stressed the unity of God and the humanity of Christ. Jesus was a man, sinless since his birth, when the Word and Christ were miraculously conjoined, the Word dwelling in him as in no other. Wisdom, a quality also of God, was found uniquely in Christ as in a temple. The Holy Spirit dwelt in Jesus who was united with God in will. By his struggles and sufferings he overcame the sin of Adam and grew in intimacy with God. No detailed theology of the generation of the Word existed in Paul's scheme, and this laid him open to charges of Modalism and Adoptionism.

A synod was convoked at Antioch in 264 to consider Paul's beliefs. Before its convening, Lucian, a presbyter of Antioch, famous as the tutor of Arius, begetter of the notorious heresy, and of his friend, Bishop Eusebius of Nicomedia, had attacked Paul's Monarchianism, but seems to have gone too far in the other direction. His history is not clear; but apparently he was denounced to Rome (he was later accused of fathering Arianism through his pupil) and condemned by Paul, who tried to get his condemnation confirmed by the Roman see. Lucian was excluded from the council but his absence was more than compensated for by a large number of Origenists who turned the tables on Paul. Synodical meetings were held in 264 and 268 and Paul was condemned, his heresy fully exposed by Malchion, another priest of Antioch. The synod appealed to the Emperor to support its condemnation, for the first time setting the dangerous precedent of appealing to the civil power. In spite of his condemnation, Paul, supported by Queen Zenobia of Palmyra, held on to his see until 272 when the Emperor Aurelian defeated Zenobia, after which he vanished from the stage.

The synod's findings rejected the use of the word *homoousion* (being of one essence, *consubstantialis*) as applied to the Trinity, a fact which caused difficulties half a century later when the Council of Nicaea wished to introduce it into the creed formulated there. Furthermore, Malchion and the synodal fathers, wishing to show that Christ was really God, compared his union with his human nature to the union between a soul and a body. The Word had the same place in Christ as the soul has in us, and so the Word, not a human soul, was united to Christ's body. This view was later rejected by orthodoxy, for it made Christ into a being different from ordinary humankind; and if he is not a complete human being he cannot, it was argued, be the representative of humanity, the 'second Adam who to the fight and to the rescue came'.

In spite of its defeats by the orthodox, Monarchianism survived in

Asia Minor, Libya and especially in Egypt for many years. The great Augustine of Hippo himself had an inclination towards Modalistic Monarchianism. The heterodoxy fathered the next, and more serious heresy of Arianism, which was to divide the Church in and after the early part of the third century and was a logical result of the Monarchian type of thinking. And many a Christian today is an unwitting Modalist in that he separates quite clearly in his thought (encouraged in this by much Church art and symbolism) God the Father as a kind of William Blake figure 'up there', Jesus the Son as a first-century Palestinian in burnous or caftan, and the Holy Spirit as a nebulous 'it' manifesting 'itself' in odd bursts of mystical or charismatic activity that have little to do with everyday living.

CHAPTER 6

Arianism

Origen who, like St Augustine of Hippo after him, was of such breadth of thought that orthodox and heretic alike claimed him as their authority, seemed to teach two doctrines of Christ. These were not irreconcilable with each other, though they helped to support both the orthodox and the heretical viewpoints. On the one hand, Origen taught that Jesus Christ was coeternal with God the Father and existed before all worlds, for since the Father is always Father, there must always have been a Son. On the other hand, since the Son is the image of the Father, he is dependent upon the Father and secondary and subordinate to him. A conception such as this last seemed to suggest that Christ was a creature.

In his opposition to the Sabellianism which he found in his diocese, Origen's pupil, Dionysius, Bishop of Alexandria, used words which implied that the Father had created the Son and that there had been a time when the Son did not exist. Lucian of Antioch, contemporary with Origen, seems to have handed on a similar view, and his pupil Arius, a priest of Alexandria, raised a storm that was to shake the Christian Church for seventy years and mutter on for centuries longer.

Arius, tall, handsome, socially attractive, with a melancholy, thoughtful face and a sweet, impressive voice which increased his eloquence as a preacher and his power as a conversationalist, seems to have been spoiled by arrogance. He made a violent protest against what he alleged to be the Sabellianism of his bishop, Alexander, who, he said, taught that 'God is always, the Son is always' and that the Son 'is the unbegotten begotten', opposing him with his own view that the Son, though the eldest and highest of creatures, had a beginning, whereas God had none. In the subsequent controversy Alexander asserted that the essence of Sonship was the receiving from a parent his own nature; therefore, as the Father is

45

eternal and unchangeable, so must the Son be. Arius retorted that the Father alone was true God, inaccessible and unique in being *arkhé*, the principle of all beings, the Logos being neither coeternal with him, nor uncreated, because he received life and being from the Father: 'If the Son is a true Son, then the Father must have existed before the Son; therefore there was a time when the Son did not exist; therefore he was created or made.' God's purpose in creating the Son was that he might be his intermediary in the work of creation. Arius was accused, probably falsely, of saying that there was a time when the Word did not exist. If he did say anything like this, he was thinking not in terms of time but of expressing the unique existence of God, for he contended that the generation of the Word took place 'before . . . time' and that the Word himself was also unique in perfection and divinity – but was, nevertheless, a creature. It was true that Christ was God, because the Father willed him to be so, but he was not God necessarily and essentially. It would have been possible, Arius contended further, for God the Son to have committed sin.

The argument became bitter and was fought by the laity as well as the clergy. Every Christian shopkeeper became a theologian and, later, Gregory of Nyssa described the money-changer who, when asked the exchange rate, replied with a dissertation on the engendered and non-engendered, the baker who informed his customer that the Father was greater than the Son, and the bath-attendant who told the would-be bather that the Son came from nothingness. Arius cleverly used popular songs and hymns sung by sailors and travellers to spread his doctrines, anticipating General Booth and the Salvation Army by nearly sixteen hundred years. When Alexander turned on him, he learned to moderate his heresy, posing as a persecuted, misunderstood and innocent believer.

Alexander called together a synod of nearly a hundred bishops from Egypt and Libya which excommunicated Arius and the thirteen who supported him at the conference. But Arius had already sought support in Palestine and Asia Minor and was given asylum by Eusebius, Bishop of Nicomedia, also a former pupil of Lucian of Antioch. Local synods in Bithynia and Palestine reversed the Alexandrian decision and rehabilitated Arius.

The rival pronouncements of the synods exploded the Christian Church into bitter controversy and quarrels, Jerusalem against Caesarea, Phoenician and Cilician Arians opposed by Tripolitanians and Antiochenes, and Bithynia hostile to Galatia. Alexander of Alexandria scattered letters defending his position to bishops throughout the Greek countries and to Sylvester, Bishop of Rome. The Emperor Constantine, who had after considerable struggles united the Empire under his rule and had recently come out strongly on the side of the Christians, expecting the Church to help preserve the unity of the State, wrote to Alexander and Arius through his adviser in Church matters, Hosius, Bishop of Cordova, telling them to reconcile their differences over what seemed to him a detail of no importance. The letter failed; and Constantine called together the first General or Ecumenical Council of the whole Church, which opened at Nicaea on 20 May 325.

About three hundred bishops, accompanied by hundreds of lesser clergy and laymen, attended. The majority had taken no side when the conference began, but violent controversy arose as soon as the small party of radical Arians, led by Eusebius of Nicomedia, stated their position. To the right of them theologically, Eusebius of Caesarea led those whose fear of Sabellianism drove them into a moderate Subordinationism and an inclination to support Arius. Opposed was Alexander of Alexandria, accompanied by a young priest called Athanasius (299–373) who was to play a major part in the eventual victory of orthodoxy and was to succeed his master as bishop (consecrated in 328 after Alexander's death in 326). To the extreme right was a minority of violently anti-Arian theologians, some of whose views undoubtedly spilled over into Modalistic Monarchianism, the error of Sabellius. Their leaders were Marcellus, Bishop of Ancyra, and Eustathius, Patriarch of Antioch.

Eusebius of Caesarea proposed that the creed used to prepare catachumens for baptism in his own see, which had been handed down to him by his predecessors, might be used as a basis for agreement. His suggestion was given a general welcome, and the Caesarian formula became the foundation of the creed accepted by the synod – not the Nicene Creed, whose present form, regarded as authoritative by the Roman, Orthodox, Anglican and some other churches, dates from 381, the year of the Second Ecumenical Council, in Constantinople. Below are quoted the Caesarian and Nicaean Creeds, ordinary type being used for expressions in them which are identical, italic type where the wording is different:

CAESARAEN	NICAEAN
We believe in one God,	We believe in one God,
the Father Almighty,	the Father Almighty,
maker of all things, visible and invisible,	maker of all things, visible and invisible,
and in one Lord, Jesus Christ,	and in one Lord, Jesus Christ,
the Word [Logos] *of God,*	*the Son of God,*
	the only-begotten of the Father,
	that is, of the substance of the Father,
God from God,	God from God,
light from light,	light from light,

life from life,
the only-begotten Son,
first-born of all creatures,

begotten of the Father before all
ages,
by whom also all things were made;

who for our salvation was made flesh
and dwelt among men,
and who suffered and
rose again on the third day,
and ascended to the Father
and shall come again in glory
to judge the living and the dead.
We believe also in one Holy Spirit.

true God from true God,
begotten, not made,

of one substance [homoousion] *with*
the Father,

through whom all things were made,
those things that are in heaven and
those things that are on earth,

who for us men and for our salvation
came down and was made man,
suffered,
rose again on the third day,
ascended into the heavens
and will come
to judge the living and the dead.

The changes were anti-Arian, but the followers of the heresy could accept all except possibly one by giving them different meanings. 'Only-begotten' for the orthodox meant 'begotten in a way different from men who can become sons of God by receiving "the spirit of adoption"'; for the Arian it meant 'the only one directly created'. 'Of the substance of the Father' and 'true God from true God', though going far towards pinning the heterodox to orthodoxy, could be interpreted as 'made of the substance and into true God by God'. 'Came down' and 'ascended into the heavens' implied to the orthodox that Christ was neither different from nor subordinate to God; and 'was made man' suggested that Jesus was true man as well as true God; but the Arians could cheerfully accept the three phrases and interpret them to fit their views.

The storm centre of the controversy was the word *homoousion*. It was disliked by some of the orthodox as well as the Arians because it was not to be found in Scripture and because it smacked of materialism (it was used, for example, to describe two coins made of the same metal) and Sabellianism. Indeed, the use of a non-scriptural word in a Church formula for the first time was of great significance. It meant that from 325 onwards the orthodox Church could enunciate dogmas which did not have the authority of Scripture and led to what was later to prove one of the great areas of division between the Catholic and Protestant wings of the Church. For the former emphasized the validity of tradition that was true to what was regarded as the spirit, though not the letter, of Scripture, and the latter insisted that the only admissible beliefs and practices were those that could be substantiated, chapter and verse, by the Bible.

Eusebius of Caesarea and other bishops suggested as a compromise *homoiusion*, 'of like substance', and thus took up what has been called a semi-Arian position. The proposal was a clever one because the word is ambiguous. It can mean 'exactly like' – that is, identical with (the orthodox belief), or 'resembling', a meaning which could be supported both by the Arians and by those who denied the consubstantiality of the Father and Son but would not allow that the Son was created, believing him to be born of the Father and yet not God. Many of the timorous orthodox were willing to accept the compromise, but Athanasius, seeing clearly that there could be no middle term between 'God' and 'not-God' swung a considerable majority of the council to reject both Arianism and semi-Arianism. Although the struggle led to the gibe that the Church was convulsed by a diphthong, the choice of words was a vital one for the whole future of Christian thought.

The Council reinforced the creed and the use of *homoousion* by an-athematizing any who said that there was a time when the Son was not; that he was created from nothing; that he did not exist before he was begotten; that he was of an essence or substance other than that of the Father; or that he was mutable or susceptible to change. All but two bishops accepted the creed and anathemas and these, with Arius, were exiled, together with, three months later, Eusebius of Nicomedia and two others who applied to withdraw their signatures.

But what seemed a victory proved to be no more than the joining of battle. Many of the eastern bishops were unhappy about the word *homoousion* and alarmed by Sabellianism which seemed to them a far more serious threat than Arianism. In 327 Arius gave the Emperor a confession of faith which, skating over the real issues, was accepted as satisfactory, and he was reinstated. The following year Eusebius of Nicomedia was not only recalled from exile but became Constantine's trusted adviser. The Emperor completely reversed his position. In 330 Eustathius of Antioch, justly accused of Monarchianism, was deposed and exiled. Eusebius of Caesarea, who in modern parlance would be termed a moderate, led a combined anti-Sabellian front but, accused among other things of adultery on the evidence of a prostitute, was replaced as leader by Eusebius of Nicomedia when he returned from exile. From 326 onwards a regular campaign against Nicene bishops was conducted, some dozen being deposed. The culmination came in 335 when Athanasius of Alexandria and Marcellus of Ancyra were removed from office and driven from their sees.

Arius died in the same year and, when Constantine followed him two years later, a kind of peace was patched up. The Empire was divided between the latter's three sons, Constans ruling the Nicene west, Constantine II, mainly under Arian influence, the east, and

Constantius becoming Emperor of Gaul. The exiled bishops, including Athanasius, were allowed to return to their sees. But the peace proved to be no more than a modern, Vietnam-type cease-fire. In 339 the Arian cause was strengthened by the accession of Eusebius of Nicomedia to the patriarchal throne of Constantinople, and a synod at Antioch over which he had great influence expelled Athanasius a second time from Alexandria. The hero of Nicene orthodoxy took refuge in Rome where he met his ally, Marcellus of Ancyra, and received the support of Pope Julius I. Eusebius wrote to Julius asking him to call a synod and judge the case himself, but when Julius did this at Rome, 340–1, the eastern bishops failed to attend. Athanasius and Marcellus were exonerated and in 341 Eusebius died.

Constantine II had died the year before, whereupon Constans continued as Emperor of the Nicene west and Constantius of the anti-Nicene east. During the next ten years the anti-Nicene party tried to bridge the gap between themselves and their opponents with a series of seven formulae to replace the Nicaean Creed and stabilize doctrine. The difficulties proved too great. In these creeds Arianism was avoided, the Nicene position was not opposed and Sabellianism was attacked, but the relationship between God and the Logos could not be satisfactorily defined. Arian formulae, probably more extreme than Arius had ever held, were condemned and exaggerations of the Nicene position were also attacked.

The Nicenes were not inactive. In 343 Hosius of Cordova presided over a Council of Sardica (Sophia) to examine once more the views of Athanasius and Marcellus. The eastern bishops withdrew on the pretext that the two defendants had been given seats in the assembly, but more probably because they saw themselves outnumbered. Athanasius was declared innocent, Marcellus orthodox, and Arian views were once again condemned. A significant by-product of the council was the decision that in future a deposed bishop might appeal to Rome, a tacit recognition of the Pope's emerging position as senior bishop of the Christian Church. In 346 Athanasius returned once more to Alexandria.

In 350 an extreme form of Arianism was put forward by Aetius, a deacon of Antioch, and his disciple Eunomius. They taught that the Son was *anomoios* – that is, totally different from the Father, fallible and capable of sin. So radical a doctrine forced the formation of a third party consisting of several groups – a right wing very close to the Nicenes led by Basil of Ancyra, who had replaced Marcellus in about 335, which accepted *homoiousios*, and others, varying in degrees of Subordinationism, known collectively as Homoeans because they adopted the formula that the Son is like (*homoios*) the Father. They were led by Acacius, a pupil and successor of Eusebius of Caesarea.

The dangers of the neo-Arian Anomoeism underlined the dangers of Arianism itself; but there still remained thirty years of struggle.

From 351 onwards Ursacius or Ursatius of Singidunum and Valens of Mursa, Subordinationist heretics, influenced Constantius' thought, and when Constantius became sole ruler of the Empire in 353, following the defeat of Magnentius, his brother's murderer and supplanter, anti-Nicene views were imposed upon all his domains. During the next few years councils at Arles, Milan and Béziers were all anti-Nicene, and opposing bishops, including the aged Hosius and Athanasius, were once again exiled (356). In 357 a council at Sirmium forbade the use of *ousia*, *homoousia* or *homoiousia* as non-scriptural, and adopted a Subordinationist formula. Its members forced Hosius, now a centenarian, to attend against his will and to sign after being beaten and tortured. For the next few years obedient councils spawned yet more formulae, including the use of the vague *homoios*, and the quarrels between Arians and Nicenes were exacerbated by their political outlooks, the former wanting the Church to submit to the State, the latter supporting the Church's autonomy. Matters were complicated by the fact that the Emperor hesitated to choose between the many contending factions.

There were occasional gleams of hope and light for the orthodox. In 358 Basil of Ancyra was victorious over Anomoeism at another Sirmium council and there was a shift towards the Nicene position. Marius Victorinus, a Roman philosopher converted to Christianity in his maturity, pointed out that the idea of *homoiousios* was self-contradictory in theological terms (even in materialistic terms, two coins made out of the same metal cannot be made of the same *piece* of metal). Yet another Sirmium council in 359 moved closer to the Nicene position. A western council at Rimini and an eastern at Seleucia in Isauria clashed, showing that the spirit of fight still remained in the Nicene camp. Hope for the Nicenes seemed to die when Constantius at last made up his mind and on New Year's Day, 360, decided for the Homoeism of Acacius as the official faith of the Empire, thus supporting historic Arianism against Catholic orthodoxy and the Nicaean Creed.

In 361, however, Constantius died. Julian the Apostate succeeded him, his cunning general amnesty to the Christians enabling heretics like the Anomoians as well as the orthodox to recover strength, and Athanasius returned to Alexandria only to be sent once more on his travels within the same year. If Julian consciously intended to 'divide and rule' his Christian subjects, the success of his policy is proved by the fact that in 362 there were five mutually hostile Christian communities in Antioch, each with its own bishop. A further complication was added to the theological tangle by the emergence of heresies concerning the Holy Spirit, for if the Son were fully divine it followed, at least in orthodox thinking, that the Spirit was divine also. The Pneumatomachian heresy denied this and was fought successfully by Basil of Caesarea, but not before it had become a cause of strife among the Homoiousians.

Before his fourth exile in 362 Athanasius held a synod at Alexandria to try to patch up his differences with the Homoiousian Meletians, followers of Bishop Meletus who, like the Donatists, had adopted a rigorous attitude to those Christians who had denied the faith in the persecutions of the first decades of the century and later repented and sought readmission to the Church. A formula was accepted that the Godhead contained one *ousia* and three *hypostases*, the latter word meaning very much the same as the former; but in Nicene thought *ousia* corresponded to the Latin *substantia* (substance) and *hypostasis* to *persona* (person). A specific doctrine of the Spirit was also agreed, that he was not a creature and was inseparable from the Father and the Son.

Hope for the Church's peace was increased when Julian died in 363 and Athanasius returned once more to Alexandria. Within months the new emperor, Jovian, died, succeeded by Valentinus I (364–75), a peaceful, tolerant Nicene Christian, who introduced a time of reconstruction and stabilization in that part of his realm over which he retained control. Unfortunately he took as associate his brother Valens (364–78) who adopted the Homoian Arianism as defined in 360 and attacked Anomoians, Homoiousians and Nicenes with equal energy. Athanasius was exiled for the fifth time. But dismal as the outlook must have seemed to the orthodox at the time, the next fifteen years were to see their triumph. The divisions within the Arian ranks were deep. The moderates among them disliked and feared the radical Anomoians. The middle Homoians were too vague for their views ever to be capable of winning over the whole Church. The semi-Arians on the right were reluctant to adopt the *homoousios* of the Nicenes because of its Sabellian undertones which damaged the individuality of the Son and made the incarnation unreal, with the result that men were unable to share in the nature of God without being absorbed into him and losing their individual identities. They were willing to use *homoiousios*. In spite of their great differences, however, there were tentative approaches by the Nicenes to the Homoiousians, though it was from the east that the eventual victory came.

There, three great allies won over the eastern bishops to the cause of orthodoxy. These were Basil (329–79), appointed Bishop of Caesarea in Cappadocia in 370, Gregory of Nyssa (335–95), his brother, and Gregory Nazianzus (329–91). The first and last of the trio were Origenists and came from their retreats in monasteries to fight Arianism which, they saw, could permanently disrupt the

Church. As Origenists they successfully fought the semi-Arians, who professed to follow Origen themselves. The tactics they used were to found monasteries as centres of propaganda, some of which included complexes of hospitals, schools and lodging-houses. They were at first suspected in the west of Arianism, and problems were created by the differences in tradition and intellectual climate, besides the handicap imposed by language; for Greek was fast becoming the monopoly of the east and Latin of the west, whereas, in the first century, Greek had been in common use throughout the Empire.

They were, however, loyal to the Nicene conceptions of *ousia* and *homoousios*, overcoming suspicions of Sabellianism from the eastern bishops by coming very close to the formula which Athanasius had used at the Synod of Alexandria in 362. They began with the distinctions in the Godhead (the Nicenes started from the one Substance). In God, they said, there is one *ousia* and three *hypostases* (they also used an alternative word, *prosopon*, person), the Father, Son and Holy Spirit. They stated further that there were not three gods but one, to be found equally and identically in the Father, Son and Holy Spirit. They thus avoided the charges of being Arians and tritheists and the Latins, for their part, by their use of one *substantia* and three *personae* as equivalents of the Greek terms, escaped the charges of Sabellianism so often made against them by eastern churchmen in the past. The Cappadocians, as the three were named, were accused of being too Neoplatonically philosophical and producing a vague, colourless abstraction far divorced from the warmth of human spiritual experience. But they broke the deadlock.

In the sixties the orthodox Nicenes must have felt that their struggles were unavailing, their labour vain, their enemies fainting not nor failing and 'as things have been they remain'. But the last phase of the Arian contention began in 370, when Basil became Bishop of Caesarea in Cappadocia. In the following year he began negotiating with Athanasius and later with Pope Damasus; and although the goal of reunion had not been attained when he died in 379, almost at once the breakthrough came. In the same year a council at Antioch of 153 eastern bishops fell into line with the western Church. The movement towards ending the schism was helped by the death of Valens in the Battle of Adrianople against the Goths, for he was succeeded by Theodosius, a convinced and energetic Nicene Christian. He at once set about imposing Catholic orthodoxy on his empire, ordering all his subjects to follow the faith in 'the deity of the Father and the Son and the Holy Spirit of equal majesty in a Holy Trinity'. Possibly his most successful step in carrying out his policy was to replace the Arian bishop of Constantinople by Gregory Nazianzus; for Gregory had already revolutionized the eastern capital, where all the churches were in

Arian hands, by the eloquence of his preaching, and it was fitting that he should preside over the Second Ecumenical Council which met at Constantinople. It is true that he resigned the see and the council chairmanship in a very short time, for he was too sensitive to the intrigues which centred on the episcopal throne. But he saw the council confirm Nicene orthodoxy and anathematize those who would not accept it, the Anomoians, Arians and semi-Arians being specifically named. And no doubt, in the monastery to which he retired, he knew of the imperial edicts of 383 and 384 which furthered the Nicene cause, followed by a third in 391, the year of his death.

Constantinople produced what is commonly, though mistakenly, called the Nicene Creed, based on a fourth-century Jerusalem formula influenced by Nicene thought. The major change from the creed of Nicaea were additions at the end: 'I believe in the Holy Ghost, the Lord, the Giver of Life, who proceedeth from the Father (and the Son [a later western addition]), who with the Father and the Son together is worshipped and glorified, who spake by the prophets. And I believe one Catholic and Apostolic Church. I acknowledge one baptism for the remission of sins. And I look for the resurrection of the dead and the life of the world to come.' The purpose of the addition was to make clear the complete equality of the Holy Spirit with the other two Persons in the Godhead and thus to combat heresies such as that called Macedonianism after its inventor, Macedonius, which denied the essential Godhead of the Spirit. Arianism denied the divinity of the Spirit, and Macedonius went further in asserting that the Spirit was 'a minister and servant' on a level with the angels.

Theodosius had established orthodoxy in the eastern empire. In the West he supported the successors of Valentinus against various usurpers and reconquered their domains for them and ultimately for himself. In the fight for orthodoxy in the West he had a notable ally in Ambrose, Bishop of Milan, who resisted the Arian Queen Empress Justina's request for a church in the city where she might worship according to Arian rules. When she tried to take the church by force, he organized a 'sit-in' of his congregation, keeping the basilica permanently occupied. Theodosius repealed measures of toleration granted by Valentinus II, Justina's young son, to the Arians, and also crushed the last remains of paganism. By 395, the end of Theodosius' reign, Nicene orthodoxy was the official religion of the whole Roman world.

Arianism survived for almost four hundred years among the peoples constantly threatening the Empire from the north. The Goths were mostly Arian, some won over by the heresy of Audius, a bishop of great purity of life if heterodoxy of doctrine, most by that of Ulfilas or Wulfilas (c. 311–80), a Goth himself and mildly Arian in

doctrine. When the Goths settled in the Empire their Arianism
was gradually assimilated to the Catholicism of their neighbours, and
disappeared late in the sixth century. The Burgundians, originally a
Germanic people, part of which remained on the right bank of the
Rhine, were at first Catholic, but then became Arian, probably
through contact with the Arian Visigoths, and the Ostrogoths,
Lombards and Vandals took the heresy with them into Italy, Spain,
North Africa and Gaul. As late as the episcopacy of John Chrysostom
(c. 345-407) in Constantinople the Arians were strong enough to
chant antiphonally songs denouncing the Catholic views; and when
the Catholics retaliated, violent conflicts broke out between the
factions and several people were killed. But by the eighth century
Arianism had disappeared – except in the minds of myriads of
Christians sitting in the pews of all the established churches, to
whom the analogy of Father and Son has suggested and continues
to suggest a human relationship of time implied by the human
experience that children always come after their parents.

CHAPTER 7

Apollinarianism

The Council of Antioch of 264, which condemned Paul of Samosata, put forward a theory likening Christ's union with his human nature to that which exists between a soul and a body. The Logos or Word had the same place in Christ as the soul has in man; so, in the Incarnation, the Word, not a human soul, was united to Jesus's human body. This was the first statement of what came to be, a century later, the heresy of Apollinarianism.

The Church was concerned in the third and early fourth centuries with Trinitarian problems and did not turn its full attention to questions of Christology until after the defeat of the Arians. This is not to say that the problem of the relationship of the divine and human in Christ was not considered at all. Both orthodox and heretic had much to say; and there were two principal schools of thought, connected with Alexandria and Antioch. Alexandria stressed the divine element in Christ's nature, at times apparently to the belittling of the human. Antioch laid emphasis on the historical study of the Gospels and consequently on the human element in Jesus's being. There was here a tendency to regard the divine and human as so distinct that some Antiochenes seemed to take up the extreme position that in Jesus there were two separate beings.

Arianism had a Christology as heretical as its doctrine of the Trinity. Since Christ was the Word of God dwelling in human flesh, he must have shared the weakness of flesh and been capable of sin, and therefore he could not be God. The first Arians and the Anomoians had believed that the Divine Word was a vital principle normally represented by and analogous to the soul in man. They held that the Logos was therefore responsible for the weaknesses – hunger, thirst, fatigue, sorrow, fear of death – mentioned in the Gospel as features of Jesus's life. These proved that the Word did not share the unchangeability of God and was therefore inferior to him. Such a doctrine was anathema to the orthodox because not only did it attack Christ's Godhead but it gave him an incomplete and mutilated humanity, a body without a human soul or, at best, a soul deprived of reason. Far from Jesus being both God and man, he was neither one nor the other.

The Arian belief was a crude attempt to answer the question as to how that which came from God and that which is human were united in the Incarnate Word and made up the unique Lord Jesus Christ. Thought about the nature of human beings themselves was vague and variable, wavering between belief in a dichotomy (body and soul) and in a trichotomy (body, soul and spirit), and there was probably as much vagueness in interpreting these terms then as there is now.

Just under a century after the Council of Antioch, quarrels broke out from about 360 onwards, even within the ranks of the Nicenes, of whom Apollinarius, Bishop of Laodicea in Syria, was one. Almost before his heresy was uttered, the Synod of Alexandria (262) anticipated an argument constantly used against it later on, implying if not explicitly stating that only that can be saved in man which has been assumed by Christ. Apollinarius was neither fool nor knave, but a man almost driven into heresy by the theological controversies of his time. He was well educated, strictly Nicene in his Trinitarian theology, a faithful ally of Athanasius in all his vicissitudes, a champion of Christianity against Julian the Apostate, a famous exegetist and tutor of the great St Jerome, translator of the Vulgate. He had a doctrine of man and of God which made his heresy a logical inevitability. Each human being consisted of body, soul and spirit (mind or reason), the third distinguishing mankind from the lower animals. Human nature was temporal, corruptible, finite and imperfect, and men could not be free from sin because of the weakness and tyranny of the flesh. Man has free will, and his freedom implies at least the possibility of sin.

God's nature, on the other hand, was divine, eternal, unchangeable and perfect. The Logos was regarded as being entirely consubstantial with God, and the Son was also absolutely and truly God.

Apollinarius was faced with two problems: that already mentioned of the existence in Jesus's being of two natures, the divine and the human; and the chance that the human side of Jesus might sin, a possibility which would make man's salvation impossible. His first difficulty was caused partly by terminology for, identifying 'person' and 'nature' in his thought, it seemed to him that if Christ had an entire human nature including intelligence, and was at the same time God, then he must have within one body two complete and contending natures, that of God and that of man. This would make him neither God nor man but an 'other' being, a hybrid. He solved this problem by allowing to Christ a human body and soul (meaning by this the lower animal soul which governs the emotions, senses, instincts and reflexes of the body) but denying the existence in him of a human soul or spirit, that rational element of mind and will which governs and guides man's actions. Its place was taken by the divine Logos, guiding the flesh he had assumed (to be like mankind), and Apollinarius denied that this in any way assumed or co-operated with a human soul. He thus thought of Christ as God clothed in human flesh, with many of the attributes of men but the ego remaining absolutely divine. In this way he met his second difficulty, for, by safeguarding the completeness of Christ's divinity, he guaranteed his sinlessness, freeing him from the duality between flesh and spirit which is so painful to mankind. But he sacrificed the reality and dignity of his humanity. Apollinarius' refusal to divide and separate the two elements which were combined in the incarnation led him explicitly to profess not only the 'communication of idioms' but the holiness and adorable character of the Body of Christ, so making it something more than human.

There were several objections to Apollinarius' theory. The first was that God clothed in human flesh is no less a hybrid than God and man in one body, and no more typical and representative of ordinary humanity. Apollinarius himself unconsciously acknowledged this in his pseudo-Athanasian work *Ad Jovianum*, in which he wrote, 'Unique is the nature of the Divine Word which was made incarnate'. Second, Christ's humanity, not being the same as ours, was useless as a vehicle of salvation – the incarnation became meaningless. Third, the Godhead was made mutable, since it became capable of the successive acts of a created intelligence (this could be answered by saying that God's mutability was part of the 'self-emptying' process of which Paul speaks – he emptied himself of unchangeableness to fit the human condition). Fourth, Christ's prayers to his Father became a meaningless charade. Fifth, his obedience, the means by which he gained mankind's redemption and by the following of which men implement it for themselves, was equally meaningless, since only an independent rational will can submit and obey. Since Christ's will was the Father's, it could not be submitted to it and there was no possibility, as there is with men, that he could choose not to obey. The only argument which could be used on the side of Apollinarius' idea was that it rejected the conception that sinfulness is an essential part of human nature.

Apollinarius was followed by several groups preaching variations of his doctrine, some moderate, some extreme. There were those who taught that Christ had a human soul but not a rational one, the Word supplying its place; others that there was nothing human in Christ save his flesh; others that the Godhead itself was changed into literal flesh. A notorious extremist was Polemon who professed synousiasm – that is, the perfect consubstantiality of the Logos and of Christ's flesh made divine.

The orthodox replied that the whole man had fallen in Adam – body, sensitive powers, intellect and will. If only a part of man was assumed by Christ, only that part was healed. Ruin was brought on mankind by Adam's misuse of his free will, and this could be undone only by the victory over temptation and right use of the free will of the 'second Adam'. Unless Christ had a rational human soul, he was not capable of free will in a human sense at all.

The heresy did not succeed against orthodoxy for anything like the same length of time as Arianism, nor did it give a quarter of the trouble. In 374 Epiphanius of Salamis, whom circumstances forced into the role of heresy-hunting which, in other ages, would have made him a professional inquisitor, held an inquiry at Antioch where the facts of the heresy were made plain to him. Two years later, Vitalis, 'bishop' of one of the Christian communities in the same city, now reduced to four, proclaimed Apollinarianism against the other three bishops and foolishly attacked Pope Damasus, who condemned Apollinarius' errors and deposed their author. A series of edicts against the heresy was issued by synods at Rome (377), Alexandria (378), Antioch (379) and the Ecumenical Council of Constantinople (381), supported by imperial ordinances in 383/4 and 388 by Theodosius who brought in the force of secular law to help in repressing the heresy.

There was also much polemical writing against Apollinarianism. The same Cappadocian doctors who won the final battle against Arianism opposed it, recognizing that the doctrine destroyed the full humanity of Christ. Gregory Nazianzus reiterated the argument that only a Christ who had all the elements of human nature could redeem all of man, and that if every phase of man's nature were not redeemed, redemption in any real sense could not be a fact. He was supported by the Antiochene school of thought which maintained that in Jesus there existed complete both the divine and human natures and the Logos dwelt in him much as God dwells in a temple. God had dwelt in the prophets and lived in Christians now, but his relationship with Jesus was unique, for Jesus freely willed (as a man) what God willed, and in him the unity had become indissoluble.

The principal exponent of Antiochene Christology was Diodorus, Bishop of Tarsus (376– before 394), an erudite, prolific writer and courageous apologist, whom Julian the Apostate regarded as his most gifted opponent. An ascetic and inspirer of Antiochene exegetics, he upheld the doctrine of the total humanity which the Word assumed at the incarnation, drawing a sharp distinction between the Son of God in Jesus and the Son of Mary and, through her, the Son of

David. Diodorus sensed that distinction might be interpreted as separation and was quick to add, 'But there are not two Sons', without being able to explain the unity satisfactorily.

Just how difficult it was to avoid heresy in Christology is shown by the career of Theodore, Bishop of Mopsuestia (392–428), Diodorus' Christological successor. Thoroughly respected and regarded as blamelessly orthodox during his life, he was posthumously held responsible for the heresies of his pupil Nestorius and anathematized 125 years after his death (553). Like Diodorus he insisted on the distinction of the two natures, human and divine, of the Incarnate Word, but was faced with the problem of how two components can make one Person – two *quids* form a *quis*. Careful not to speak of two Lords or two Sons, he used the term 'conjunction' to express the unity. The word had limitations, suggesting as it did the uniting of two different things – for example, that of man and woman in marriage rather than the 'one flesh' which the two form as a result of this. Theodore tried to safeguard 'the communication of idioms', attributing to the human nature in Christ the title of Son of God, though not that nature's weaknesses to the Divine Word. But since his aim was to ensure the full humanity of Christ and make him assume everything that had to be saved, he was led to reflect less on the mystery of God who emptied himself to become man than on the raising of man to achieve his destiny and fulfilment in God.

The questions raised by Theodore's formula were threefold. First, did it sufficiently respect the unique character of the incarnation? Second, did it not draw too close a comparison between the incarnation and the presence of God in the Christian soul through sanctification by sacramental grace? Third, did the word 'conjunction', however close the union it intended to convey, really avoid the danger of dividing Christ? But the questions were not asked loudly enough to disturb Theodore's peace or reputation during his life, and, if his pupil Nestorius had remained an ordinary monk living quietly in his monastery near Antioch, might never have been heard at all.

Theodore was overlapped by Cyril, Bishop of Alexandria (412–44), who was one of Apollinarianism's most vehement opponents. He maintained that in Christ the divine and human natures were both complete and that the latter included the rational element. The unity of Christ was through the Logos who became incarnate in Christ and took on the general characteristics of man. The humanity in Christ was not so much an individual man as humanity in general. Salvation was accomplished by the personal Logos who assumed impersonal human nature, thus uniting it with the divine nature and enabling it to become a partaker of God and of immortality.

Theodore and Cyril were to some extent shadow-boxing, for the Apollinarians, knocked reeling by the many ecclesiastical and imperial edicts aimed at them, had withdrawn from open fight and gone underground. The heresy survived until the 420s, kept alive by forged books written under the names of the most respectable and orthodox churchmen, such as Pope Julian and Athanasius. These deceived many, including some eminent thinkers, and did orthodoxy some harm. But, difficult though the relationship of the two natures in Christ was – and is – to define, Apollinarius' hybrid was clearly not the right answer to the problem. Anathemas and edicts were not essential for its eventual defeat; in the long run, common sense would have been enough.

CHAPTER 8

Nestorianism

If heresy is a cause of damnation, then the fourth and fifth centuries must have appeared as a series of crises to the orthodox. Major heresies such as Nestorianism, Eutychianism, Monothelitism and Pelagianism, together with some minor ones, writhed like a nest of snakes in the undergrowth of theology. Their movements have been likened to a fugue, but had nothing of the neat patterning and balance of music, being reminiscent rather of discord and cacophony. If the pagans of the first century were amazed by the love which Christians bore one another, those of later centuries could have been equally astonished at the loathing and intolerance the upholders of loving God and their fellow-men displayed towards their associates whose formulae for defining the indefinable differed from their own.

For clarity's sake it is best to take each heresy in turn and trace it to its conclusion, though the same characters and councils often dealt with several heterodoxies simultaneously.

Nestorianism is the most important of the fifth-century heresies because of its widespread missionary work in the Middle and Far East, the results of which have not completely died out to this day. It has been seen already that Theodore of Mopsuestia, although dying in the peace of the Church in 428, was posthumously anathematized for having been a Nestorian before his pupil, Nestorius. He taught that God dwelt in Christ as in a son, but in a unique manner, the union of the two being compared to that between man and wife. Theodore explicitly talked of there being only one Person, but his language implied two.

In the year in which Theodore died, Nestorius, who had begun his career as a monk in a monastery near Antioch and had become a priest and famous preacher, was summoned by the Emperor, Theodosius II, to become Patriarch of Constantinople. He proved a violent, headstrong, overbearingly zealous persecutor, attacking indiscriminately everything which savoured to him of heresy – Arians, Novationists, Macedonians and Quartodecimans. Wishing to safeguard the true human nature of Christ against Apollinarianism, he attacked the use of the word *theotokos* (Mother of God), often applied to the Virgin Mary and up till then unquestioningly. God, he said, could not be born of a woman who could not bear a son older than herself, and the term implied that the human in Christ was swallowed up in the divinity. 'She who received Christ', 'she who bore Christ' (*Christotokos*), or 'the mother of Christ' were possible alternatives. He was accused, almost certainly unjustly (it was subsequently difficult to find Nestorianism explicitly stated in the formulae and liturgy of Nestorian churches), of asserting not only two natures but two distinct Persons, divine and human, in Jesus Christ. He defended himself in the *Book of Heracleides* in which he accused Cyril, Bishop of Alexandria, of making Jesus without nature – that is, not completely human. He did not in so many words repudiate *theotokos* but its use in implying that the Virgin, as the source of God, was herself a goddess. He could not say 'God was three months old'. He could say, 'A child three or four months old was God'.

Nestorius wrote:

> The Church teaches that God the Son was not united to an already existing being but that Christ's human nature, when first created by God, was not given one moment's purely human existence. From the first moment it existed, not as a single independent existing essence or nature, but as the human nature of the Word.... It was *his* nature, not as our garments are our garments but as our hearts are our hearts, united to his eternal Godhead with a union so close that the only analogy we can find is the union in man of soul and body.... As the reasonable soul and flesh is one man, so God and man is one Christ.

And he distinguished between acts of the human nature and acts of the Divine Person: 'Mary is literally and truly the Mother of Jesus, therefore he is true man. Jesus is true God, therefore she is Mother of God' (in this respect only).

Nestorius appeared to the orthodox so to express himself that, while he recognized one Son and one Christ in two natures, he explained their union as one that was little more than a moral union of two distinct beings. The Divine Personality of Jesus was missing. If Nestorius' doctrine had been adopted as orthodox, in time Christ would have been a mere man, although one inspired to a superlative degree by the indwelling of the divine Logos. This is again a position held mentally if not stated by many members of main-line Christian denominations today who are Nestorian in thought, though quite unaware of it.

Nestorius, tactless and belligerent himself, was unlucky in his opponent. Cyril, ambitious for leadership and jealous of the other great eastern sees, Antioch and Constantinople, may have deserved the canonization he was later given for the orthodoxy of his theology, but scarcely earned it for such qualities as temperance, forbearance, humility and Christian charity. Nor was he made less enthusiastic in attack by the fact that his critics had complained about him to Nestorius. He reacted sharply against Nestorius' assault in his use of the word *theotokos*. 'If our Lord Jesus Christ is God,' he retorted, logically enough, 'how can it be that the Holy Virgin who gave birth to him is not the Mother of God, Theotokos?' The primary fundamental fact was the divinity of Christ. Cyril was deceived into using Apollinarianist apocrypha circulating under orthodox names to justify his position, but managed to interpret their heretical formulae in an orthodox fashion. He used the phrase 'hypostatic union' in its earlier sense of 'real, true union' – the indissoluble unity between God and man which came about in the incarnation. This unity resulted through the Logos' incarnation in Christ and his taking on the general characteristics of man. Christ was therefore not so much an individual man as humanity in general. Salvation was accomplished by the personal Logos who assumed impersonal human nature, thus uniting it with the divine nature, with the result that human nature becomes partaker of God and of immortality.

The war opened with a battle of correspondence. Cyril enlisted the aid of Pulcheria, eldest sister of the Emperor Theodosius II and the power behind the throne, and Eudoxia, his wife. Both he and Nestorius appealed to the Pope, Celestine, Cyril proving the better tactician in translating his letters to Rome into Latin – the reply to one of Nestorius' was held up for some months because no one could be found to understand Greek. Cyril was also more deferential while Nestorius was already in ill-odour with Celestine for having given support to some Pelagian heretics. At a synod held in Rome in 430 the Bishop of Rome condemned Nestorius, ordered him to recant or be excommunicated and, told Cyril to carry out the sentence. Nestorius replied that 'the man Jesus is the temple, the vesture of the Word' and denied that it could be said with accuracy that the Word suffered during the Passion – 'God did not die'. Another synod at Alexandria in the same year also condemned Nestorius for his failure to use *theotokos* and for his separation of the divine and human natures in Christ in such a way that Christ was viewed as a 'God-bearing man' and that 'Jesus is, as a man, energized by the Logos of God'. Apart from his reluctance to use *theotokos*, Nestorius had not taught this, though it was the logical conclusion of his thinking. Cyril summarized the case against his opponent in a long document ending with twelve anathemas or propositions.

Nestorius, obdurate and protesting, demanded an ecumenical council to decide the question. A snowstorm of letters flew between Alexandria, Constantinople, Rome and other of the principal sees. Bishops intrigued and lobbied the imperial court.

When the Ecumenical Council, the third, was convened at Ephesus by imperial decree in 431, Cyril, with some two hundred bishops who supported him, arrived first. Nestorius sent contemptuous replies to a threefold summons to appear before them before his own supporters arrived, and was condemned and deposed in his absence in hearings which lasted but a single day. Memnon, Bishop of Ephesus, stirred up the city mob in violence against him. Five days later, John of Antioch with about forty other bishops who supported Nestorius arrived and organized themselves into the 'legitimate council'. They condemned, deposed and excommunicated Cyril and Memnon as Arians and Apollinarians. Some ten days after, Pope Celestine's representatives arrived and, the majority council being reconvened, excommunicated Bishop John and his party. Confusion was worse confounded at the council by the intervention of some of the imperial civil servants, attempts at bribery, and the feelings of the common people who displayed the usual Greek passion for things philosophical and theological.

Both sides appealed to Theodosius who temporarily confirmed the depositions of Cyril, Memnon and Nestorius and, dismissing the council, rebuked it sternly for failing in its task of reconciliation. He tried himself to bring the factions together. There was a partial peace in 433 when John of Antioch accepted the condemnation of Nestorius and Cyril agreed to a creed submitted by John which was the same as a formula agreed at Ephesus by the counter-synod of eastern bishops, with one small addition. A synthesis of two rival theologies, it expressed a 'union without confusion' of the two natures in Jesus, declaring him to be 'true God and true man, consisting of a reasonable soul and a body'. The term *theotokos* was accepted by John. Both he and Cyril had to deal with extremists in their respective parties who disliked the creed for different reasons.

Only Nestorius' deposition, confirmed by Pope Sextus III who succeeded Celestine, proved permanent. Sent first to a monastery near Antioch, after four years he was exiled to the Egyptian desert where he survived until 451, often in great physical and mental distress and writing copiously in defence of his theology, perishing eventually in wretchedness and obscurity. To the last it was not clear whether he did hold that the divine and human were present in Christ in such fashion that there were in him two distinct beings or persons rather than two natures concurring in one person (*prosopon*) and one substance (*hypostasis*), the orthodox view.

Seeing that the hunt was up, Cyril, with some support from others, tried to condemn posthumously as Nestorians Diodorus of Tarsus and Theodore of Mopsuestia, but the Emperor commanded that none who had died at peace with the Catholic Church should be pursued after death.

Throughout the fifth century Nestorianism continued to be condemned. The Ecumenical Council of Chalcedon, held in 451, the year of Nestorius' death, condemned his heresy, even Theodoret of Cyrrhus, a great Antiochene theologian and supporter of Nestorius, reluctantly agreeing to a formal condemnation, something he had refused to do until then. The creed of the Council of Chalcedon, proclaimed in the presence of the Emperor, Marcian, stated a belief in 'one single Christ, Son, Lord, Monogenic [meaning here, born of one human parent], without confusion, without change, without division, without separation, the difference of natures being in no way suppressed by the union, but rather the properties of each being safeguarded and reunited in a single person [*prosopon*] and a single hypostasis'. In 482 the Emperor Zeno, in his edict 'Henoticon', an attempt to heal breaches between factions in the Church, condemned Nestorius among others and revered the memory of Cyril and his twelve propositions, concluding with an appeal to unity on the basis of the Nicene Creed as the one official definition of faith.

Nestorianism, although conquered within the Empire, carried Christianity to the bounds of Asia. The way for its path to the East had been unwittingly prepared for it years before Nestorius became Patriarch of Constantinople. In 410 there existed a Church of the Eastern Syrians, with a hierarchical centre at the Persian capital, Seleucia-Ctesiphon, and an intellectual centre and school for training clergy at Edessa, which was in Roman territory. Like other churches, it was torn by Christological disputes. Rabbula, its bishop from 415 to 436, favoured Cyril, but was succeeded by Hiba or Ibas, who leaned towards Nestorius, and its school under Narsai was attached to the Antiochene or Nestorian tradition. But although it had asserted its canonical independence from the western Church in 424, the Syrian communion swung again to orthodoxy, and in 457 the greater part of the school escaped across the frontier to Nisibis, which had been in Persian hands since 363. That part which remained in Edessa closed in about 489. Narsai, who did not die until 502, aged one hundred, reorganized the school at Nisibis, protected by the local bishop, Barsumas, who was anti-Cyril.

The Nestorian Christology triumphed in Persia and was duly accepted by a general synod of the churches of the Persian Empire held in 486 at Seleucia. The orthodox were expelled and Nestorius was not condemned, but, apart from these measures, it is not easy to find where the Persian heresy existed; although the orthodox came to be treated as heretics and a certain Henana, reverting towards the Cyrilline position in 585, was excommunicated and his followers persecuted with a ferocity worthy of orthodoxy. The parting of the Eastern Syrians was schismatic rather than heretical, owing to politics more than religion; for the kings of Persia found a useful ally in a Christian church in their dominions at odds with Constantinople and Rome, especially as it grew almost to rival the power and influence of the more westerly churches. Far from apologizing for their own heresy – if it existed – the Syrian Nestorians regarded the Catholics as the heretics.

If Europe owes its Christianity to the zeal of Catholic missionaries, the east was in the debt of Nestorians – 'was' because eventually the eastern churches all but disappeared. Within the Persian Empire itself, Nestorians won converts from Zoroastrianism, including some even from the ruling classes of the Sassanid Persians. Before the Arab Mohammedan conquests, Christianity spread widely along the caravan routes to the Far East, churches being founded in Merv, Herat and Samarkand. Travelling in the Indian Ocean, 520–5, the Alexandrian traveller Cosmas tells of churches of Persian origin in Socotra, an island in the Arabian Sea near the Gulf of Aden, and in Ceylon. The Hephtalite Huns of Central Asia asked for a bishop to be sent to them in 549.

Mohammedanism did not at once annihilate Nestorianism. In fact, Christians were sometimes freer under Mohammedans than they had been under the Zoroastrians. There was a Nestorian community in Baghdad, capital of the Abbasid caliphs, under their own Catholicos or Patriarch, strong enough to arouse the jealousy of the Moslems by their eminence as officials and physicians. They taught their new masters much Greek civilization, translating into Arabic some of the writings of the Greek philosophers. These, lost by the West for almost a millennium, were restored to it in translation at the Renaissance.

It is thought that there were Christians in India before Nestorianism. However, later churches were founded by missionaries from Persia, Mesopotamia and Syria. Contacts were made through commerce, for the Christian communities were to be found on the coast and in cities. In China, the first missionary, named Alopen, was welcomed by the tolerant Tai-tsung, ablest monarch of the T'ang dynasty, at his capital city of Ch'ang-an (now Hsianfu). The Chinese Church was never numerous but boasted a Metropolitan, monasteries and Christian literature. A hostile imperial edict in 845 reduced numbers sharply, and monks sent out in 980 could find no traces of Christians in the country.

Early in the eleventh century the Nestorians made fresh gains. In about 1100 a prince of the Keraïts, Turks of central Asia, asked for baptism. The Onguts, Tartars who lived to the north of the Yellow River, were evangelized together with some among the Uighurs, through whose territory trade routes ran between the west and China. One of Genghis Khan's sons married a Christian Keraït princess, and his grandson, Hulagu, not only had a favourite wife who was a Christian but is believed by some to have been baptized himself. Under the Monguls Christianity recovered in China, the Nestorians having an archbishopric at Cambaluc (modern Peking). William of Rubruck, a Franciscan, found Nestorian Christians when he visited the Great Khan in China in the thirteenth century.

When, however, the Mongol rulers were expelled from China, Christianity died out before 1500. It disappeared also in Persia when the Mongols became Moslems. Socotra ceased to be Christian, no one knows how or when. Nestorians throughout Asia survived only in tiny pockets, although in South India they applied to their patriarch as late as 1490 to send them bishops. In the sixteenth century some became Uniates, giving allegiance to the Pope. In the nineteenth a few existed in Persia known as Assyrian Christians, continually reduced by conversion and massacres by Turks, Kurds and Moslems.

The Church of the East has today perished save for scattered remnants in Iran, Iraq and the United States to which many, including their Patriarch, emigrated in the nineteenth and twentieth centuries. The only other possible survival of a form of Christianity that once appeared capable of winning the East for Christ is the Syro-Malabar Church flourishing today in South India. That may owe its origin to Nestorian missionaries, but it is by no means certain.

CHAPTER 9

Eutychianism and Allied Heresies

Heresy breeds heresy by over-reaction to it; and in about 447 there broke out in opposition to Nestorianism a series of disputes of which the main protagonist was Eutyches. He was the aged archimandrite of a monastery of over three hundred monks near Constantinople, had influence at court and was in touch with all the anti-Nestorians of Cyril's party who could not accept the formula agreed on by Cyril and John of Antioch in 433. Eutyches denounced this creed as Nestorian. He was attacked himself by Theodoret, the theologian who was not to condemn Nestorius until 451 and then unwillingly, in his work *Eranistes*, then accused Eusebius, Bishop of Dorylaeum, of Nestorianism and was counter-accused of teaching that there was only a single nature in Christ. His case was argued before a Constantinople synod presided over by Flavian, bishop of that city. Questioned as to whether he admitted that in Christ there were two natures after the union (the incarnation), and that Christ was consubstantial with humanity according to the flesh, Eutyches gave a grudging acceptance to the latter doctrine but largely negated it by his views on the former. Christ, he maintained, was *of* two natures, but not *in* them; before the union there existed the two natures, divine and human, but after it the two so blended that there was one nature only, and that fully divine. Jesus was *homoousion* with the Father but not with man.

Eutyches was deposed from every priestly office and excommunicated as 'a reviler of Christ' – scarcely a fair description of one who had over-emphasized the Lord's divinity. But his heresy did make nonsense of the doctrine of the Atonement which is one of the central themes of Christianity. To deny that God was in Christ is to make the Passion a merely individual human suffering, insufficient to atone for the sins of the world (Nestorianism) : to deny the reality of Christ's human nature is to make the Passion of no relevance to humanity and to devalue Christ's life on earth. This becomes apparent, not real, and useless as inspiration and example. Unless Jesus is of the same nature as humanity, consubstantial with it, he cannot be the 'second Adam' – nor could he have suffered, nor would it be true to say that he was tempted in all points as we are yet without sin, nor could mankind follow the example of his life any more than the life, say, of a Greek god or of an angel.

The orthodox position is that the divine and human natures must exist in Christ as both eternally distinct and uniquely united. If not, they would either be so mixed that Christ would be neither true God nor true man but a hybrid compounded of both; or else the Godhead would so have absorbed the Manhood that in every respect that mattered the incarnation would be no more than a largely irrelevant phase in the existence of God. The third possibility, that Jesus was a mere man, though one uniquely inspired by God, was rejected by orthodoxy because it was realized that the greatness of God was such that no man, however inspired, could attain a position in which he understood God completely and could communicate him wholly and unerringly to humanity.

Eutyches had literally friends at court in the persons of his godson and an influential eunuch, Chrysaphius. The Emperor, Theodosius II, was persuaded to summon a general council to re-hear the case. In 449 a council packed with Eutyches' partisans, nicknamed the Latrocinium, or Robber Council, and presided over by Dioscurus, who had succeeded Cyril as Bishop of Alexandria, met at Ephesus. Pope Leo (440–61), a man of strong personality, was represented by two legates, and his anti-Eutychian views were expressed in a lengthy letter to Flavian, known as the 'Tome of Leo'. In it he asserted the view expressed as early as Tertullian's day and commonly held in the west concerning the two natures of Christ. In Christ Jesus there was neither manhood without true Godhead nor the Godhead without true manhood, and in him two full and complete natures came together in one person 'without detracting from the properties of either nature and substance'.

The Robber Council was well named. Theodoret was forbidden to attend, Leo's 'Tome' was refused a hearing, and so great was the gathering's violence and the intimidation by imperial troops that Flavian later died of the ill-treatment he received at it. The council gave its allegiance to the creed of Nicaea, Dioscurus excommunicated Leo, appointing an Alexandrian priest to replace him, deposed Flavian and dubbed Nestorians Eusebius of Dorylaeum, Theodoret and some leading thinkers of the school of Antioch. The victims at once appealed. Bishops of Italy and Gaul and the court of the western Emperor, Valentinian III, reacted sharply against the violence of the Latrocinium, and Leo was swift to condemn it and annul its decrees. The task of the orthodox was made easier by Theodosius' unexpected death in 450. Chrysaphius, Eutyches' patron, was disgraced and executed. Pulcheria, who succeeded Theodosius, married Marcian, who was loyal to the Pope, the noisy bishops sank into docility, and, after some delays, in 451 Pulcheria summoned the Fourth Ecumenical Council to meet at Chalcedon. A record number of bishops, nearly six hundred, attended, almost all from the east. Leo was again represented by legates, and the imperial commissioners presided. The proceedings of the Robber Council were entirely annulled, Flavian was posthumously exonerated and restored, and Dioscurus, remaining an obstinate Eutychian, was deposed, excommunicated and exiled to Paphlagonia. Eutyches was declared a heretic. The 'Tome of Leo' was approved, and a creed, condemning Apollinarianism, Nestorianism and Eutychianism, was agreed upon. This read as follows:

... there is to be confessed one and the same Son, our Lord Jesus Christ, perfect in Godhead and perfect in manhood, truly God and truly man, of rational soul and body, of the same substance with the Father according to the Godhead, and of the same substance with us according to the manhood, like to us in all respects, without sin, begotten of the Father before all time according to the Godhead, in these latter days, for us and for our salvation, born of the Virgin Mary, the Mother of God according to the manhood, one and the same Christ, Son, Lord, Only-begotten, in two natures, inconfusedly, immutably, indivisibly, inseparately, the distinction of natures being by no means taken away by the union, but rather the peculiarity of each nature being preserved and concurring in one person (*prosopon*) and one substance (*hypostasis*), not parted or separated into two persons, but one and the same Son and Only-begotten, divine word, the Lord Jesus Christ; as from the beginning the prophets declared concerning him, and the Lord Jesus Christ has taught us, and the creed of the holy fathers has transmitted to us.

But Monophysitism, as the Eutychian heresy came to be called, did not die. Emperors hesitated to attack it, for not only were those who ruled for the next half-century inclined to it themselves (the differences between it and orthodox doctrine grew increasingly smaller and later led to attempts on both sides to bridge the narrow chasm) but, anxious to unite their eastern dominions against external threat, they also found it necessary to make concessions to it. This resulted in strife with Rome and the west. Part of the eastern dominions also became permanently Monophysite, as will be seen below. The Egyptians, for example, remained loyal to Dioscurus, and his orthodox replacement was imposed upon them only after fighting in the streets of Alexandria and intervention by the army. Even when he died, another Monophysite, with the delightful sobriquet of Timothy the Cat, succeeded him for a time until, following the assassination of his orthodox rival, he was exiled. There was a struggle in Palestine between orthodox and Monophysite factions, and in Syria Peter the Fuller, the first Patriarch of Antioch (464–90) favourable to the heresy, occupied the see four times, having been driven out thrice and reinstated by brawls and intrigues, one of his orthodox substitutes being removed by murder. Nationalism in Ethiopia, Nubia (modern Sudan), Armenia and elsewhere strengthened the Monophysite cause, and it cannot be denied that the best men for religion and piety and the strongest characters in the Christianity of the fifth century were to be found among the Monophysites.

In 476 the Emperor Basilicus issued his 'Encyclion', in which he condemned both the 'Tome of Leo' and the Council of Chalcedon. Six years later Emperor Zeno published his document of reconciliation called the 'Henoticon', referred to previously. This was deliberately open to various interpretations and favoured the Monophysites, some of the more moderate of whom accepted it. But it condemned Eutyches as well as Nestorius, and the more extreme Monophysites rejected it, as did Pope Felix III on the different ground that it was a rejection of Chalcedon. He broke off communion with Acacius, Bishop of Constantinople, who supported it, and Zeno's attempt to impose it on the Church led to a schism between its eastern and western halves which lasted from 484 to 519. Zeno's successor, Anastasius I (491–518), was favourable to the Monophysites who, under him, were successful in occupying many episcopal thrones.

When Justin I came to the eastern imperial throne in 518, he founded a house which lasted for a century and sought union with the western Church. He and his successors were ready to enforce orthodoxy even if it meant schism in some parts of the east. His nephew Justinian, the great law-giver and builder, succeeded him in 528. Justinian prided himself on being also a theologian, favouring orthodoxy, but his influence was modified by his wife Theodora, who was an enthusiastic Monophysite.[1]

Justinian was a great persecutor of some heretics, and in his reign one of the first Christian heterodoxies came to an end. The Montanists, who had lingered on from the middle of the second century, harried by the Emperor, reached a point where they could stand persecution no longer. Loyal to their tenets to the last, they

---

[1] Some authorities, such as Danielou and Marrou, op cit p 357, state that it was Justinian who was Monophysite and Theodora who was orthodox. It can at least be said with certainty that both views were supported by the imperial couple.

chose death rather than surrender. They gathered themselves into their churches which they then fired, perishing to the last man, woman and child in the flames.

But the principal theological question in Justinian's reign, that of Monophysitism and its descendent heresies, was not to be settled so simply. The heresy had been given its historical shape, from which there were many, more radical, variations, by a great thinker, Severus, who after making a deep impression during a sojourn in Antioch, in the period 509–11, became its bishop in 512. He was a scholar and a man of action, logical in thought and tireless in controversy, whose life ended sadly in exile in Egypt in 538. But although a Monophysite, he rejected Eutyches as a heretic as erroneous as Nestorius, as well as considering the 'Tome of Leo' and the Chalcedonian definition as Nestorian. Severians identified *physis* (the nature) with the *hypostasis* and the person, and in emphasizing both the divinity and the unity distinguished the two natures in a way that was logical rather than real. But the difference between Severianism and orthodoxy was narrow, and Severus' heresy has been described as an attitude, not a doctrine.

Since the Catholics were as anxious to dissociate themselves from Nestorius as the 'orthodox' Monophysites from Eutyches, there were continual efforts by both sides to approach each other. Some help was given in this by a theologian, Leontius of Byzantium, who defined *hypostasis* as 'that which exists by itself', and applied this to the incarnate Word. Contention continued principally about the acceptance by the orthodox of Chalcedon and a good deal of Cyril's teaching and terminology, including his twelve anathemas.

In 532–3 Justinian attempted to bring together the two sides at a conference. He tried to satisfy the Severians by producing a formula of faith devised by some Scythian monks thirteen years earlier, 'One of the Trinity suffered for us in the flesh', an article approved by Pope John II who quoted in support one of Cyril's twelve anathemas – 'Anathema to him who does not confess that the Word suffered in the flesh'. This was the first official recognition of Cyril's document by Rome. But the Emperor's attempt at reconciliation was spoiled by the intransigence of the Severians. In the years that followed he mingled repression of them with peaceful overtures. Since they accused the orthodox, trying to renounce Nestorianism, with restoring at Chalcedon the good name of three 'Nestorians', Theodore of Mopsuestia, Theodoret the theologian and Ibas of Edessa, in 544 Justinian, some say under the influence of Theodora, issued on his own responsibility a document called the 'Three Chapters'. Previous to this, Theodora, striking a blow for Mono-physitism, had in 540 contrived to have Pope Silverius arrested on a charge of treason and replaced by Vigilius on condition that he renounced the Council of Chalcedon. Justinian's document was another encouragement for the heretics, for it condemned groups of writings attributed, perhaps wrongly, to Theodore, Theodoret and Ibas, and this condemnation, together with the renunciation by Vigilius of Chalcedon, was intended to reconcile the Monophysites and the orthodox.

It had the opposite effect. Some western bishops condemned it as an endorsement of heresy and an attack on dead men who could not defend themselves. The Monophysites accused Justinian of personal loyalty to Chalcedon and were unmoved, although the Bishop of Constantinople gave an unwilling assent to the 'Three Chapters'. Justinian seized Pope Vigilius and kept him, old and sick, under pressure of threats alternating with persuasion, from 547 onwards. Vigilius resisted, yielded, recanted, yielded again, not explicitly enough to please Justinian, but eventually published a formula in 554 which satisfied the Emperor, declaring the 'Three Chapters' heretical and anathematizing Theodore of Mopsuestia in retrospect.

In 553 Justinian assembled the Fifth Ecumenical Council at Constantinople. It deposed and banished Vigilius, who refused to attend, and gave independent judgement on points under debate, but it did not excommunicate him or break with Rome, making a somewhat unreal distinction between the Apostolic See and the person of the Pope occupying it. However, the Emperor freed the old man when he conceded the legitimacy of the council and condemned the 'Three Chapters'. The council also condemned them but accepted the decrees of Chalcedon, though it slanted them towards the views of Cyril of Alexandria. These, it has been seen, subordinated the human element in Christ to the divine, and in this way a tendency to a modified Monophysitism has become part of the official doctrine of the Roman Catholic Church.

But if he hoped to reconcile Chalcedonians and Monophysites, Justinian was disappointed. The latter, notably the Egyptians, would accept nothing less than the condemnation of Chalcedon, some Italian and Gallic bishops on the orthodox side refused to recognize the authority of the Constantinople council, and any hope of reunion between the factions disappeared. Justinian was forced back into a policy of repression, decreeing death for heretics who reverted after recanting. He did not, however, act against Monophysites with either energy or consistency, and the heresy tended to emphasize several of the more radical variations on its theme which had developed over the years.

The Emperor adopted one of these himself, Aphthartodocetism, which taught the incorruptibility and impassibility of Christ's human body. Since this body was divine, the heresy said, it underwent no change from the time of its conception in Mary's womb, and was free of all passions, including those which are natural and blameless. Though Justinian still claimed loyalty to Chalcedon, he was planning to impose this extreme belief upon the Church when, in 565, death removed him.

His successors returned to orthodoxy. Justin II (565–78) first tried appeasement and persuasion to union but, when these measures were rejected by the Monophysites, reverted to persecution. Tiberius II (578–82) was relatively mild and Maurice (582–602) openly tolerant, but none of these attitudes was successful. Although the repressive measures of Justin I and the actions of Justinian had threatened the heresy with extinction, only time removed open Monophysitism from the west; and because of the conclusions reached by the Fifth Ecumenical Council, moderate Monophysites found themselves accepted within the Catholic Church.

Pope Gregory I (590–604) was nevertheless grieved by the large number of heretics he saw within Christendom. And in the seventh century over-emphasis on part of the Cyrilline tradition led to other daughter heresies, Monoenergism and Monotheletism; for if too much emphasis was laid on the divinity of the incarnate Word, its full humanity was in danger of being lost in several different ways. According to orthodox belief, there was both a divine and human *energeia* (activity) in Christ, and another theory of the *energeia* became the first of the secondary heresies. It was first put forward by Patriarch Sergius of Constantinople. In 634, the year in which the Mohammedan conquests began, he suggested to the Emperor Heraclius (610–41) that the selfsame Christ and Son works divine and human deeds by one divine-human operation (*energeia*). This view was supported by documents allegedly written by Dionysius the Areopagite, converted at Athens by St Paul, but in reality composed between 475 and 550. Sergius' doctrine brought about a temporary union between the orthodox and the Monophysites in Egypt, but was immediately subjected to attack from other quarters. The patriarch tried to pacify the disputants in the debate he had inspired by suggesting that the question of one or two *energeias* be dropped. Surely all would agree, he continued, that in Christ there was only one will (*thelema*). He sent his theory to Pope Honorius (625–38) who agreed, and Heraclius, backed for once by rare agreement between Rome and Constantinople, issued an edict called 'Ecthesis' forbidding the discussion of two *energeias* and declaring one will.

The emperors desperately needed a formula upon which the Church could agree so as to present a united front against the Mohammedan threat, though it was yet too early to realize how gargantuan that threat would prove to be. Heraclius seemed to have found it; but the theologians had other thoughts. In 641 Pope

Severinus, successor to Honorius, declared for two wills in Christ, divine and human, for if Christ is truly man as well as truly God he must have a human as well as a divine will; for to deny him a human will is to deprive him of full humanity. The two wills were, of course, always in agreement.

If the basic Christian contention that Christ is perfect God and perfect man united in one Person is true, Severinus was surely right. If it is believed that God assumed complete human nature, this must include the will, for it is in the free exercise of the will that the dignity of human nature is to be found. Moreover, to be completely and truly human, that will must operate in its own proper sphere – Christ's obedience had to be exactly that of the free will of a human being submitting itself voluntarily to the will of God yet quite distinct from it. There is confusion in English in the use of the word 'will', which sometimes means the act of choosing, sometimes the thing chosen. We can say, 'Your will is mine', meaning 'I choose what you choose', but the fact that the two wills choose the same thing does not make them one.

In 648 Emperor Constans II, faced with the loss to the Mohammedans in only fifteen years of Damascus, Antioch, Jerusalem, all Mesopotamia, Alexandria and the whole of North Africa, to name but some of their conquests, tried to bring peace to his 'church militant'. He issued his 'Type' forbidding further debate on the subjects of energies and wills. But there were turbulent priests before Thomas à Becket. In the following year Pope Martin at a Roman synod defied the Emperor's prohibition *ex cathedra*, repudiated both the 'Ecthesis' and the 'Type', declared for two wills in Christ, condemned and excommunicated the Patriarch of Constantinople for Monotheletism (doctrine of the one will in Christ) and wholly opposed the imperial edicts of 638 and 648. It is not altogether surprising that Constans haled Martin to Constantinople and treated him savagely. The wretched Pope was stripped, led through the city with an iron collar round his neck, thrown into a dungeon and finally exiled to the Crimea, where he died in 655. A Greek monk, Maximus the Confessor, an outspoken opponent of Monotheletism, was likewise imprisoned, tortured, mutilated and exiled. It was not until well after Constans' death that Pope Agatho was able to hold a synod at Rome, attended by 125 bishops, which condemned the heresy of the one will.

The Sixth Ecumenical Council met in 680–1 at Constantinople and made the condemnation of Monoenergism and Monotheletism the decision of all the orthodox. There it was categorically affirmed that in Christ there were two energies and two wills. This was the end of the debate over the relationship of Jesus Christ to the Father and the Holy Spirit within the Trinity and that of the human and divine within the personality of Jesus. Today Roman Catholics, the Orthodox Churches and most Protestants agree with the findings of the ecumenical councils. The minorities who disagree are possibly not as insignificant as they have been in the past, and the findings of psychology may decree that the last word has not yet been said.

In parts of the east and south of the old Empire, Monophysitism has survived until this day. Armenia, much of Syria, most of Egypt, Nubia and Ethiopia boasted Monophysite churches, some of which still exist, though in nothing like the numbers and strength which they once possessed.

The hero of Monophysitism was Jacobus Baradaeus (James the Ragged, or the Beggar), who was born about 490. Consecrated bishop by Theodosius, the imprisoned Patriarch of Constantinople, he might have claimed before Wesley that the world was his parish or, rather, diocese, for he wandered on foot for some thirty years until his death in 578 from Nisibis to Alexandria, clad only in a ragged horse-cloth, adopting this disguise to escape the imperial police. Yet he managed to call together a synod of Monophysite bishops at Alexandria, extended and strengthened the organization of his church, giving it a sense of unity, and finally gave it an autonomous hierarchy validly instituted in the line of the Apostolic Succession. James is said to have consecrated from twenty-seven to eighty-nine bishops and ordained a hundred thousand priests. He cut all ties with Catholic orthodoxy and gave the name Jacobite to a church which has survived to this day. He was helped in Egypt by the fact that the Copts, descendants of the ancient Egyptians, who spoke their own vernacular, had a strong antipathy to the Byzantines. So great was the dislike of the Copts for the Melchites, the Greek-speaking imperial party, and their attempts to impose Catholic orthodoxy, that they almost welcomed and actively assisted the Saracen invaders in 642.

Yet before the advent of Islam, Monophysitism had triumphed almost completely over orthodoxy in Egypt in the fifth and sixth centuries. In its triumph, however, lay degeneration. As so often happens with heresy, separation from the parent belief led to divisions within the offshoot creed, and by the year 600 there were said to be twenty or more Monophysite sects in Egypt founded on over-subtle theologizing.

All these divisions led to anarchy. In about 556, for example, there were four Monophysite patriarchs together with an orthodox claimant disputing the episcopal throne of Alexandria. Attempts to reach unity failed. In 575 the Egyptian Monophysites chose a Syrian patriarch under whom to unite, but he was not accepted by many, and an appearance of unity brought about by a council in 580 was short-lived. Just before the Mohammedan conquest the Byzantine imperialists were planning to crush Monophysitism and, though inspired largely by nationalism, they might well have succeeded. In the 630s Cyrus, Patriarch of Alexandria, had persuaded many Monophysites to submit to the Catholic Church by a formula which affirmed Christ to be 'in two natures' but accomplished his divine and human works by 'one theandric operation' (theandric = pertaining to both God and man). He was attacked for this by the orthodox Sophronius, a Palestinian monk, who complained that the expression was the old Monophysitism disguised.

When the Arabs invaded Egypt, capturing Alexandria in 641–2, they at first tolerated all variations of Christianity, although restrictions and discriminatory taxes were laid heavily on all not of the faith of Islam. The lot of the Monophysites was better in some respects than under the Byzantines, for they were at least left to enjoy their faith in peace. But the Christian Church as a whole was reduced to an insignificant minority within a generation of the conquest. The faithful fled to Sicily and southern Italy. Those who remained defected to Islam in large numbers, for the Prophet's victories seemed to prove that God was with him, not the Church. The Christians who remained loyal were so restricted that no propagation of their faith was possible, and their numbers could be maintained or increased only by births within their communities, growing increasingly rigid and conservative. Yet the Arabs employed Christian artists and architects who had considerable influence on their art-forms; and when the Fatimids (Shiah Moslems) took over Egypt, in the period 950–75, restrictions were at first eased and at least one caliph had a Christian wife. Caliph Hakim, a Moslem fanatic and possibly mad, brought in a period of persecution during the first quarter of the eleventh century, and by its close there were not to be found in the whole of North Africa the three bishops necessary for the consecration of an archbishop. Yet a faithful minority of Christians persisted, mainly in monasteries, holding their services in Coptic although producing some Christian literature in Arabic, which had become the vernacular.

Thereafter periods of toleration and persecution followed, the latter being particularly acute between 1300 and 1350. The Coptic Church declined, experiencing corruption within because of persecution, which led to attempts by its members to keep on good terms with their Moslem rulers. This inspired competition for official favour by aspirants to Christian high office and interference by Mohammedans in the internal affairs of the Church. Quarrels were common, there were no new creative movements in the Church and it grew steadily weaker. In 1517 Ottoman Turks conquered Egypt. Under them some Christians grew wealthy and prominent as secretaries and administrators, arousing Moslem jealousy and, from time to time, inspiring renewed persecution.

For the next three or four centuries there were further assaults on the heretical Christians of Egypt and the east by Catholic missionaries, mainly Jesuits, who tried to win them to submit to the Pope. But the largest church in Egypt remained the Monophysite, and, in the second half of the nineteenth century, its numbers were increasing, though by births not conversions. The increase has been maintained in the present century, balanced to some extent by steady if slow defections to the Islam which dominates Egyptian society.

As in Egypt so in other eastern countries Monophysitism was linked with nationalist feeling against Byzantine rule. From the sixth century onwards this led its adherents to strive increasingly for a separate church altogether, rather than a different attitude within the Church. The Jacobite Church in Syria, supporting Syriac speech and culture against the Greek, had been founded by that Jacob Baradaeus who had had so much influence throughout the east, and Syrian merchants, fleeing from persecution by the orthodox, carried its doctrines to Mesopotamia, Persia and lands eastward. In Syria itself the Jacobites evolved a system headed by a patriarch at Antioch which extended into other lands, including Cyprus and Central Asia; though a quarrel between the Coptic and Syrian Monophysite churches led to a break in relations between them from 575 onwards. By the twelfth century the Syrian Jacobite Church had about twenty metropolitans and a hundred bishops. The next two centuries saw marked literary activity, culminating in so outstanding a work by a scholar, Barhebraeus (1226–68), that at his death he was honoured by Orthodox, Nestorians and Armenians as well as by Monophysites.

In the fourteenth century the Syrians were, like the Egyptian Christians, weakened by internal quarrels, Moslem persecutions and a continuing rivalry with orthodoxy. This has lasted to this day for, from the death of the Monophysite Patriarch of Antioch in 539, there have always been two patriarchs in the city, a Jacobite and an orthodox. There was also a 'Babylonish captivity' of rival Monophysite patriarchs from 1292 to 1495, leaving, when the schism was healed, only some fifty thousand poor families as adherents of the Church. A number of these were won over to allegiance to Rome in subsequent centuries to form the Syrian Uniate Church, and today Jacobites, Greek Orthodox, Roman Catholics and Uniates are rivals for the allegiance of such Syrian Christians as remain.

The Armenian Church remained faithful to Nicaea against Arianism. But, partly through the nationalist desire for freedom from Byzantine rule, it supported Monophysitism against Chalcedon and broke with orthodoxy in 491, confirming the rupture by anathemas fired from Chalcedon at synods held in the 520s and 552. This was partly because of Monophysite proselytizing from Mesopotamia and Syria. In 562 the Byzantine emperor Maurice tried, with only temporary success, to impose orthodoxy on part of Armenia which had come under his control, but the rest of the country remained Monophysite as a symbol of its independence. Georgia, originally theologically allied with Armenia, became orthodox, its Catholicos, Kvirion, being excommunicated by the Armenian Monophysite.

Although pressed on all sides through the centuries by, successively, orthodox, Zoroastrians, Moslems, Turks, Mongols and Turks again, the Armenian Church proved resistant in the mountain fastnesses north of Mesopotamia. From about 950 to about 1075 the Armenians were ruled by the Bagratid dynasty under the suzerainty of the Caliph of Baghdad. They were followed by Turkish invasions which split the country into several principalities under Turks or Kurds. The Mongols succeeded them from about 1235.

An independent Armenian kingdom existed from about 1075 until after 1350 in Cilicia in Asia Minor to the west of Armenia proper. This came into contact with the Greek Orthodox Church and, through the Crusades, the Roman Catholics. It had closer relations with Rome than with the Orthodox Church, and many Cilician Armenian Christians in due course submitted to Rome. The withdrawal of the Crusaders and the disappearance of their principalities in Syria and Palestine led to the collapse of the Cilician Armenian kingdom. Turkish invasions drove its inhabitants into exile east, west and south, where they maintained their religion and customs living in isolated communities within other nationalities, like Jews. The Armenian Church was much troubled by separatist movements within it, principally of Paulicians, Nestorians and Jacobites. Yet it retained its vitality.

The Paulicians, so called because they accepted only the Gospels and Pauline epistles, were first heard of after 650 in the district south of Armenia. They had many Gnostic features, being dualists and believing that matter, the world and the flesh were evil, created by the evil God of the Old Testament, spirit and soul being the work of the good God. They divided themselves into the 'Perfect', who were celibate, sometimes vegetarian and initiated by adult baptism in running water at the age of thirty, and 'Hearers', who were baptized at the end of their lives. They rejected veneration of the Virgin Mary, the invocation of saints, icons, incense, candles and all material symbols. They held a Eucharist and Agape (love-feast), celebrating the former at night with the use of water, not wine. There was no hierarchy in their church, only one grade of ministry being recognized. Christ was born of the good God, but passed through Mary's body like water through a pipe, drawing nothing from her. His birth and death were illusory and his true work was that of a teacher.

In spite of pressure and proselytizing, most Armenian Christians were stubbornly faithful to their church and produced some Christian literature of high value. After the break-up of the Mongol rule, Armenia was divided into a number of principalities, and from 1380 Timur's (Tamberlaine's) Tartars repeatedly ravaged the country. After the death of Timur in 1405 the Turkomans succeeded him, followed by the Persians in the early sixteenth century. In 1439 the union of the Armenian Church with that of Rome was solemnly proclaimed at the Council of Florence (there had then existed an Armenian Uniate Church for nearly a century) but most of the church held aloof from it. Perhaps because of the years of unsettlement, the Armenian communion at this time was in a sorry state of violence and dispute. But in spite of their troubles within and without, the Armenian Christians continued to train, ordain and consecrate clergy and bishops and produced a notable theologian, Gregory of Datev (c. 1346–1410), a loyal Monophysite who strongly opposed union with Rome. He presented the historic Christian tradition from the Monophysite viewpoint, notably in his *Book of Questions*, completed in 1397. Matters improved when the Ottoman Turks, making Constantinople the capital of their empire after its capture in 1453, gave the Armenian patriarch civil jurisdiction over all their Armenian subjects.

Struggles between the Ottoman Turks and the Persians brought further severe suffering to the Church, but in the seventeenth century there was a spiritual revival. Monasteries were renewed, schools were built, evangelistic preaching flourished. Moses of Datev, formerly an itinerant preacher, reformed the supreme leadership of the Armenian Church when he became its Catholicos in 1629. New Julfa in Persia became a centre of religious devotion and learning till its almost complete destruction in the Afghan invasion of 1721. In 1652 a Jerusalem synod promoted reform, and printing enabled an Armenian version of the Bible to be distributed widely. The church continued to live a comparatively uneventful and settled life under its Turkish masters until the nineteenth century when the intrigues of the Great Powers led to further sufferings. In 1828, Russia, acquiring a portion of Armenia from Persia by conquest, and in 1878 another from Turkey, reorganized the church under the Tsar. After the Crimean War the Armenians in Turkey were given a constitution which improved the lot and quality of the clergy, church and civil life.

The intrigues of the powers, notably Russia and Great Britain, brought nothing but trouble to the Armenians. The Turks, afraid of Armenian nationalism backed by either Russia or Britain, massacred thousands of them in the mid-90s, and the Russians forbad the use of their language and confiscated church property in those parts of the country they controlled.

Some recovery took place in the early twentieth century, but the Armenian Church was troubled by a religious movement something like the old Paulicianism and declared by the church to be heretical, and from without by missionary activity by Roman Catholics who attracted many to the Uniate Church and Protestants who founded evangelical churches. These were at first excommunicated by the Armenian Patriarch of Constantinople, although, later, relationships became friendlier.

Christianity was introduced into Nubia in the reign of Justinian in both its Catholic and Monophysite forms. In about 535 the Emperor and his wife Theodora both sent missions into the land, but Theodora stole a march on her husband by intercepting his mission. First in the field, her Monophysites gave a permanent colour to Christianity in that country, where it continued for many centuries. Its king was still building churches in the eleventh century; by the thirteenth, however, mosques were springing up and Christianity beginning to wane. It continued until after 1500, but Moslem merchants increasingly imported their religion with their goods, and Nubian Monophysitism quietly disappeared. By that date every trace of the old Jacobite Church in central Asia and nearly all Persia and Mesopotamia had as completely gone.

Monophysitism was established as a minority religion struggling with Judaism and paganism in the Himyarite country (modern Yemen) and helped to a position of strength for a time by the establishment of Ethiopian rule over southern Arabia. But the Persians conquered the land in 570, Islam in turn conquered the Persians, and Christianity vanished as completely as in Nubia. In the Lebanon it survived but not in its heretical form. After 1516 the remnants of the Monothelites joined the Roman Church.

The only other country where Monophysitism has survived is Ethiopia (Abyssinia). It experienced a slower growth of civilization but maintained a notable vitality. Little is known of its beginnings. It had a tradition of foundation by the 'Nine Saints', apparently Monophysite Syrian monks who entered the country perhaps at the end of the fifth century, possibly as refugees from Catholic persecution, possibly as missionaries. Ethiopia's Monophysitism was also strengthened by its dependence upon Egypt – the head of the Ethiopian Church was appointed by Alexandria until 1951. An attempt to win independence from Egypt in the twelfth century had failed. The thirteenth century saw a revival through literature, while on the military front Islam was pushed back in a series of campaigns. Monasteries, Christian strongholds of propaganda, were built, the numbers of monks increased and converts won from paganism both on the frontiers of Ethiopia and within the land itself. Attempts were made to raise standards of morality, one abbot being courageous enough to excommunicate the king.

In the sixteenth century, there was an effort made to draw the Ethiopians into communion with Rome, supported by Portuguese who had been called in to help the Africans against the Turks. Early in the next century an Ethiopian ruler sympathetic to the Jesuits did reunite most of the Ethiopian Church with Roman Catholicism, only to inspire a nationalist reaction which drove out the missionaries and severed the connection. Protestant attempts met with as little success, and the Ethiopian Church has kept its Monophysite doctrines to the present time—one example of a declared heresy which has survived the assaults of history and all the efforts of the orthodox to end it.

CHAPTER 10

Pelagianism

The sixth Ecumenical Council at Constantinople in 681 brought to an end the period of dispute about the place of Jesus Christ in the Trinity and the relationship of the divine and human nature in his being. Thereafter, whatever heretics might say, orthodox belief on these issues had been clearly stated, and any departure from its norm was heterodox at least.

This is a convenient point at which to summarize the safeguards that the Church had established by which orthodoxy might be ensured and heresy defined. There were first the creeds. These were originally declarations of faith made by the convert to Christianity at his baptism, and, as such, were simple statements of a minimum belief. In the hands of the councils they became theologically complicated definitions of orthodoxy. The two which came to be generally accepted are the comparatively simple Apostles' Creed, based on the Old Roman Creed which goes back to very early days, perhaps the first century; and the so-called Nicene Creed, which is used in the form agreed on by the Council of Constantinople of 381. The statements of the two creeds were not intended to be spiritualized or allegorized in any way. They were meant to be and were, in fact, taken literally up to comparatively modern times. It must be acknowledged that now these creeds are repeated Sunday after Sunday by many who regard themselves as faithful and orthodox Christians but who do not accept as literal truths such phrases as 'born of the Virgin Mary' and 'the resurrection of the body'. Yet no official authorization has been given by any of the major denominations which use the creeds that any of their phrases may be spiritualized or allegorized. Strictly speaking, a believer who uses them in this way is at least heterodox and may be heretical, even though he will find himself in the good company of many theologians and clergy.

The second safeguard was the canon (rule or measure) of

Scripture. Three influences moulded the formation of the New Testament as it is accepted today. First, there had to be agreement as to which writings were sufficiently edifying to be read publicly at church services. Second, some heresies, notably that of Marcion, used incomplete and mutilated New Testament books, and the Church had to decide what writings might be regarded as authoritative and in what form. Third, when during the Diocletian persecution the Emperor ordered the Christian sacred books to be destroyed, both he and the Church had to know, for their different reasons, which books were sacred and which were not. It was not until the fifth century that the canon of New Testament scripture was finally established, after periods when some books which in the end found a place were omitted and others were included which were ultimately rejected.

The third defence against heresy was the doctrine of the Apostolic Succession; that is, of the unbroken line of the consecration of bishops beginning with the Apostles and continued through those upon whom they laid hands and their successors. This guarantee of orthodoxy was given largely against the claims of Christian Gnostics to possess an esoteric knowledge communicated orally by Christ to the Twelve, a secret teaching which the ordinary churchman did not at first have and into which he needed to be initiated. The orthodox pointed out in reply that the Apostles had consecrated certain known successors, and that these had consecrated others. If any secret knowledge existed, it would have been handed on to the people chosen to be bishops and overseers of the Church. Apostolic Succession is still a touchstone by which the Roman and sections of other episcopal churches judge the right of certain Christian communions to be regarded as 'proper' Christians. The two objections to it are, first, that properly consecrated bishops, such as Jacobus Baradaeus, the Monophysite, were heretics and founded heretical churches; and, second, that a man consecrated out of the succession may either be entirely orthodox or revert to orthodoxy. In soundness of doctrine and holiness of life he may be indistinguishable from the most regularly consecrated bishop.

The fourth safeguard was that of the infallibility of the Pope. While this did not become a Roman Catholic dogma until 1870, it had existed possibly for centuries, and was certainly the logical conclusion of a process which had begun in the age of the councils. Once the struggle for leadership between Rome and Constantinople had been resolved by the schism between the Roman and Greek Churches, and once the papacy had established its position as the spiritual ruler of the Holy Roman Empire, what the Bishop of Rome decreed to be orthodox became so and deviation from it heterodox if not worse.

The four safeguards sorted themselves out neatly. Who or what had sired the creeds? The Church. Who or what had settled the canon of Scripture? The Church. Who came to be head of the Church on earth? The Pope. Therefore the order of authority became clear. Over all is God. He, through the Holy Spirit, rules through his vicar or representative on earth, the Pope, who is the head of the Catholic Church (the Roman Church is also guided by the Holy Spirit to elect the man whom God has chosen to lead them). The Holy Father is infallible when he makes pronouncements *ex cathedra*, surrounded by his College of Cardinals, that is with the support and assent of the representatives of the whole Church, on matters of faith and morals. The Pope is not able, as Protestant critics sometimes unfairly assert, to make arbitrary statements which must then be accepted as gospel. New dogmas are not added to the faith until they have come to be generally accepted by the body of the Church, thoroughly debated by its authorities and the time is felt to be right for their promulgation. All these factors are within the province of the guidance of the Holy Spirit, part of whose function is to guide believers into all truth. But since the Pope is the one infallible authority upon earth, he has the final say in matters of interpretation of Scripture and the creeds. So, in the western Church, that which is agreeable to the body of dogma by the Roman Church is orthodoxy, and that which does not agree is heterodox or heretical.

Some non-Roman Episcopalians would accept the authority of the Church as supreme, although, while recognizing the Pope's position within the Roman communion, they would regard him as not infallible and hold that an ecumenical council would have authority over him. (Roman Catholics would argue that nowadays it would be impossible for a Pope and council to be at loggerheads.) Other Episcopalians and very large numbers of Protestants would regard the Bible, especially the New Testament, as the supreme authority, arguing that the apostolic writings came before the Church, and that it is to those writings that we owe such knowledge as we have of the Church's beginnings. But who interprets the Scriptures? The unhappy divisions of Protestantism and the 'lunatic fringe' sects show what happens if the interpretation is left to private judgement, and if it is the Church that decides the meaning of holy writ, surely the Church's authority is greater than that of the Scriptures? It is yet another debate which is unlikely to be resolved either way.

The end of the Christological debates was also the end of the most important early eastern heresies. A return in time must now be made to consider two western heresies, the first insignificant except for its conclusion, the second important in geographical extent and in its reflection of a certain type of thought and personality.

Little is known of Priscillianism which originated in Spain and was named after its originator, Priscillian (?–385). It seems to have been a form of Christian Gnosticism or its first cousin, Illuminism (the claim to have received a special enlightenment), allied with asceticism. It caused so great a furore locally that news of it reached Rome, leading Pope Leo the Great (440–61) to write telling the Spanish bishops how to counter it. Priscillian was condemned by regional councils at Saragossa in 380, Bordeaux in 384 and Trèves in the same year, and, with his followers, was condemned to death at the clamorous request of the bishops by Maximus, the emperor who had usurped the throne.

Martin (321–401), Bishop of Tours, who was present at Trèves (and later canonized), protested against the heretics' being brought before the secular power at all, insisting that excommunication was a sufficient punishment. He refused to leave the city until the Emperor promised to spare them. No sooner had he departed, however, than the bishops persuaded Maximus to behead Priscillian and one follower. Thus, in 385, the first heretic died at the hands of a secular power.

But the Church's conscience had not yet become accustomed to the shedding of blood as an expression of the love which Jesus preached. Martin expressed that conscience by vowing never again to communicate with any of the bishops who had procured Priscillian's death and excommunicated every one of them. Some time afterwards, wishing to obtain pardon for other Priscillianists who had been condemned to death, he acceded to Maximus' request that he should restore relations with the excommunicated bishops, on condition that the Emperor ceased his harrying of the heretics. But he was never happy about his giving way or sure that the end had justified the means. Another saint, Ambrose, Bishop of Milan (374–97), while believing that heretics should not be allowed to practise their religion, also opposed bloodshed and refused to communicate with the bishops who had been responsible for Priscillian's death.

Far more important than Priscillianism was the heresy associated with the name of Pelagius, said to have been a British monk. He came to Rome in about 390 where he was scandalized by the loose living of many of the citizens. He was himself a man of exemplary life, ascetic, spiritual and admirable in his dealings with penitents who sought his help. He had a lay friend and supporter, a lawyer named Coelestius, probably an Irishman, described as a man 'of incredible loquacity', and Julian, Bishop of Eclanum in Campania, southern Italy, later formed a third in the unholy trinity of the Pelagian heresy.

Pelagianism was – many say still is – a heresy of a western type which could not have happened in the east. Indeed, the west became obsessed with it. It caused the stir it did largely because the principals on both sides had personalities which saw self-evident truth in their own spiritual experiences. They could not have been more out of sympathy with each other and, one feels, would have considered any subject they debated from opposite viewpoints. The problem that exercised them was one which panders particularly to disagreement, for those who debate it usually approach it from one of two sides and find it difficult to hold a balance, not to overstate their case and see their opponents' side of the question. The debate can be summed up in the single phrase, 'predestination versus free will'.

The eastern half of the Church was concerned with questions of the nature of God. The Latin west, much more practical and social and less mystical, was interested in the nature of man. The east accepted that man's will was free and the individual able to do what God commanded. The saintly and learned John Chrysostom, Bishop of Constantinople from 397, summarized the east's teaching when he preached that men can choose the good and when they do the grace of God comes to help them do it. Ambrose of Milan spoke for the west when he taught that all men were tainted by the sin of Adam who passed on his fallen nature to all his descendants. No one is conceived without sin, therefore even the new-born infant is cursed with 'original sin'. God's grace has to take the initiative in the work of salvation, man's freedom of will replying to and co-operating with it. St Augustine (354–430), Bishop of Hippo, Pelagius' principal opponent in the dispute, whose nature and experience, as will be seen, was so different from his, was more detailed in his doctrine. When creation began, he said, evil did not exist. God created men and angels both rational and free to choose. This capacity for free choice is man's greatest quality and danger, for while he can exist without being wicked, only he and the angels can become wicked. Adam could have remained sinless but deliberately sinned through pride, which is the belief carried out in action that man's will is to be followed rather than God's. For Augustine, with the intense sexual awareness that was part of his nature, sexual lust was the special expression of man's degraded will. Once he has fallen man can never be free, for even his efforts to extricate himself are selfish and self-willed. The only freedom that then remains to him is to continue to sin. The original (that is, 'root') sin, which fallen Adam has transmitted to mankind, is a universal tendency to sin and an inability to choose God. Even the infant dying at the moment of birth is therefore guilty, and all men need a second birth. This can be given them only by an act of God, and in this lies his grace.

As he was born of a virgin, Christ did not inherit the sin which accompanies normal human begetting. He lived and died without sin and, as the second Adam in whom all could be made alive, gave mankind a fresh start. God has predestined some to salvation, others to the punishment their sin deserves. (This doctrine is quite unacceptable to anti-Predestinationists – how can a god be called just, good and loving, who has created men for damnation? And such damnation!) God has predestined the exact number of the elect to be saved through grace. These fortunate ones can still sin, but they are granted perseverance so that repentance will follow sin, and eventually they will reach a stage where they will be able not to sin. The culminating blessing of the elect will be that they will not be able to forsake good, the highest freedom of all, and will attain eternal life. To the elect, God's grace will prove irresistible.

Baptism washes away original sin and sins committed before it, and Augustine therefore advocated infant baptism. God's grace can inspire men to do good, which he rewards as if it were of their own making, and they may be gradually transformed by grace – yet still not be given perseverance and salvation. An individual never knows if he is of the elect, for knowledge might lead to pride, the greatest and most fundamental sin of all.

Augustine was what has been called a 'twice-born' character – that is, a man capable of great sins or extreme goodness and able to swing from one extreme to the other. Always restlessly searching for truth, he became a Manichee at nineteen and remained one until he was thirty, when he turned Neoplatonist, a disciple of Plotinus, meanwhile leading a private life which he felt to be sexually depraved but from which he could not break free. The story of his conversion to Christianity is well known. It was the culmination of a process which had continued for a long time, but it happened suddenly, dramatically and so powerfully that the man who had looked upon himself as a great sinner became transformed in a moment to one in whom others saw the development of a great saint. Conscious that God had acted upon him from without, Augustine's doctrine of election sprang from the experience of his own helplessness in controlling his sexual appetites and his conviction that a power greater than and external to himself had taken control.

Pelagius was entirely different. He was a moralist, not a theologian (as his misunderstandings of St Paul's epistles in his still extant commentary prove), and there does not seem to have been a trace of the mystic in him. He was a typical 'once-born' character, unimaginative in sinning and as incapable of great or shocking wickedness as he was of outstanding virtue or saintliness. He can be pictured as a solidly respectable individual, with no skeletons in his cupboard and conscious of his own integrity and ability to mould his life and control his appetites and no less his fate. He was an ascetic, conscious that he was progressing in the good life in his own view and that this progress had been achieved by his personal struggle, effort and will-power. His experience led him to believe the opposite to Augustine. By the exercise of their natural powers and their own efforts men could avoid sin, become morally perfect, even sinless, and acquire heaven. They had unconditional freedom of the will to resist sin or yield to it at pleasure, although it was true that the help of God enabled them to resist more effectively. God's grace, his first and greatest gift to mankind, was man's nature and free will with its sin-resisting potentiality. Men could live without sin by training their wills, and some had done so before and after Christ came. At birth each human being began with a clean sheet, for Pelagius denied original sin – Adam bequeathed to his descendants not an inherited taint but a bad example. Death and concupiscence did not result from his fall – some Pelagians even believed that Adam was created mortal. Pelagius seems to have believed in traducianism, that the human soul is propagated along with the body.

These beliefs led to a different understanding or virtual dismissal of many accepted Christian tenets. The freedom of the new-born infant from original sin led to a dislike by Pelagius and a still greater one by Coelestius of infant baptism, which became pointless. Election disappeared, predestination became a mere foreseeing of merit. Grace had a different meaning altogether. The cross no longer spoke of redemption, and atonement became unnecessary, while Christ turned from a saviour into a teacher, giving as the second Adam a good example to be followed where the first had given a bad. Forgiveness of sin through faith became the 'let-off' of punishment by a weakly, kindly schoolmaster, not a renewal of grace. The Law was given equality with the Gospel as a guide to heaven, and the whole of Christianity was reduced to a caricature of itself.

For a time Pelagius' views were either not clearly enough expressed to arouse comment or did not attract the attention of powerful enough opponents. Alaric's capture of Rome in 410 displaced a number of its inhabitants, among them Pelagius and Coelestius, who arrived in Africa in 411. The spark which was to set off the powder-keg of Pelagian controversy seems to have been a sentence in Augustine's *Confessions,* much read at this time, which ran, 'Give what you command, command what you will'. This seemed to Pelagius to smack of what was later called Quietism, religious passivity which waits for God to take action. Such moral listlessness was anathema to his active, disciplined mind and habits.

He remained only a short time in Africa, moving eastwards and leaving behind him in Carthage his ally, Coelestius. The lawyer applied for ordination in 412 but was refused on account of his heretical teachings and excommunicated. He seems to have held that

Adam's sin injured himself only, not the whole human race; that every child is born as free as Adam before the fall and can do right and fully keep God's commandments if he chooses, and that some before the time of Christ were sinless. These doctrines were, as has been seen, associated with Pelagius himself. Coelestius seems to have been more extrovert and less discreet in preaching them than his mentor. He followed him to the east and was eventually ordained presbyter at Ephesus.

Pelagius arrived in Palestine and aroused the hostility of St Jerome (345–420), author of the Vulgate and a vitriolic opponent of heresy. Yet a synod at Jerusalem took no action and referred the matter to Rome; and another at Diospolis (Lydda), in December 415, declared Pelagius innocent of heresy in spite of the opposition of Jerome and Orosius, a young Spanish priest and disciple of St Augustine. The exoneration did not last a year. The council was blamed for mishandling a problem of which it had no experience and Pelagius accused of duplicity in making some of his replies with mental reservations. Two further local councils at Carthage and Mileve in Numidia condemned him, their verdict shortly afterwards confirmed by Pope Innocent I. Carthage spelled out the orthodox position against Pelagianism in four points:

1. Death in Adam was the result of sin.
2. New-born children needed baptism on account of original sin.
3. Grace is needed not only for knowledge of God's commandments but also for strength to obey them.
4. Without grace it is impossible to perform good works.

Upon Innocent I's death within a few months, Pelagius appealed to his successor, Zozimus, who declared him blameless. The Pope wrote to the African Church declaring that Pelagius and Coelestius had never been separated from the Catholic truth, an important letter in that it is the first instance of a document emanating from the Pope being proposed as a standard of orthodoxy. The following year Zozimus reversed his decision, and his condemnation was reinforced by another plenary council of all Africa presided over by Aurelius, recognized as the chief of the bishops of the continent. Unconvinced, Coelestius continued to preach his doctrines in Sicily and, later, in Asia Minor where, in the event, he unwisely enlisted the support of Nestorius, still Bishop of Constantinople.

Augustine of Hippo now began writing his first refutation of Pelagianism, a work which was to occupy a large part of the remainder of his life – thirty-five books in all, excluding letters and sermons. The orthodox called Emperor Honorius to their aid. He declared Pelagius and Coelestius heretics, liable to punishment. Eighteen bishops who would not condemn them were deprived of their sees. Popes Boniface (418-422) and Celestine (422) repeated the condemnation. However, the battle was not over. Although Pelagius took refuge in silence and Coelestius in the east, a new champion, Julian, Bishop of Eclanum, took the field. He was a pugnacious and skilful debater who attacked St Augustine and waged war against him until Augustine's death twelve years later. He was condemned and exiled from Italy and first sought refuge with Theodore of Mopsuestia who, it must be remembered, was without orthodox blame and without reproach during his lifetime. Next, he accompanied Coelestius in seeking the protection of Nestorius at Constantinople.

Meanwhile, Britain had patriotically adopted the heresy of her native monk, to the concern of orthodox British bishops. They invited St Germanus of Auxerre and Lupus of Troyes to come over and put matters to rights. A public debate was held at St Albans before 'an immense multitude', at which the Pelagians were routed and the country saved for orthodoxy by the winning of a battle which was also, locally, the winning of the war.

Nestorius' protection did the Pelagians more harm than good, for when the Ecumenical Council of Ephesus condemned his heresy, it followed this up with a blanket condemnation of the Pelagianism to which he had given protection, naming as heretics with him Pelagius, Coelestius and Julian. But Pelagius was anathematized only for his negative themes, his denial of inherited sin and need for divine grace. His positive insistence on the need of the active exercise of man's will was accepted.

Julian continued his activity on behalf of his beliefs, even applying unsuccessfully to Pope Sixtus III in 439 for readmission to the Church. He did not hesitate to use personal arguments against the champions of orthodoxy, quoting Augustine's earlier allegiances and writings against him; and he embarrassed the orthodox by carrying some of their assertions to extreme logical conclusions. If original sin was transmitted at conception or birth, this condemned Christian marriage. If infant baptism was absolutely and universally necessary, this entailed eternal damnation for unbaptized children who died without personal sin as well as all those myriads of unbelievers who perished in 'invincible' ignorance; the small number of elect saved under predestination denied God's love, goodness and justice and the effectiveness of Christ's redemptive sacrifice. These were called quibbles by the orthodox, but they are difficulties to this day and should not be underrated. There were also contentions on the Pelagian side never adequately answered by orthodox theologians. In denying, for example, Pelagius' assertion that Adam's death was not a punishment for sin but due to his corporeal nature (a view held surely today by every Christian with a smattering of biological knowledge), they did not explain how or why Adam was not originally destined for bodily death.

A more dangerous heterodoxy because more reasonable from an orthodox Christian's view, and seemingly supported by much personal experience, was semi-Pelagianism, more accurately called anti-Augustinianism. Experience for some 'once-born' Christians seemed to support a modified Pelagianism, for, although 'twice-born' characters feel their wills to be impotent and victory in overcoming sin and personal shortcomings to be initiated solely through God and given them from outside through Jesus Christ, this is not true of the spiritual bourgeoisie. They are without deep inner conflict and have no great sense of a flood of victory or release from the burden and power of sin after a crisis of conversion experience. They are conscious of progress or lack of it by their efforts and self-discipline or absence of them. For such believers men attain the good life by their own efforts assisted by God.

The principal exponent of semi-Pelagianism was John Cassian of Marseilles, who had founded monasteries in southern Gaul in about 415. Driven by the demands of dialectic in his writings against Pelagianism, Augustine sometimes went almost, if not altogether, too far. He wrote that above what he called the freedom of indifference was the freedom of sinning no longer, by which redeemed mankind is given a share in the freedom which is part of the nature of God. The doctrine did away with the opposition between grace and free will, but Augustine exaggerated his position and, in doing so, could later be claimed to be the spiritual father of Wyclif, Luther and other reformers.

His writings caused a reaction in monastic circles, especially those of south Gaul, for they seemed to belittle the life of self-denial and discipline and to nullify all moral effort. Some Catholics also felt that there was a basic immorality in the view that, unless God chooses, no sinner can take even the first step, and, if God wills it, none of the elect can escape salvation (or the damned damnation). Cassian's view was very like that held traditionally in the eastern part of the Church: God and man were concerned in a co-operation between grace and free will operating mysteriously and intimately in the work of salvation. Cassian looked at the problem of personal salvation psychologically. He agreed that man could not merit salvation; but, while rejecting the Pelagian contention that man's nature was uncorrupted and grace unnecessary, he allowed that by natural good works he could in some sense deserve grace. Men had the free will and the power to co-operate with the grace of God, could come to him of their own free will without any prevenient grace of God. Men were not unable to will or to do good, and God strengthened even the smallest spark of will towards goodness. Once in a state of salvation, the saved individual could attain final perseverance without special help from God.

These notions were criticized on the ground that man instead of God was given all the credit for salvation. Cassian believed also that it was God's will that all men should be saved. Some of his followers, however, put forward strange arguments to justify the eternal damnation of unbaptized infants: this happened because God had foreseen the lack of faith they would have shown, had they lived.

Vincent, a monk of Lérins, also in southern Gaul, supported Cassian, attacking Augustine's teachings as 'novelties' and putting forward his famous but challengeable definition of Catholic faith as that 'which has been believed everywhere, always and by all'. Augustine, however, had his champions, notably Prosper of Aquitaine, a layman leading the monastic life, who defended him untiringly in writings from 428 to 435 and tried to get support, which was given in the most prudent moderation, from Pope Celestine.

Augustinianism hardened under controversy into Predestinationism, which was a heresy. Augustine himself was never called heretical, but some of the more extreme of his supporters maintained that those not among the elect could multiply their efforts and good works all in vain, for God would choose to withhold his grace and thus prevent them from persevering in goodness. Faustus, Bishop of Riez, a former Abbot of Lérins and an opponent of Augustinianism, accused a priest named Lucidus, a strict Augustinian, of Predestinationism in about 474, first refuting and convincing him, then having the heresy condemned in councils at Arles and Lyons. Faustus was too naïve a theologian to walk the tightrope between the divine grace and human nature successfully, his language suggesting at least a semi- if not a neo-Pelagianism.

In 519 the anti-Augustinianism of the Provençal monks was challenged by those same Scythian monks who had made a contribution to the Monophysite crisis, and ten years later the Catholic Church made its final pronouncements on Pelagianism and semi-Pelagianism at a synod held at Orange. Caesarius, Bishop of Arles, educated at Lérins and familiar with both Augustine and Faustus, met semi-Pelagianism with a moderate Augustinianism, approved afterwards by Pope Boniface II, and from then on the official doctrine of the Catholic Church. Man, the council stated, inherits a nature corrupt in body and soul, and is unable to do anything whatever towards salvation by his natural powers. He has lost all power to turn to God because sin has so weakened his free will that 'no one is able to love God as he ought, or believe in God, or do anything for God which is good except the grace of divine mercy come first to him'. Nothing was said, however, about the

'total depravity' of mankind through Adam's sin, and man's will was
not so impaired by Adam's fall that, healed by grace and helped by
Christ, it can achieve salvation. But those who asserted that man's
will could anticipate God's action, or that faith could begin or belief
be willed apart from the free gift of grace, or that choice of good be
made apart from it, were condemned.

Not only is grace essential before men can move at all towards
faith and salvation, but it is necessary also after men have turned, if
they are to persevere in the good life. Grace inspires the desire for
baptism and does not merely elect souls, for all who are baptized
are capable of salvation. 'All who have been baptized can and ought,
by the aid and support of Christ, to perform those things which
belong to salvation if they labour faithfully'. The fear of being
among those to whom the gift of perseverance was not given was
consequently removed from all baptized Christians. Those who
taught that any man was predestined to evil by the divine power
were anathematized.

By stating a moderate position, useful later in arguing against
some Protestant beliefs, and avoiding extremes on one side or the
other, the Council of Orange escaped swimming in waters which
could not fail to be troubled. But it did not solve the fundamental
and insoluble question, 'How can a loving and just God create men
who he knows will not respond to his grace nor avail themselves of
the salvation offered in Christ, and thus be condemned to everlasting
damnation?' Nor did it destroy the Pelagian cast of thought which
is to be found in much Anglo-Saxon Puritanism, which regarded
success in business as God's reward for the scrupulous honesty that
marked the Puritan's dealings upon earth. Furthermore, the supreme
pleasure of heaven would be given them as recompense for their
avoidance of the inferior pleasures offered by the world, the flesh
and the Devil.

It may not be an exaggeration to say that all religious activity
which is done solely from a sense of duty and not from the love of
God is Pelagian; for it betrays a mind which believes that heaven
can be won by human effort. Yet to do one's duty or even to know
that one ought to do it is, perhaps, the result of grace. The circle
of the debate, like most theological debates, is never-ending.

CHAPTER 11

To Wyclif and Hus

Schism is not heresy. It is, however, its first cousin, and important breaches need to be mentioned in passing, for often there were principles of doctrine behind them. Novationism, Donatism and Meletianism were three faces of a single schism, based on the contention that consecrations and baptisms by unworthy ministers were invalid.

During the persecution by the Emperor Decius in 250, thousands of Christians apostasized but sought readmission to the Church once the danger was past. Cornelius, Bishop of Rome, was prepared to readmit them, but Novatian, an impeccably orthodox presbyter of the Roman Church, opposed leniency and was appointed rival Bishop of Rome, rebaptizing those who sided with him. The movement was heretical in so far as it allied with the Montanists, and lasted till the fifth century in Rome and somewhat longer in Constantinople.

The Donatists took up a similar position after the Diocletian persecution fifty years later. A 'traditor' who had given way under persecution was consecrated Bishop of Carthage in 311, and one who had remained faithful was consecrated rival bishop to him and was succeeded by Donatus in 316. The Donatists, claiming at one time as many as 270 bishops, maintained their separate identity probably until the Moslem invasion of the seventh century, successfully resisting pressure by both the Catholic Church and the imperial power. The Meletians were an Egyptian branch of the Donatists, taking their name from Meletus, a bishop. The Donatists were in the main orthodox, although some of them were tinged with Arianism, and the Meletians adopted the Monophysitism of the Coptic Church.

Augustine wrote copiously against the Donatists, helping to establish the principle, which has remained that of the western Church, that sacraments are not dependent for their validity upon the moral character of the men by whose hands they are administered but are valid in themselves, deriving their efficacy from God. It is obvious to Christian thought that this must be so, because an apparently upright priest may be merely a successful hypocrite, whereas an obviously culpable one may be fighting hard against the sins which beset him, and only God can know the hearts of men. The receiver of the sacrament, too, must be able to trust its efficacy for himself, whatever the character of the administrator.

The iconoclastic quarrel which tore the Church apart from 726 to 843, in which one side wished to destroy all representations in sculpture and paintings of Jesus and the saints, was a result of the fears of many Christians that their use broke the second commandment, 'Thou shalt not make unto thee any graven image'. Perhaps Moslem criticism of Christian 'idolatry' reinforced their fears. The details of the struggle are of no relevance to a history of heresy except that those who wished to retain the use of images accused their iconoclastic opponents of being Monophysites; for, they said, they denied the reality of the incarnation and humanity of Christ. In refusing to depict him as a man, they implied that he was God but denied that he had ever really become man. The result of the conflict was that the Greek Church used sculptured figures as well as pictures – a small contributory factor to the eventual schism between the Roman Catholic and Orthodox Churches. In the course of the quarrel, a council at Chalcedon in 754 condemned the use of images, a decree supported by an edict of Constantine V which said that offenders should be punished as heretics. This was one of several 'temporary' heresies which were later accepted by the orthodox as normal faith and practice.

Different dates are given for the Great Schism between Rome and Constantinople, leading to the division of the imperial Church into the two communions of Roman Catholicism and Orthodoxy, 1054 being the year that is widely accepted as the date of the final breach. The reasons were political rather than doctrinal and, as such, are not the concern of this book. Although patriarchs and popes thundered anathemas and excommunications at each other, and accusations of heresy accompanied their broadsides, rivalry, ambition and extravagant claims were the ever-recurring motifs in the quarrels of the centuries. There were differences in eastern and western teachings about Purgatory, but these were not significant; and even the dissension over the *filioque* clause, now to be discussed, would have been no bar to the unity of Catholic and Orthodox or their reunion after the schism, had the will to Christian love been in their leaders.

In 589 a council at Toledo took a step which resulted in an accusation of heresy by the east. It added the words 'filioque' ('and the Son') to the clause of the creed which reads, 'I believe in the

Holy Ghost...who proceedeth from the Father', an addition now accepted throughout those parts of the western Church that use the creed, though not officially for some centuries after Toledo. The Spanish Church made the addition as a safeguard against the Arianism of the Visigoths, and its use was exported to France and Germany, where Charlemagne employed it to support an accusation of heresy which he made against the Greeks. They counter-charged, alleging heresy by the west on two grounds. The first was that any alteration to the creed had been expressly forbidden by the ecumenical councils, and only another council could authorize the addition. The second was that the expression was theologically suspect and could upset the balance between the unity and diversity of the Trinity. The single essence of the Godhead must not be over-emphasized at the cost of the distinction between the Persons. By the statement that the Holy Spirit proceeds from the Son as well as the Father, the Greek Church felt that the latter's monarchy was weakened and that the distinction between the Persons was sacrificed to the divine simplicity of the common Essence. If an addition had to be made at all, the words, 'proceedeth from the Father *through* the Son' would supply what both sides believed. When the eastern bishops under Photius, Patriarch of Constantinople, met at a synod in that city in 867, they accused Rome of heresy not only on the grounds of the *filioque* clause but for insisting on the celibacy of the clergy, a practice which seemed to them to smack of the Manichean view that matter and the flesh were evil, and for confining confirmation to bishops.

All the above movements are of great importance in the general history of the Church but of little relevance to the history of heresy as such, the story of which in the western Church must now be resumed.

For some centuries heresy was not the business of large movements, as the Christological heterodoxies had been, but of individuals and small sections of believers. Spain, largely isolated from the rest of Europe by Moorish conquests, was the scene of one local heresy. Elipand, Archbishop of Toledo and the leading Spanish ecclesiastic, tried to insist upon the full humanity of Christ by maintaining that, although in his divine nature he was the Son of God, in his human form he was a son only by adoption. Felix, Bishop of Urgel, also in Spain, agreed with Elipand in spite of the Pope's reproof of the latter for his heresy of 'Adoptionism'. But in 792, at the Synod of Regensberg, Felix renounced the belief, and two years later, at the Synod of Frankfurt, summoned by the Emperor Charlemagne, the Spanish Christology was formally condemned. Felix, meanwhile, despite his renunciation, was energetically defending Adoptionism, in debate against Alcuin, invited by Charlemagne from his native

Yorkshire to encourage learning among the Franks. The Frankfurt condemnation made no difference to Felix's views, and in 798 a council at Rome repeated it. In 800 Felix and Alcuin debated in front of Charlemagne at Aix-la-Chapelle. Once more Felix professed himself convinced and renounced the views he had held, but he was not trusted and was kept confined until his death in 818. Alcuin tried to convert Elipand to orthodoxy, but the Archbishop remained obstinately heretical, together with other bishops of Moslem-controlled Spain. Yet it was about this time that the Gallic Church accepted the *filioque* 'heresy' from Spain, as the use of the clause was approved by a synod held at Aix in 809.

In 831 Paschasius Radbertus, a monk of Corbie near Amiens, proposed the doctrine of Transubstantiation in a treatise on the Eucharist, a teaching which was to lead to much controversy at the time and heresy later. The bread and wine, he wrote, remain unchanged to the senses, but by a miracle the substantia (underlying essence) transforms into the very body and blood of Christ which was once on earth. This change takes place only for those who believe it and accept it in faith, and is not effective for the unbeliever. Christ on the altar repeats the sacrifice of the cross, suffering and dying once again. Raban Maur (Hrabanus Maurus), Abbot of Fulda and a pupil of Alcuin, denied the physical identity but accepted that the body of the risen Lord was present, though not physically. To receive the body of Christ is to be united with him by faith so as to form a single body with him. Gottschalk, a former monk of Fulda, agreed with Radbertus that the body and blood of Christ are physically present but as an objective reality, quite independently of the faith of the communicant. Ratramnus, another monk of Corbie, maintained that the true fruits of the Eucharist are spiritual power and healing. The body of Christ must be present spiritually, not physically, if these spiritual fruits are to result from the sacrament. The doctrine was not finally settled for the Roman Church until the Fourth Lateran Council in 1215 made Transubstantiation *de fide*.

Gottschalk caused a greater stir by carrying some of Augustine's teachings to extremes. He wrote that, for reasons which are beyond man's comprehension, God predestines some to eternal life, and these fortunate ones cannot escape it. On the other hand, those who are not predestined to life eternal are predestined to eternal death. These views ran counter to the ruling of the Council of Orange of 529 and were opposed by Raban Maur and Hinemar, Archbishop of Rheims. They were willing to allow that God foreknows the sins of those not elected to salvation, but denied his foreordination of them. In 848 Maur, then Archbishop of Mainz, expelled Gottschalk into Hinemar's province, where the unfortunate scholar was deposed from the priesthood and imprisoned in a monastery. Powerful friends were unable to help him. Hinemar was vindicated at a council held in 860 and a few years later Gottschalk died, unreconciled with the Church.

Another heterodox ecclesiastic of the early ninth century was Claudius, Bishop of Turin, who denounced the veneration of images and the cross, and prayers to the saints for their intercession. He declared that the Pope should not be called apostolic because he sat in the seat of an apostle, but only he who did an apostle's work.

Contemporary with Claudius was a much more dangerous, because more erudite, and wittier scholar, John Scotus Eriugena, or Eruginus. An Irishman, famous for his jests, he was protected by Charles the Bald. In the controversy over predestination and free will he put forward the remarkably modern view that, since for God who is eternal there is neither past nor future, so that he sees everything and everyone simultaneously, foreknowledge and foreordination cannot be disjoined. God knows only what he does. Scotus also held that evil has no real existence, that creation consists of a series of emanations from the Godhead and that reason is superior to authority. He was saved from charges of heresy by the power of his patron, but even so he was forced to flee for refuge to King Alfred in England, where he is said to have been stabbed to death at Malmesbury by irate scholars armed with iron pens. After his death his views were condemned at two synods held in 855 and 859.

Apart from these and, perhaps, other individuals too obscure for their names or fates to have been recorded, the Church remained untroubled by heresy until after the First Crusade, which took place in 1096. Partly inspired by the wish of the Pope to restore unity between the eastern and western divisions of the Church by recapturing the Holy Places which belonged to the whole of Christendom (a wish eventually made impossible of fulfilment by the sack of Constantinople by the Crusaders themselves in 1204), the Crusades were for many reasons a disaster for Christianity, although they had some beneficial results. One of their evil effects was to accustom men to killing for the sake of religion. To slaughter heretics because they held a different form of belief was only a step beyond slaying Moslems because they held a different faith; and in the twelfth and thirteenth centuries the conscience of the Church, which had been expressed by St Martin of Tours in his concern for the life of Priscillian, became as calloused as that of any savage heathen. Not for six or seven hundred years was the Church to restore tolerance to its counsels, and since at the moment of writing Catholics and Protestants are murdering each other in Northern Ireland in the name of the Lord of Love, perhaps it has still not succeeded in doing so.

At the beginning of the eleventh century heresy began once more to be a matter of movements rather than individuals, though movements rarely take shape without leaders. These leaders came mostly from urban populations, from merchants, artisans and peasants, aristocratic churchmen being inclined to maintaining the *status quo*, which favoured them. Tanchelmus (Tanchelin), for example, came from Antwerp and preached in the district of Utrecht, whence his views spread to the Netherlands and along the Rhine. He attacked the Roman Church as it was constituted, denied its authority and that of the Pope, and taught that some of the sacraments were useless and all of them invalid if administered by immoral clerics. He was accused, perhaps falsely, by his opponents of preaching a doctrine of free love, saying that irregular relations between the sexes affected only the body and not the soul and are therefore permissible. He was imprisoned by the Archbishop of Cologne, and killed after escaping from him in 1115.

Contemporary with Tanchelmus was the far more important and exotic Abélard, hero – or villain – of the romance with Héloïse. Born about 1079, he was brought up by devout parents and developed into an attractive, charming, brilliantly intellectual individual, an enthusiast for debate, a stimulating teacher who drew students to him like a magnet, a restless seeker of knowledge and a sensitive and sincere Christian for whom faith and reason were allies. But he was also arrogant, and his habit of defeating his elders and teachers in debate did not endear him to them. Some of his sentiments were modern in spirit such as, 'By doubting we come to inquire, and so to the truth'. He was eventually condemned for heresy on account of some of his opinions on the Trinity, the Atonement, free will and original sin.

In his view of the Trinity Abélard, by reacting against the philosophy of Nominalism (the doctrine that general or abstract words do not stand for objectively existing realities and are only names given to individual physical particulars which alone have objective existence), which tended to make three Gods of the Trinity, verged on Monarchianism and laid himself open to the charge of Sabellianism.

Abélard's doctrine of the Atonement was that, since God had forgiven sin before Christ came, the satisfaction made by Jesus was unnecessary for the forgiveness of sins. Forgiveness as an act of God's grace is offered freely – there is no need to make satisfaction for sin, and gratitude and love for God awaken in men when they realize this. Men see in Jesus Christ what man should be, by this are made conscious of their sin and the love of God, and respond in love which inspires good living, thus bringing about 'new creatures'.

Abélard rejected the Augustinian doctrine of original sin, holding that mankind does not share in the guilt of Adam's sin, but that all men share in the punishment meted out to Adam. The weaknesses in men incline them to sin but in themselves are not sources of guilt, and men also have tendencies to good. Sin or absence of sin lies primarily in the motives with which men act, not only in the deeds that result. Reason, the gift of God, can reveal what is good, and since every human being can co-operate with the grace of God and use his will to follow the good revealed by reason, he can escape his share in Adam's punishment by good works.

Bernard of Clairvaux, considered a model Christian by his contemporaries, regarded these doctrines of Abélard's as subversive to the faith. Abélard had already appeared before a council at Soissons in 1121 because of his heterodox opinions, and in 1140 Bernard caused him to be convicted of heresy at a council at Sens. Abélard appealed to Rome, but the Pope confirmed the condemnation and excommunicated him. He was given refuge by the monastery of Cluny, and he and Bernard were happily reconciled before Abélard's death in 1142.

Also active early in the twelfth century were Peter de Bruys in Languedoc and Henri de Lausanne in France. Peter was an ascetic, leader of a fanatical sect called the Petrobusians, who profaned churches, overthrew altars and burned crosses. He rejected infant baptism, rebaptizing any who joined him, and the Eucharist. Church buildings and ceremonial, prayers for the dead and reverence for the cross were all anathema to him. Since the cross had been the instrument of Christ's death, he believed Christians should loathe rather than revere it, and implemented this article of his faith by destroying any crosses he could find. He met his death through burning by an enraged crowd.

Henri seems to have had a larger following, called Henricians, and was less extreme than Peter. He believed that sacraments lost their validity unless administered by ascetic priests who led a life of poverty, and attacked contemporary clergy for their love of wealth and power. He was attacked in his turn by Bernard of Clairvaux, who had a keen nose for heretics, and was handed in chains to the ecclesiastical authorities.

Another of Bernard's victims was the Italian, Arnold of Brescia, a friend of Abélard. He was a priest of pure life with an uncompromising ideal of poverty, who believed that no cleric from the Pope down should hold temporal power or own property. Sentenced for heresy at the Council of Sens in 1140, he was granted absolution by Pope Eugene III. He added political rebellion against Eugene's successor, Hadrian IV, to his heterodox religious opinions and was hanged in 1155, leaving a few followers, who later joined the Waldenses.

The Waldenses, or Vaudois, were founded by Peter Waldo, a

wealthy merchant of Lyons. Inspired by religious idealism, he disposed of his fortune and in 1176 gathered round him a band of itinerant preachers, mostly simple and illiterate men and women. They imitated the disciples who, at Christ's bidding, went out in couples without money, change of clothes or shoes, and existed on what the charitable gave them.

At first favoured by the Pope, the 'Poor Men of Lyons' or 'Poor in Spirit', as they called themselves, disregarded restrictions placed upon them, attacked papal corruption and preached many heretical doctrines. These included the priesthood of all believers, men and women; any good Christian could preach, absolve from sin and administer the sacraments. Masses and prayers for the dead, indulgences, confession, penance, church music, chanting of prayers, saying of prayers in Latin, and adoration of saints and of the blessed Sacrament were rejected. Lying, swearing oaths even in court and homicide of every kind were deadly sins. Those who preached crusades were damned.

Waldensian ministers were called Majorales or Perfect, renounced marriage and property and spent their time preaching. All Waldenses, lay or cleric, were missionaries, and, because of their energy and single-mindedness, the sect spread rapidly through most of western Europe.

Waldo was refused recognition by the Third Lateran Council in 1179 and in 1184 was excommunicated. Internal conflicts and external pressures resulted in the breaking away of sects differing in minutiae of organization and doctrine from the parent heresy, while other Waldenses regarded themselves as an orthodox though reforming movement inside the Catholic Church. Pope Innocent III, seeing the popularity and appeal of the poverty of the Poor Men, in 1208 took a good deal of the wind out of the movement's sails by forming his 'Poor Catholics' who, controlled by the Church, could follow those practices of the Waldenses of which the Church could approve.

Although the ecclesiastical and civil authorities regarded the Waldenses as heretics – as, indeed, they were in their many departures from orthodoxy – they tried to win them over by persuasion and used force only if this failed. Apart from their heterodox opinions they were blameless in their lives, being humble, industrious toilers with their hands, who dressed simply, were temperate in all their appetites, sober, truthful, slow to anger, eschewing the gathering of wealth, and avoiding taverns, dances and similar worldly pleasures. But neither the Church's tolerance nor their own inoffensive manner of life saved them. Some were burned at Strasburg as early as 1212, they were condemned by the Lateran Council of 1215, and by 1250 the full strength of the Inquisition, which had been instituted by then, was levelled against them. So many of them were in prison by the end of the century that the Catholics were begged for food for them, and in 1393, at Grenoble, 150 of them were burned in a single day. The heretics survived by taking refuge deep in the valleys of the Italian Alps. But even there they were not safe, for Innocent VIII organized a crusade against them in Dauphiné and the Savoy.

At the Reformation the Waldenses associated themselves with the Calvinist or Reformed Church, largely because of their geographical proximity to Switzerland. This made it easy for Farel, an early Reformed pioneer, to evangelize them and for their pastors to visit Basle, Berne and Strasburg. The Waldenses were enthusiastic for the Reformation, which caused a revival among them and a turning to Calvinist principles, expressed by them in a Confession of Faith issued in 1655. Persecution by Roman Catholic princes never ceased, but somehow a remnant of Waldenses survived, even when most of their villages in France were destroyed by order of the national Parlement.

In the nineteenth century, when the kingdom of Italy granted a measure of civil liberty to them, the Waldenses were removed from their remote villages to cities, helped financially by their fellow-Protestants in Great Britain and the United States, and later in the same century contingents of them emigrated to Uruguay and Argentina, where they counter-attacked by founding missions to Roman Catholics.

A heresy contemporary with the Waldensian, attracting far more attention and potentially far more dangerous to the Catholic Church, was one already mentioned in an earlier chapter, that of the Cathari (the Pure Ones) or Albigenses (from Albi, a town in southern France) or Patarini, or Paterenes – although this seems to have been a name given to all heretics. It was the Cathari who brought about the full development of the policy of persecution by which the Catholic Church came to defend itself against potential threats to its existence. Churchmen alone were not to blame, for, whatever its faults, the Church was a strong influence for unity and stability in the political system at a time when it most needed support, and also for civilizing Europe in its historical development. To lay rulers heresy was not only false doctrine which haled souls who believed it to the everlasting fires of hell, but a subversive movement which could topple their thrones.

Yet there was reluctance to execute and it was only slowly that the Church's conscience became calloused. From 385, when Priscillian was done to death, there were few killings, and many of those had been condemned by orthodox Christians. Robert II, King of France (971–1001), lived up to his sobriquet 'The Pious' by executing some heretics on his own authority. The Archbishop of Milan protested against the actions of the Milanese mob who seized and burned some Cathari. Peter Damian (c. 1007–72) wrote proudly that saints lay down their own lives for the faith but do not destroy heretics. In 1144 Wazo, Bishop of Liège, more successful than the Archbishop of Milan, rescued some Cathari the mob wished to burn, since 'God their Creator and Redeemer showed them patience and mercy'. When a few years later the Emperor Henry III executed some heretics, the opinion was expressed that if Wazo had still been alive, he would have acted like Martin of Tours in the Priscillian incident. In 1145 Bernard of Clairvaux, that uncompromising enemy of heresy, wrote that heretics should be won by reason rather than force, and it has already been seen that he reasoned and was reconciled with Abélard, although he demanded the imprisonment of Arnold of Brescia. Regrets were expressed by one writer, when the latter was executed, that he had not been bloodlessly punished. In 1162 Pope Alexander III said of some Cathari sent to him that 'it was better to pardon the guilty than take the lives of the innocent', and in 1165 the differences between Catholics and Cathari were threshed out peacefully in public debate at Narbonne.

The Cathari, however, became too numerous to be tolerated. A large part of the population of southern France joined the heresy, which attracted adherents also in northern Italy, northern Spain, and some in northern France and in Flanders, while there were a few even among the Slavs and in Constantinople. They were found mainly in the cities. The reason for their success was that the orthodox Church was weak, its clergy mostly ignorant, luxurious, corrupt, indolent and profane. Those who were not illiterate compiled indecent books, and simony and concubinage were rife. The Cathari, both clerics and laymen, were ascetic, self-denying and so much morally superior to the orthodox clergy that they attracted the idealistic in an age when there was much yearning for spiritual fulfilment, exemplified by the orthodox movements which gave birth to the Cistercians, Dominicans and Franciscans.

The beliefs of the Cathari that descended, as has been seen, from those of the Gnostics, Bogomils, Paulicians and Manicheans, were perhaps debatable in days before doctrine had settled, but intolerable in an age when orthodoxy had been fixed. They may be summarized as follows:

1. *Dualism* There are two eternal powers or principles, a good and an evil. The evil principle, not the good, is the creator of this material world. Some Cathari taught that the former was a rebellious creature of the First Principle, others that he was a coexistent principle, the source of all evil as the other is of all good. A variant doctrine was that the good God had two sons: one, Satanal, who rebelled; the other, Christ, who is the Redeemer. A practical

result of the doctrine was that the Cathari Church was regarded as being the creation of the good God and founded by Jesus, while the Roman was a product of the evil principle.

2. *Mankind* A mixture of the two opposing and irreconcilable principles. Man was originally a spiritual being, but, tricked by the evil principle, was thrust into a material body created by the bad God.

3. *The Soul* Created by the good God, this must be liberated from its imprisonment in matter. Every concession to the flesh made the imprisonment stricter and more oppressive, a belief which had important results for the practical life of the Cathari. Some of them believed in the transmigration of the soul.

4. *Procreation* This was anathema. Though marriage was permitted, it was regarded by some Cathari as more evil than adultery.

5. *The Incarnation* The incarnation of God in Jesus was obviously impossible, since matter was evil. His birth, physical body, crucifixion, resurrection and ascension were all illusions. He had neither true manhood nor was he God, but merely one of the pure spirits appearing on earth to deliver man from the delusions of the flesh by example and teaching. He came to redeem the fallen and enable them to return to their maker.

6. *The Bible* The Cathari found support from the Bible by picking and choosing, for they rejected parts of the Old Testament as having been written by the evil principle; while in the New, they laid undue emphasis upon St John's Gospel.

7. *Church Membership* They had two divisions, the 'Perfect' who had received the 'Consolation' (*consolamentum*), a spiritual baptism. This was administered by one who had already received it and granted to the recipient forgiveness of sins upon death and immediate entry into the kingdom of the good God and eternal life. The price paid was: complete celibacy, those unmarried remaining single and those married being required to separate; long fasts, with total abstinence from eggs, meat and milk; no ownership of property; and pacifism. The 'Perfect' formed the clergy, of which there were three orders – Majors (bishops), Presbyters (priests) and deacons, but the Church of the Cathari lacked the comprehensive and efficient structure of the Catholics.

The second division, of ordinary members, was that of the 'Believers' who might marry, hold property and remain outwardly in the Roman Church, even receiving its sacraments from priests and obeying its laws. Presumably the Believers were allowed mental reservations, for all three, sacraments, priests and laws, were rejected by the Cathari. These ordinary members received the consolation in old age or on their deathbeds.

8. *Worship* They had no church buildings and, because of their disbelief in the reality of the crucifixion, did not use crosses or crucifixes. They read from those Scriptures they accepted, heard sermons and, after a washing of the feet of those attending by the presiding 'Major', they shared a common meal of bread blessed, broken and distributed to the seated believers. There were other meals of bread, wine and fish, and a special Easter Communion of bread and wine.

Their enemies accused them of the grossest immoralities, as all sects meeting privately from fear of persecution have been accused from the early Christians meeting in the catacombs onwards. They could have been better accused of ignorance, for most of them were peasants and artisans – although a few scholars among them produced vernacular literature, including translations of the Bible.

In 1167 the Cathari were powerful enough to hold a council at Toulouse, presided over by their own bishop; and in 1179 the Third Lateran Council proclaimed a crusade against them – the first against fellow-Christians, however heretical – offering two years' indulgence as an inducement. A crusading army mustered in 1181, but it was disbanded after some initial success and allowed the Cathari to recover. Innocent III tried to stir enthusiasm, but was thwarted by the indolence or obstinacy of Count Raymond VI of Toulouse and by the preoccupation of King Philippe Auguste of France with his problems with the English.

In 1206 St Dominic (c. 1170–1221) preached to the Albigensian heretics in Languedoc with such success that he founded an Order of Preachers, the Dominicans, accepted by Honorius III. Had the fervent and instructed preaching and example of the devoted lives of these dedicated men had their way, southern France might have been peacefully recovered for the Catholic Church. But in 1208 Peter of Castelnau, a papal legate, was murdered in the dominions of Count Raymond of Toulouse, perhaps at his very court. The crime horrified western Europe. Innocent III once more proclaimed a crusade, promising the same indulgences and privileges for sixty days' campaigning in Languedoc as for service in Palestine. More than 200,000 Crusaders met at Lyons in 1209 under the capable leadership of Simon de Montfort. Not only were they fired by religious zeal, but the nobles of northern France wanted to reduce the power of the south and obtain some of its wealth for themselves, hoping for plunder on a much larger scale than the ordinary Crusader regarded as his right.

For twenty years the most civilized and, in the opinion of some, the happiest and gayest part of Europe, the land of the troubadours, was subjected to pillage and wholesale destruction. The town of Béziers was stormed early in the campaign and its inhabitants massacred. An oft-repeated story concerning the slaughter is that Arnaud, Abbot of Citeaux and papal legate, when asked how the orthodox were to be distinguished from the heretics, replied, 'Kill them all – God will know his own'. The crusade was carried on throughout the reign of Louis VIII (1223–6) and into that of Louis IX (1226–70), until the complete submission of Raymond VII of Toulouse at the Treaty of Paris in 1229. He professed loyalty to the Catholic Church, married his daughter to one of the King's brothers, agreed to the findings of an ecclesiastical council held at Toulouse, and later gave evidence of the sincerity of his repentance by burning eighty heretics at Agen in 1249 – his last public act on earth.

The Toulouse Council forbade the laity possession of the Bible, especially in the vernacular, except the Psalms and passages to be found in the breviary. It also systematized and elaborated the Inquisition, probably the most potent and certainly the most feared instrument ever used by the Catholic Church to cauterize heresy.

The remnants of the Cathari fled to the Balkans, where they formed the greater part of the population until the fifteenth century. Eventually the Turkish religion absorbed them and they disappeared as an organized body.

Few heresies could survive against the power of the orthodox, once the Catholic Church flexed its muscles. Heretics were weaker or fewer. Even if locally stronger they lacked the organization to oppose the juggernaut hierarchy of Rome backed by the civil power. Formal condemnation put them outside the law. When faced by eloquent and persuasive preaching like St Dominic's, the weakness of their opinions, illiterate as many heretics were, was often revealed to them. The Inquisition and the use of the civil arm were finally too much for them. By about 1350, the heresies of the twelfth and thirteenth centuries were mostly dead. Yet they remained rooted in southern France like weeds, emerging in later centuries in full strength as will be seen.

The Inquisition has been mentioned, and for convenience' sake its history and organization, as well as the progress of the actions against heresy undertaken by governments, are summarized here. In 1184 Emperor Frederick Barbarossa made outlawry the punishment for heretics. Thirteen years later Pedro of Aragon was the first to institute death at the stake as their fate. Aquinas (1224/5–c. 1274) lent the weight of his great scholastic authority to action by secular powers when he wrote that heretics were not to be tolerated but excommunicated and handed over to the civil power for execution. Aquinas was some six years old when Pope Gregory IX reorganized the Inquisition, inspired, according to some historians, by Raymond of Pennaforte, Confessor to the King of Aragon, who visited the

Pope in 1230 to enlist his help against heresy. Three years afterwards Gregory transferred the control of proceedings against heretics from the bishops' courts to special commissioners chosen from Franciscan and Dominican friars. Innocent IV (1243–54) added the use of torture, to be administered by the secular authority, but this proving impracticable, inquisitors and their assistants were allowed to absolve one another for using torture to 'promote the work of faith more truly'.

A suspect, however powerful or distinguished, once hauled before the Inquisition, was judged guilty unless he could prove his innocence. This was an all but impossible task, so heavily were the dice loaded against him. The evidence of wives, children, servants and persons heretical, excommunicated, perjured and criminal could be used against a man, secretly and without their having to face him, their charges being communicated to him only in summary form. Perjury was pardoned if it was the outcome of zeal for the faith, obedience to a superior was forbidden if it hindered the inquiry, and those who helped inquisitors were granted the same indulgences as pilgrims to the Holy Land. Any advocate acting and any witness giving evidence on behalf of a suspect laid themselves open to charges of abetting heresy. No one was ever acquitted, a released person always being liable to rearrest and a condemned one to a revised sentence with no retrial, at the discretion of the inquisitor. All proceedings were in secret. Legally torture could be inflicted only once, but was repeated as often as necessary on the pretext that it was the same torture continued, with intervals between the sessions.

Only the sentences were made public, on Sundays at high mass in the cathedral, attended by the civil authorities. Penitents confessed and abjured their heresy publicly before going to their penance (not called punishment or penalty), consisting of periods of imprisonment up to life sentences, the wearing of crosses, flogging and going on pilgrimage. The obdurate and relapsed were taken outside the church and handed to the magistrates with a recommendation to mercy and instruction that no blood be shed. The supreme hypocrisy of this was that if the magistrate did not burn the victims on the following day, he was himself liable to be charged with abetting heresy.

Heretics who repented at the last moment after condemnation to death were given life imprisonment, and relapsed heretics were burned without mercy. But the object of the Inquisition above all other considerations was to obtain a confession, as this strengthened the Church's authority – the burning of an obdurate represented the victory of an individual over ecclesiastical sovereignty and its failure in spite of all its power.

The organization of the Inquisition was thorough. Districts were set up corresponding to the Provinces of the Mendicant Order to which the inquisitor appointed for each district belonged. Each such official had a staff of agents who acted as police, spies and torturers. The Inquisitorial Court went on circuit preceded by a delegate who preached in the local church exhorting his congregation to repent if they harboured heretical opinions, and promising pardon to those who did and who laid information against others. In France, Germany, Italy and, later, Spain, under the notorious Torquemada, the Inquisition was established. England escaped except once during Edward II's reign, when it came for the suppression of the Templars. Elsewhere it was the boast of the Dominicans that they had preached with such success in Abyssinia as to have founded the Inquisition there. The institution decayed in the fifteenth century, owing partly to the success of its work (if heretics, men kept their thoughts locked in their minds and without communication there can be no movements), and partly to the rise of nationalism which caused rulers to dislike jurisdiction from powers outside their domains.

To return to national measures against heresy, in the twelfth century the Emperor Frederick II brought in death by burning throughout the Empire, and in Sicily. France formally promulgated the same penalty in 1270, thus legally recognizing a practice which had been in use for years. The English statute, *de heretico comburendo*, was not enacted until 1401 – one disadvantage in being an offshore island is that the refinements of civilization take somewhat longer to arrive.

Scarcely had one crusade against heretics come to an end than another began. Floris IV, Count of Holland, was enjoined by the Pope to attack the Stedingers, or Stedhengi. These were a Germanic people living near the Weser River who had refused to acknowledge the temporal jurisdiction of the Archbishop of Bremen. He accused them of heresy before Pope Gregory IX, who preached a general crusade against them, although there seems to have been little if any evidence of doctrinally heretical opinion among them. They were attacked by the combined forces of the Duke of Brabant and the Counts of Cleves and Holland in a fleet of three hundred ships, and in a savagely fought battle from four to six thousand 'heretics' were killed and the rest drowned in the Weser or scattered to the four winds.

The Archbishop of Narbonne in 1243 'strenuously carrying out the apostolic commands [of Innocent IV] delivered more than two hundred heretics of either sex to the flames'. Other examples of Christian love could doubtless be culled from the obscurer pages of history if one had the heart or the stomach to search for them.

Even within the ranks of the picked troops of orthodoxy heresy was to be found. Before the death of St Francis of Assisi the order he founded had begun to depart from the simplicity and poverty of its first days. After it, the Franciscans divided into three camps:

extremists, who wanted a complete relaxation of the rule of poverty; the moderates, who wished to maintain something of the original rules but wanted to develop scholarship and win influence in the Church; and the other extreme, truest to the ideals of Francis, who wished to stay loyal to the starkness of the first fellowship. These were known as the Spirituals or Zealots. Had they confined their strictures to their laxer brethren they would probably have escaped attention, but they criticized corruption in the Church and papacy. They were much influenced by the writings of one Joachim of Flora (Fiore), founder of the small strict order of St John of Flora, who died in 1202. Although the papacy had condemned some of his works in 1225, one of the Spirituals, John of Parma, wrote a preface to a new edition of Joachim's *The Everlasting Gospel* in 1254. This proclaimed the coming of a new religion to replace Christianity which, it suggested, had failed. The world was destined to pass through three cycles – the first of the Father, the second of the Son, and the third, about to begin, a perfect millennium in which there would be no need of Eucharist or sacraments, ruled by the Holy Spirit. In 1259 the whole of Joachim's works was condemned by the Church, and any who favoured his views were suspect.

Some extreme Spirituals seceded from the Franciscans, calling themselves the Fraticelli, or Little Brothers, and efforts to restore unity were vain. They held the 'heresy' that Christ and the Apostles had no property, and for this wickedness nine were burned at Viterbo during the papacy of Urban IV (1261–4). In 1297 Peter John Oliva produced another book of apocalyptic prophecies proclaiming that the whole Church system was to be superseded. The Fraticelli regarded this as divinely inspired. Pope John XXII carried on the persecution against them in 1316, not surprisingly as they had proclaimed him Antichrist or, at best, the forerunner of Antichrist, and the Roman Church that harlot of Babylon mentioned in Revelation. The sacraments and the Church, they added, were obsolete, for the whole Church had apostasized and they alone possessed the ministry and the sacraments.

Four Spirituals were burned in 1318, many more executions following. Their heresy was a variation of the theme that Christ and the Apostles held no property. They taught that it was unlawful for a Franciscan house to possess a granary or wine-cellar – hardly a burning topic, one would have thought, in any sense of the word. The General Chapter of the Franciscans seemed to support the Fraticelli in 1322 when it declared that Jesus and the disciples *had* stood for absolute poverty. Pope John XXII was swift to react. In a bull, *Cum inter nonnullos*, published on 12 November 1323, he declared that the Franciscan view was a perversion of Scripture, false and heretical, and ordered the Inquisition to treat as heretics all who held this doctrine. In 1337 a Spiritual was burned at Venice, one of many who eventually died for the trivial opinion. Some kind of peace was restored to the Franciscan order when finally, in 1517, Leo X divided it into two bodies, the Spiritual party taking the name of Observants or Recollects.

Loosely connected with the Franciscans were the Beghards (male) and Beguines (female). They were originally varieties of religious lay people, mostly women, who lived quiet, virginal lives, some living in their homes, others in communities. They often professed to be Franciscan tertiaries. As time passed, vast numbers of wandering mendicants began to call themselves by these names. In 1311 Pope Clement V took action against them at the Council of Vienne because they were channels for the spread of heresy. After 1317 many of both sexes were burned, chiefly in that hotbed of heresy, the south of France. In 1325 the Pope condemned a tract by a Franciscan, which encouraged 'the pestilential sect called Beguines'. The charge of spreading heresy was more just than usual; for many of the Beghards and Beguines belonged to a sect called the Brethren of the Free Spirit who were pantheists, hunted down by the Inquisition, like the contemporary German Luciferans. In spite of their harrying by the authorities, this type of heretic survived until the fourteenth century, a remnant perhaps even into the sixteenth.

The Brethren of the Free Spirit was but one of a number of mystical movements which blossomed in Germany about this time. Another, the Brethren and Sisters of the Common Life, was orthodox, but the Friends of God, though less suspected by the authorities, had at least one member, Nicholas of Basle, burned as a heretic. Possibly the greatest German mystic, Meister John Eckhart (c. 1260–c. 1327), a Dominican, was accused of heresy partly because of Franciscan rivalry with his own order. Protesting that he was orthodox, Eckhart appealed to the Pope. He died before a verdict was given, but after his death Pope John XXII branded as heretical seventeen propositions in his works, and there is little doubt that he had leanings towards pantheism.

It has been seen that the Franciscans, who may be regarded as part of the élite of the Church and were often inquisitors, could be judged guilty of heresy and die at the stake. Not even the Pope was always able to avoid a charge of heresy. Boniface VIII, coming to the papal throne in 1294, quarrelled with Philip the Fair, King of France. A haughty letter from the Pope asserted that all kings whatever, the King of France as well as others, by divine command owed allegiance to him not only in religious matters but also in secular and human affairs. Philip replied with extreme bitterness. Boniface retorted with the bull *Unam sanctam*, in which he asserted that the whole human race was subject to the Roman pontiff and that all who differed from this doctrine were heretics and could not be saved. In 1303 Philip, in an assembly of his nobles, publicly accused Boniface of heresy, simony and the practice of magic and dishonesty, and urged the calling of an ecumenical council to depose him. The Pope in his turn excommunicated the King and all his adherents. Falling temporarily into the hands, however, of a force of French allied with Italians of the Colonna family who had also quarrelled with him, and struck on the head with an iron gauntlet, Boniface, though rescued, died, not of the blow but of rage, frustration and chagrin.

In 1324, the year that Wyclif was born, Marsilio of Padua wrote *Defensor Pacis*, a work implicitly condemning persecution for heresy, for its author argued that the infliction of temporal pains and penalties or any coercive jurisdiction was not within the province of the clergy, whose business it was to warn off with spiritual penalties or persuade, not to punish or compel. The conscience of the Church had not yet, therefore, become entirely hardened, although only an individual here and there was bold enough to speak out and, as Wyclif's followers proved, those who protected them did so from political self-interest rather than pity or Christian tolerance.

John Wyclif had a brilliant career at Oxford where he was Master of Balliol and the foremost scholar among contemporary dons. He showed his independence of mind by being a philosophical Realist (one who holds that general ideas, such as love and beauty, have an objective existence) in an age when its opposite, Nominalism, was currently popular, and was much influenced by Plato, via Augustine, Duns Scotus and Robert Grosseteste, the reforming Bishop of Lincoln. During his Oxford career he lived the life of puritan asceticism which was to mark his days in the parish of Lutterworth where he spent his last seven years. His favour with the Crown is shown by the appointment, made in 1374, which was a royal one, and, until his views grew too extreme, he was under the protection of John of Gaunt, the King's uncle.

Although he had been critical of some existing beliefs at Oxford, it was not until his parish life gave him leisure to write and organize that Wyclif became famous (or notorious). He attacked the wealth of bishops and clergy, maintaining that all endowments should be abolished and that they should live on voluntary offerings. All property belonged to God, who lent it temporarily on the condition of faithful service, and the right to it forfeited if the service was unfulfilled. If an ecclesiastic was unfaithful he could be removed by the civil power. In an age of greedy clergy and papal exactions from England on a large scale, such teachings were favoured by the wealthy laity. Not as welcome was the extension of the doctrine to themselves that they might be deprived of their riches if they misused them.

Wyclif asserted that popes could err and that, since to be a worldly pope was to be a heretic, such a man could be removed from office by laymen, if necessary. He rejected the dominion of both Pope and Church. Believing in the omnipotence of the arbitrary will of God he conceived of the Church as consisting of those predestined to salvation. It was an invisible and unknown body, for, since it is God's choice which determines membership, no visible church or its officers can admit to or bar from it, nor can anyone know who the saved are. Connection with the visible Church and priesthood is no guarantee of salvation – only God 'knows his own'. Later Wyclif developed the doctrine of the priesthood of all elected believers, and taught that in certain circumstances laymen could officiate at the Eucharist. The Scriptures, which became for Wyclif the only law of the Church, saw no difference between bishops and priests. Dominion of any kind was founded on grace only and clergy should be honoured solely for their characters and example, especially since the virtue of the sacraments they administered depended on the worthiness of the minister. Wyclif was particularly critical of monks and friars.

Without rejecting any of the seven sacraments Wyclif nevertheless saw no necessity for confirmation. He accepted the Real Presence of Christ in the bread and wine of the Eucharist, but in 1380 denied Transubstantiation on philosophical grounds. Though retaining a belief in Purgatory, he repudiated indulgences, masses for the dead and the cults of saints, relics and pilgrimages. Intelligent sincerity in worship was of more value than formalism and elaborate ceremony which might, in his view, endanger worship. In preaching, he avoided the usual artifices of the time, fables, stories of miracles and lives of the saints, and drew his material from the Bible.

Wyclif quickly aroused the hostility of the Archbishop of Canterbury and the Bishop of London, but was protected by John of Gaunt until his views became altogether too radical for the royal duke. He was fortunate in that he was allowed to die in his bed in peace.

By the time of his death Wyclif had caused the Bible to be translated into the vernacular. This was because he believed the Scriptures to be the supreme authority under God, and held that not only should all clergy know them but that even unlearned and plain men were to be able to understand them. They were used also by the poor preachers (given no formal title) introduced by Wyclif, who preached wherever they could gain a hearing, in churches or markets or on village greens, recognizable by their uniform of undressed russet cloth reaching to their bare feet, and the long staves they carried. They took such food and shelter as were offered them and, besides denouncing the corruption of the Church and clergy, taught in the vernacular the Lord's Prayer, the Ten Commandments and the Seven Deadly Sins, as well as extracts from the Bible, especially the Gospels and Epistles. Wyclif wrote tracts, sermons in outline and paraphrases of the Bible for their use. At first a number of priests and men of good class were to be found among the poor preachers; later they were mostly laymen drawn from the poorer strata of society. They attracted a large number of adherents who came to be known as Lollards (from a Middle English word meaning 'a mumbler of prayers'). These were at first protected by many of the local gentry until official opposition to them became too intense for the safety of sympathizers.

Persecution was as intense as it was inevitable. Not only were the ecclesiastical authorities attacked directly by the poor preachers in a way which, if successful, would have destroyed their power and influence, but many beliefs and practices unquestioned for centuries were denounced. The Peasants' Revolt in 1381, the result of economic and social unrest, was falsely ascribed to Lollard-inspired disaffection and frightened those among the prosperous who had protected the Wyclifites. A council at Oxford in the same year condemned many of Wyclif's teachings, in 1382 the 'Earthquake Council' at Blackfriars repeated the condemnation and in 1383 the Archbishop of Canterbury took action against Lollards at Oxford. In 1384 Wyclif died peacefully, and in 1401, under the intensely orthodox Henry IV, England belatedly followed the example of continental powers by making the stake the legal penalty for heresy. Five years later Parliament passed a savage act against the Lollards, and in one year more the Archbishop of Canterbury condemned Wyclif's doctrines and unauthorized translations of the Bible, and prohibited unlicensed preachers. These measures were confirmed by a London synod in 1409 and some Lollards were burned. Henry V (1413–22) took ruthless and ferocious measures against the heresy. The year after he ascended the throne, some Lollards met at Little Lincoln's Fields in London, were attacked by royal troops and many of them were captured. Thirty-seven were hanged and seven burned.

In 1415 the Council of Constance condemned Wyclif on 260 different counts, and ordered his bones to be exhumed and thrown out of consecrated ground. However, this order was not put into effect until 1428, and then it took a papal command to enforce it. The bones were burned and the ashes thrown into a running stream. This burning of bones of heretics who had died in peace, a usual practice of the Inquisition, was not simply a petty revenge, linked as it was with the forfeiture to the Church of the heretic's possessions and dispossession of his family and heirs.

In spite of continued persecution, Lollardism survived and even recovered a little in Henry VII's reign (1485–1509). It is impossible to say how strong it was or how influential, but it left enough seeds to flourish anew when the Reformation came, though under different names.

If Wyclif was the English Morning Star of the Reformation, John Hus was the Bohemian. By his burning at the stake at the instigation of a council which, if not ecumenical, was at least European, he possibly caused a greater pre-Reformation blaze. Born about 1373, Hus went to Prague University, where he was an average student, was ordained priest before 1403 and became dean of the faculty of philosophy and rector of the university. His private life was exemplary.

He was not the first Bohemian to move towards reformation. The country had already been influenced to some extent by the Cathari and Waldenses, and Hus had been preceded by John Milič who announced in Prague that the reign of Antichrist in the person of the Emperor Charles IV was beginning. Milič had been sent by the Holy Spirit to reform the Church in Bohemia, and advocated daily or frequent communion as a means to this end. He had a disciple, Mathias of Janov, who saw in the current papal schism a sign of the end of the world. He also advocated frequent communion, and held in common with later Protestantism a dislike of excessive veneration of saints, of monks, ecclesiastical ritual and Greek philosophy. The Holy Spirit and the Bible were the guide to faith for the Christian, and there should be a return to the piety and simplicity of the early Church. Not only was Bohemia being stirred by individual preachers like Milič and Mathias, but there was a groundswell of religious revival that was spreading throughout the country.

There had been political connections between England and Bohemia which led to a circulation of Wyclif's writings in the latter country, and in 1403, not long after Hus's ordination, the University of Prague condemned, by a majority vote, forty-five propositions taken from them. Hus may well have been familiar with the Englishman's work as a student, and the condemnation made little difference to his own reforming opinions. The previous year he had been appointed rector of the Holy Innocents of Bethlehem in Prague and attracted large congregations by his earnestness and eloquence. He was keen to reach the ordinary Bohemian and preached in Czech as well as Latin, in this way encouraging the national feeling which was now stirring in the land. He won popularity not only with the masses but also with the aristocracy, and he was the Queen's confessor. Naturally enough the clergy whom he attacked were critical of him, and some of the conservative-minded were troubled by his radical views.

Yet Hus was, in the main, orthodox. His opinions were less extreme than his contemporaries judged them to be, and some scholars maintain that Hus was in error only in his opposition to papal supremacy. But that was enough to put any man beyond the pale in the eyes of true believers; one must not attack the Establishment and particularly its head. Hus's revolt, however, was ethical rather than theological, and he yearned for a reform in morality rather than a revolution in the Church. He fulminated against worldly and corrupt clergy from the parish priest to the Pope, asserting that many popes had been heretics. Christ, not Peter (and, by implication, his successors), was the rock upon which the Church was built. Hus followed Milič and Mathias in advocating more frequent communion. He appealed to the Bible as establishing the law of Christ by which men's beliefs and conduct should be ruled, overruling the ordinances of men. He allowed private interpretation of the Scriptures and preached that it was lawful for men to resist authority for conscience' sake. Popes and others were to be resisted if they hindered people from following Christ. Only the predestined elect, not sinners, belonged to the true Church. The efficacy of sacraments depended on the worthiness of the minister. Circumstances led him to denounce indulgences, as will be seen below.

There were considerable political tensions in the Bohemia of Hus's day, not the least being the struggle which was to last until and beyond the formation of Czechoslovakia in the twentieth century between Czechs and Germans. In 1409 Hus supported Wenceslas, King of Bohemia (1378–1419), when he gave the Czech 'nation' in the University of Prague a vote worth three times as much as the German. The Germans migrated in a body to the University of Leipzig, accusing Bohemia and Hus of heresy, which made him the champion and hero of the Czech students. For a time his influence and that of Wyclif's writings were dominant in the university. But Pope Gregory XII had prohibited Wyclif's writings in 1408 and was to do so again in 1412. His successor, John XXIII, did likewise the following year. And the Archbishop of Prague, hostile to Hus, obtained a decree from Gregory ordering the surrender of all Wyclif's writings for burning. Hus refused to give them up.

In 1410 many of Wyclif's books were burned. He and his followers having been excommunicated by the Archbishop as heretics, Hus appealed in due course to John XXIII. But he destroyed his own chances of reinstatement by the increasing vehemence of his preaching. Supported as he was by Wenceslas, he felt himself safe in denying the worth of priestly absolution and asserting the authority of Scripture as a test of belief; and he finally scuttled his chance of successful appeal by denouncing the indulgences sold by the Pope's emissaries in Prague to raise money for a crusade against the King of Naples.

Indulgences were the immediate cause of the eventual Protestant breach with Rome, and it is convenient to outline here the theological doctrine behind them. It was believed that Christ himself, the Virgin Mary and many of the saints had accumulated a 'credit balance' of merit in their lives which could be drawn upon by those weaker brethren who had run up a deficit of sin and had earned a lengthy period in Purgatory. The popes, holding the power of the keys through Peter, were able to draw upon this treasury of merit and distribute it among those sinners who needed a lightening of their sentences in Purgatory – they could exchange some of the treasure they had accumulated upon earth for the heavenly treasure of the saints. Salvation could not be bought; but punishment could be bought off, even entirely, if the contribution in money or service was large enough.

Hus's condemnation of indulgences alienated the theological faculty of the University of Prague and brought his excommunication by the Pope and an interdict upon the city. He left Prague in 1412 but continued preaching, mainly in the open air, supported by the Czech people. He and Wyclif were becoming known far beyond the boundaries of their countries, and the Emperor Sigismund, Wenceslas' brother, was concerned to bring the unrest to a peaceful end if he could. He had played a considerable part in organizing the Council of Constance and in good faith promised Hus safe-conduct if he would present his case to it. Pope John suspended the excommunicaton. But the Germans, still smarting under their treatment by the Czechs in the University of Prague, swayed the council against Hus, and on the plea that no faith should be kept with heretics, and in spite of the suspension by the Pope of the excommunication (perhaps because of it, for the Council of Constance insisted on its right to judge the Pope), Hus was at once imprisoned.

The council had already condemned Wyclif and his writings, and among the counts on which they tried Hus was the accusation that he had supported the English reformer's teachings. Hus denied that he had followed Wyclif in every respect, but refused to condemn every article in his work which the council had anathematized. Nor would he recant his own teachings, such as the statement that if a pope, bishop, priest or king were in mortal sin, his office was forfeit. He maintained he had been accused of holding positions he did not hold, was willing to be informed by the council of his errors and would submit to its judgement if this did not offend God and his conscience. But the Scriptures alone were a test of doctrine.

Since the council had met to assert the authority of the Church over the rival pontiffs who had caused the Great Schism within it for so many years, its members regarded themselves as the supreme ecclesiastical power. If they had met to adjudicate between popes, they could scarcely allow a mere priest to claim the right of an individual to hold opinions at variance with those accepted by themselves as the representatives of orthodoxy. Hus was condemned in spite of his claim to innocence, refused to abjure his errors, was silenced, degraded from the priesthood and burned on 6 July 1415.

His death made him even more of a national hero to the Czechs. He met it with pious fortitude, as did his disciple, Jerome of Prague, almost a year later. Two Hussite parties, moderate and extremist, formed after his death. While Hus was still in prison, some of his followers began administering communion in both kinds to their parishioners, a practice which he approved, though did not consider essential. These Utraquists, or Calixtines (from the Latin *ultraque* = both, and *calix* = chalice), tended to be aristocratic and moderate, wanting continuation of their communion practice, free preaching of the Gospel and a moral priesthood. In other respects they accepted the practices of the Roman Church which could not be shown to be against the will of God and the Bible. They formed the moderate party, declaring to the Council of Constance in 1415 after Hus's death their orthodoxy and submission to the Pope, bishops and priests and willingness to submit any difference between the council and themselves to the arbitration of the University of Prague. The council at once suspended the university and prohibited communion in both kinds, threatening King Wenceslas and the Archbishop of Prague with penalties if they did not take heresy in hand. There was, however, peace until 1418 when, after the dissolution of the council, Pope Martin V ordered Sigismund and Wenceslas to restore all Catholic priests to the parishes from which they had been driven.

There was then a popular rising in Prague which spread to the country and the peasants and gave rise to the more extreme party of the Hussites. These were called Taborites, from the Bible name of Tabor which they gave to their principal mountain-fortress. They rejected everything not warranted by the Bible, and soon gave rise to further socialist-religious sects knowns as Adamites, Nicolites and Horebites. In 1420 the Calixtines agreed on the Four Articles of Prague which stated that:

1. Free preaching of the Word of God in the popular tongue should be allowed.

2. Communion was to be administered in both kinds.

3. Ecclesiastical domains should be suppressed. Priests were to be simple apostolic pastors, not owning worldly possessions.

4. Public sins of priests, especially simony, were to be punished by temporal penalties.

The first of the four articles opened the way to preachers of many kinds of heresy in Bohemia in the following years—Cathari and Waldenses as well as the different Hussite sects. Sigismund, seeing that a war of religion and race was inevitable, invaded Bohemia in 1420. But not only was his feudal army trounced by the Czech peasantry who met the Germans with methods of war completely strange to them, but the heretics in the next decade carried the fight into German territory, overrunning Austria, Silesia, Saxony, Lusatia, Brandenburg, Bavaria and Hungary. The Council of Basle (1431–43) gave certain concessions, allowing the chalice to the laity, and in theory brought the wandering sheep of Bohemia back into the fold of the Catholic Church. The Calixtines accepted the invitation to send representatives to the council, and the Four Articles of Prague were accepted as a basis for compromise. But the Taborites would not accept reconciliation with the Church. Civil war resulted between the Calixtines and themselves, ending in the defeat of the Taborites at the Battle of Lipan in 1434. There was a patched-up peace between the Catholics and Hussites, but it did not last long. Sigismund unwisely stirred up a Catholic reaction, emphasizing the antipathy between Czech and German, and Pope Pius II (1458–64) put an end to the artificial unity by declaring the agreement reached at Basle illegal. Thereafter Bohemia separated from the rest of Christendom, Hus and his followers having had a permanent effect upon her. The Bohemian Parliament gave the Utraquists equality with the Roman Catholics; and in the mid-fifteenth century the Unitas Fratrum (Bohemian Brethren) was formed from Utraquists, Taborites and Waldenses, the spiritual ancestor of the Moravian Brethren.

The Hussites became like later Puritans, rejecting festivals and pictures and laying great emphasis on sermons. They held that the real body of Christ was not present in the Eucharist, which was a kind of representation. They rejected confirmation. After the Reformation some returned to Catholicism, others became Calvinists, the heretical Church as a separate entity disappearing from history.

Almost sixteen years later, on 30 May 1431, Joan of Arc was burned as a sorceress and heretic. Her story is too well-known to need retelling here. Her heresy was not in essence different from that of Hus and many others in that it was, basically, the maintaining of her own judgement against that of the Church. In canonizing her on 18 April 1909—possibly the only case of a convicted and executed heretic's being given this honour—the Church admitted that in one case at least its judgement was wrong and that of an individual right.

A few words must be said in conclusion about Girolamo Savonarola (1452–98), for his career emphasizes that the supreme heresy of the ages preceding the Reformation was opposition to papal authority.

Savonarola won fame as a preacher after a quiet decade of life n the reformed Dominican monastery of San Marco, Florence. In about 1491 he began to affect the city by his teaching that God's judgement was soon to be visited on the earth, and two years later became prior of San Marco and head of the local Dominican province. Events supported him. The Florentines at war with France suffered heavy losses, the ruling family, the Medici, was distrusted, and Savonarola's preaching that the evils experienced by the city were God's punishment for its sins and frivolities seemed justified. When the Medici were expelled and the French king, over whom Savonarola had some influence, left the city, Savonarola was hailed as a true prophet and won general popularity as well as gaining influence with the city government.

In 1495 a series of Lent sermons led to startling repentance and reforms in the lives of ordinary Florence citizens, bonfires being made of 'vanities'. Puritans always make enemies, and Savonarola's reported him to Pope Alexander VI. The Pope sent him an invitation, expressed courteously at first, to come to Rome to answer for himself. Savonarola asked to be excused on grounds of ill-health and the furtherance of the reforms he had begun. In October the Pope ordered him to stop preaching. Although Savonarola obeyed, he continued personal persuasion with marked results.

In Lent, 1496, he was allowed to preach again, and in the same year the Pope tried to bring the preacher under control by grouping San Marco with a number of Dominican houses more directly subject to Rome. Savonarola defied the order, and in the following Lent preached boldly against the evils of the Church, making thinly veiled allusions to Alexander. The enmity of the Borgia pontiff was increased by political hostility, for Florence had combined with France against a league of Italian states, of which the papacy was a member.

In May 1497, Savonarola was excommunicated by Alexander because of his refusal to come to Rome and also to include San Marco in the combination of Dominican monasteries subject to the Pope. Savonarola remained defiant, whereupon the Borgia threatened Florence with an interdict if they did not silence the preacher and send him to Rome to be tried. Savonarola called upon the sovereign powers of Europe to summon an ecumenical council, declaring that Alexander was neither true pope nor true Christian; but, at the request of the Florentine city fathers, he stopped preaching.

A Father Francis, of the order of minor Observants, a tool of Savonarola's enemies, challenged the Dominican to a trial by ordeal, calling him heretic, false prophet and schismatic. The ordeal was that Francis and Savonarola were to enter a fire, Francis maintaining that he, a poor sinner, would perish, but that Christian charity teaches me not to withold my life if, in sacrificing it, I might

precipitate into hell a heresiarch, who has already drawn into it s
many souls'. Savonarola rejected the trial, but it was accepted on h
behalf by a fellow Dominican.

On 7 April 1498, the scene was set for the trial in the publ
square of Florence, to be undergone by one Dominican and o
Franciscan only. Almost the whole population of the city turned ou
to watch; but, frustrated by hours of procedural wrangling an
drenched by a deluge of rain, the fickle and illogical crowd turne
against Savonarola. Within twenty-four hours he fell from the zenit
of popularity to the nadir of public detestation. Alexander ser
judges from Rome with instructions to find Savonarola guilty, an
the torture with which the trial opened wrung from him a confessio
of all the crimes and heresies imputed to him. He and two follower
were executed in May 1498, some saying that they were first hange
and their bodies then burned, others that they were burned alive.

So, twenty years before Luther, died one more martyr whose re
heresy was a disbelief in the supremacy of the papacy when that offic
is in the hands of a wicked man. Savonarola was the victim of on
who has been called the Nero of pontiffs, destitute not only c
religion but of any vestige of virtue and shame. Popes can sometime
hide their true selves from readers of history under the anonymit
of adopted names like Innocent or Pius; there are few who do no
think of Alexander VI rather as a Borgia himself and father of th
infamous Cesare and Lucrezia. Nor can there have ever been ;
clearer case of evil confronting good than when Rodrigo Borgi;
brought about the death of the sensitive and idealistic Savonarola
more worthy of canonization than of the stake.

CHAPTER 12

Luther and Lutheranism to 1600

There are said to be over three hundred biographies of Luther in which he is characterized as everything from saint to villain, according to the author's viewpoint. To a reader of his life and times trying to be impartial and objective he seems to have been above all things a human being with great strength of character, courage and many virtues, together with marked weaknesses which led him to say and do things which shocked some of his followers at the time and his critics in centuries afterwards. But he was the man for his times. Where a Wyclif and a Hus lived just too early to profit by changes in the spirit of European thought and the new inventions of printing and paper, Luther came on the scene when they were established. He was the first reformer to be supported by many factors which, though they had existed earlier, had been undeveloped. Their coming to maturity, allied with new technology and the circumstances of the time, made him pre-eminent among rebels against the Roman Church, and his personal spiritual problems and their solution caused him to become, without at first intending it, the inspirer of *the* Reformation with a capital R.

In spite of Calvin's greater logic and genius for systematization, compared with which Luther's development was muddled, opportunist and piecemeal, it is the German, not the Frenchman, with whom the Reformation is primarily linked. This is not only because he was born twenty-six earlier—a period long enough at that time for Europe to move intellectually and spiritually an appreciable distance further into the modern age—but because as well as being the first to break successfully with Rome on a large scale, he showed a heroism and a warmth which can inspire admiration and even affection among those who read his story today. It is difficult to feel affection for Calvin.

The success of Luther's heresy was the result of a number of factors operating at the time. A notable mystical movement in Germany early in the fourteenth century had effects which worked like leaven through society, preparing it for discontent with a materialistic Church and hierarchy. It produced a number of works, one of which, *Theologica Germanica*, had a marked effect on Luther. Theological interest was widening and interest awakening especially in the Bible with emphasis on the New Testament and the thought of St Paul, and in the works of St Augustine. The inventions of printing and paper made the dissemination of books wider and heresy more difficult to destroy. For where the burning of a heretical manuscript, product of many weeks' painful copying, could mean the final disappearance of that expression of heterodox thought, especially if its owner were burned too, it was almost impossible to destroy every copy of a printed edition. The pre-Reformation dissenting movements, although suppressed, had been strong enough to linger on. Zeal for moral reform was widespread, and even the most orthodox Catholic could see that the papal court at Rome was staffed by men whose open contempt for standards of Christian morality made a mockery of their professed religion. Papal history of the period reminds one constantly of the *Decameron* story of the Jew who having resisted conversion until he visited Rome, then asked for it on the grounds that a religion which could continue in spite of the monstrous infamies practised by its chief adherents must be true. The rise of the middle classes in Europe meant a wider public for the books coming off the new printing presses. Equally, the rise of a spirit of nationalism meant an increased willingness on the part of rulers of states to support their subjects and accept support from them in resistance to papal financial exactions.

Possibly the most important factor of all in preparing Europe for reformation was humanism, of which there were many facets, some devoutly Christian, others entirely pagan though dressed, perhaps for safety's sake, in Christian clothes. Humanism rejected asceticism and contempt for the world and exalted the good things of human life and the world – culture, literature, philosophy, art, nature, the wonder of man in his physical beauty, powers of reason and ability to achieve and to understand and master the world. Humanists developed their critical powers and were often cynical, paying lip service to Christianity by going through the motions of worship and outward assent which it demanded of them and careful not to flaunt their unbelief or their frequent lack of morality by expressions or behaviour more brazen than society would tolerate. They loved life far too much to leave it via the stake.

Since humanism was largely a product of Christianity which taught that man was so infinitely valuable in the eyes of God that God in Christ had died for him on the cross, it is not surprising that by the end of the fifteenth century, Christianity had to a large extent captured humanism. Such men as Marsilio Ficino (1433–99), leading member of the Platonic Academy at Florence, Pico della Mirandola (1463–94), profoundly influenced by Savonarola, the Frenchman d'Etaples (c. 1455–1536), the Germans, Roelof Huysmann, alias Rudolf Agricola (1443–85), and Johann Reuchlin (1455–1522), whose grand-nephew, Philip Melanchthon, became a prominent Lutheran, the Englishmen, John Colet (c. 1467–1519), Thomas More (1478–1535) and the Dutchman, Erasmus (c. 1466–1536), all contributed to the thought of the day in such ways as to prepare or support the Reformation, even though most of them were or would have been appalled by the idea of a complete breach in western Christendom. Between them they translated the Bible into French, pointed out errors in the Vulgate, published a new edition of the Greek New Testament with a Latin translation, sought from primary sources to know the Christian faith as it came fresh from Christ, mocked superstition, sought moral reform and deprecated formalism and corruption. The return to the original Greek and Hebrew of the Bible by Humanist scholars resulted in the complete alteration of the meanings traditionally ascribed to certain passages, and this was enough to destroy the authority of many medieval developments and additions. One of their chief weapons was satire. Sebastian Brandt's *Ship of Fools*, the anonymous *Letters of Obscure Men* and Erasmus's *The Praise of Folly* set Europe laughing at the follies and vices of the Church as well as other institutions of the day. Erasmus in particular, by attacking the miraculous powers ascribed to images, indulgences, vain repetitions of the Psalter, prayers to the saints, monasticism, the efficacy of pilgrimages and the sanctity of ignorance and dirt, made himself so hated and feared by contemporary churchmen that, had he not been protected by the Pope and the Emperor, he would undoubtedly have perished at the hands of the Inquisition. A century earlier such works as his, if written at all, would have been read by a mere handful of men, those who were wealthy enough to buy them. Printing enabled tens of thousands to read them and laugh together, in strong contrast to times when a single critic might have had to face torture and death for voicing his opinion.

Martin Luther was born on 10 November 1483, at Eisleben in Upper Saxony, eldest of seven children in an orthodox Catholic peasant family. Taught partly by the Brethren of the Common Life, he went to Erfurt University where he took his MA in 1505, intending to study law. While on a country walk he was felled by lightning, an experience which led him to vow to become a monk. Almost at once he entered an Observant Augustinian house, chosen because only the most rigorous discipline, he felt, could satisfy him and bring him to salvation. In 1507 he was ordained priest, but in spite of disciplining himself far beyond the requirements of his order, his morbid fits of depression gave him no peace to balance his overwhelming sense of sin. A business visit to Rome in 1510 on behalf of the Augustinians distressed him because of the corruption he saw there of Pope and clergy. On his return he became doctor of divinity and town preacher of Wittenberg, appointed by the Senate, was ordered by his superiors to teach theology at the university, and, although accepting orthodox doctrines, he felt uneasy about some of them. Predestination, for example, seemed to him to make God capricious.

But at some time between 1515 and 1517, after many 'dark nights of the soul', Luther, lecturing on the Epistles of St Paul, had his need met by a single text–'the just shall live by faith' (Romans 1 : 17). There does not seem to have been a moment of enlightenment as with many to whom their brand of truth is flashed by God like a lightning-bolt, but the growth of doctrine over months, affording Luther the characteristic teaching which revolutionized his life and was the inspiration of the Reformation, justification by faith.

Luther's doctrine was that Christ was the judge of mankind. But the judge had himself experienced the anguish of separation from God expressed in his cry on the cross–'My God, my God, why hast thou forsaken me?'–and had suffered with those he condemns. So Luther felt that Christ knew and understood what his dark night of the soul meant to him. The cross became to Luther the means by which God reconciles the world to himself, purging away and healing sin, and enabling him to offer forgiveness freely to men. All that man needs do is to accept the gift of forgiveness in faith, which is not intellectual assent but a response of his whole being to the love of God in Christ and complete confidence in God's longing to save the sinner. This response knows that God is judge who rightly condemns but has provided in Christ a Saviour whom the sinner can recognize as such and by means of whose sacrifice on the cross God's justice and his longing to save can be reconciled with each other. Luther was bold enough to add the word 'alone' to 'by faith', although there was no scriptural warrant for it, for it seemed clear to him that penance, good works or any other expressions of piety could not earn God's favour or justify men. These were effectively the results, not the cause, of justification.

Luther continued to have fits of depression to the end of his life, but his new-found doctrine gave him the means to deal with them and a message so vital that he was compelled to preach it to others. Although his teaching contradicted some beliefs and usages of the time and although he urged the moral reform of the Church in his sermons, there was nothing at first serious enough to lead to a breach with Rome. This came gradually, but when it did come, it came catastrophically and completely, leading to a division in Christendom which has never been healed and which opened the way to others.

In 1516, when the Pope had granted indulgences to those who paid to see a collection of relics assembled at Wittenberg, Luther had questioned the efficacy of indulgences in a series of sermons and declared that the Pope had neither the power nor the authority to release souls from purgatory. The following year, Tetzel, a Dominican and salesman of no mean calibre, hawked indulgences throughout Germany partly to raise money for the building of St Peter's, and partly to pay a debt incurred by Albert of Brandenburg, a Hohenzollern, in buying for himself the Archbishopric of Mainz. Luther's own account of Tetzel's claims included such items as that

> . . . he had such grace and power from the pope that if any man had defiled or impregnated the Virgin Mary he could forgive the sin, as soon as a fitting sum was deposited in the chest; the red indulgence-cross with the pope's banner . . . was as efficacious as the cross of Christ; if St Peter were here now, he could have no greater grace or power than he had himself; . . . he had released more souls with indulgences than St Peter with his preaching; when a coin was placed in the chest for purgatory, as soon as the penny fell ringing upon the bottom, the soul immediately started for heaven; the grace of indulgence was the very grace whereby man was reconciled to God; there was no need to feel grief, or sorrow, or repentance for sin, if a man bought the indulgence, or the letter of indulgence. Tetzel also sold the right to sin in future time . . . everything might be done for money.

On All Saints' Eve, 31 October 1517, 'the birthday of the Protestant Reformation', Luther nailed ninety-five theses attacking indulgences on the Wittenberg Castle church door, a usual procedure in challenging to debate. Points he made among others were that indulgences did not remove guilt, that the Pope could remit only penalties he had himself imposed on earth, that he had no jurisdiction over purgatory, and that the saints had not accumulated surplus merit. There are times when a document or deed is an expression of a widespread feeling within a society and acts as a catalyst precipitating what had been universally but inarticulately felt. Such were Luther's theses. To their author's surprise they were circulated in Latin and German throughout Germany and Luther was drawn into controversy.

Pope Leo X summoned the monk to Rome in 1518 to answer charges of heresy and contumacy, but when the hearing was transferred to Augsburg, where the imperial diet was unfavourable to papal claims and requests, Luther refused to retract. He appealed first to the judgement of the universities, then to the Pope 'better informed', then from the Pope to a general council. A papal bull or indulgences had meanwhile been issued which met some of Luther's objections, Tetzel was disowned and died, some say of fear inspired by the sternness of the papal legate towards him, others of chagrin the Pope was conciliatory through political motives, and Luther promised to refrain from debate if his enemies did likewise.

He was absolved from his promise in 1519 because a former friend, Dr Eck of Ingolstadt University, an adroit and experienced campaigner in debate, challenged a statement of Luther that the primacy of the Bishop of Rome had not existed before St Gregory' time. Studying to defend himself, Luther concluded in *De Potestat Papae* (On the Power of the Pope) that the papal power was no rooted in divine right, though it should be accepted as a matter of expediency. The Church was not the visible sacerdotal and sacramental edifice but the body of the faithful whose faith would bring the rest, sacraments and the power of the keys. 'I do not know' concluded Luther, 'whether the Christian faith can bear it, that there should be any other head of the universal church on earth than Chris himself.' Such views alarmed his friends because by them Luther clearly crossed the border from heterodoxy to heresy – he wa rebelling against the institution which had claimed for a thousand years to administer the sacraments of salvation.

Luther, however, was brave to the point of foolhardiness. He wa willing to debate his views at Leipzig, the university of those who had fled from Hus and among whom the memory of the Hussite wars wa still strong. Eck's skill drove Luther to several declarations which left no doubt that he was a heretic and a spiritual anarchist. He had already denied the supremacy of the Pope. Now he affirmed tha several of Hus's doctrines were 'Christian and evangelical' and had been unjustly condemned, that therefore the Council of Constanc had erred, and that the authority of general councils was consequently suspect. They had, moreover, sometimes contradicted each other Articles of faith must come from Scripture and could not be established by Pope or Church – against the authority of the Church was to be set that of the Bible interpreted by the individual believer The confrontation ended with Eck's return to Rome to obtain a bul of excommunication and Luther's to Wittenberg to write his three treatises: 'To the Christian Nobility of the German Nation Respecting the Reformation of the Christian Estate: an appeal to the laity chiefly directed against abuses'; 'De Captivitate Babylonica', a Latin appeal to theologians; and 'Concerning Christian Liberty', sent to the Pope. He also wrote a 'Sermon on Good Works' and 'The Papacy at Rome', the five works together containing his distinctive convictions.

From these works a composite picture of Luther's basic premise may be made. He was no systematic theologian and his beliefs were hammered out red-hot on the anvil of controversy, shaped in response to the exigencies of the times, not worked out in coolness and detachment. They are therefore full of unresolved questions and weaknesses obvious to any theologian who carried them to their logical conclusions. Luther's faith, arising out of his experience and enlightened by his discovery for himself of justification by faith as the way to peace with God, was of the heart, not of the head.

His doctrine of the Church was that it is an invisible body of believers consisting of all who are justified by faith. Within this body all are priests, ordained by baptism, and there is, therefore, no superiority of clergy over laity, the only difference between them being one of office. It followed, therefore, that the Pope, cardinals, bishops and other dignitaries of the Church have no right to the temporal and spiritual powers claimed by them. They are, in fact, subject to the jurisdiction of the civil authorities whom God has ordained to safeguard the good and punish the bad, whether they be clerics or laymen. Monastic life is no better than the ordinary living of a Christian farmer or housewife, and monastic vows, which have no scriptural authority, breed only pride and contempt for the 'ordinary' Christian.

The supreme authority for the Church is the Bible, and its beliefs and practices must be tried by the touchstone of Scripture. 'One thing and one thing alone is necessary for life, justification and Christian liberty; and that is the most holy word of Christ, the Gospel of God.' The papal claim to the exclusive right to interpret the Bible is erroneous on two counts: first, many popes have been unbelievers and are therefore incapable of interpretation; second, every true believer, since he is a priest, is competent to do so. Luther is at his weakest here, for his own treatment of Scripture was inclined to be cavalier, and he exhibits the weaknesses ever since inherent in Protestantism's treatment of the Bible. First, he discriminated between different parts of the Bible as being of greater or lesser value, rejecting Revelation completely. Every student of the Bible does the same (the genealogies of Matthew 1 and Luke 3 are obviously of lesser spiritual value than the Sermon on the Mount), and in doubtful matters subjective interpretation and emphases clash, as is evidenced by the proliferation of Protestant sects, many mutually exclusive, all claiming scriptural authority. Second, Luther emphasized not so much the literal word of Scripture as the Living Word, Christ, revealed by it. It may be generally agreed that this is a right emphasis, but it, too, can give rise to that subjectivism mocked by Voltaire when he said that God created man in his own image and man has ever since been repaying the compliment.

Since Scripture is the supreme authority, only those sacraments for which it gives grounds are permissible. Communion is one. The laity are to receive the bread and wine which are real, not merely clothed in their 'accidents'. Christ is present in the elements as fire is present in a red-hot iron (a doctrine known as Consubstantiation), but Luther permitted a belief in Transubstantiation for those who wanted it. The Mass is not a good work or a sacrifice, but a gift of God, a promise of the remission of sins to be received by confident faith in the promise of God whose Son's body and blood were given and shed for the recipient.

Baptism is scriptural and valuable, infant baptism permissible and total immersion (since it symbolizes death to sin and a sharing in Christ's resurrection) preferable. The rite itself does not justify, but rather faith in the promises which accompany it. Infants are justified by the faith of those who bring them and the prayers of the Church. Penance and confession have no authority in Scripture, but confession, which can be made to any Christian, not necessarily a priest, has its place in Christian life. Confirmation is a useful ceremony of the Church but not a sacrament, nor is marriage, which should not, moreover, be denied to priests. Ordination as a rite practised for many centuries is not to be condemned, but it was invented by the Church of Rome and is unnecessary since every Christian is a priest. The 'indelible character' of ordained priests is a myth. Nor is extreme unction condemned, although its efficacy depends on the faith of the recipient.

Since man is justified by faith, the value of good works and what constitutes them must be given their rightful place in Christian living. Good works do not make a good man, only faith, which results in good works—Luther, though describing the Epistle of James as 'right strawy', would not have denied that 'faith without works is dead' (James 2:20) although some of his extremist followers went as far. The noblest good work is to 'believe in Christ', and other good works can include one's daily tasks and all normal activities 'that help nourish the body or are generally useful', the Christian doing everything he has to do, however ordinary or routine, to the glory of God and to please him, not to accumulate merit and gain rewards. Good works are not limited to prayer in church, fasting, almsgiving, confession, pilgrimages and the invocation of saints.

Luther's most revolutionary step was his absolute denial of the Pope's rights or authority. He showed that the papal claim to the sole right of calling a council was disproved by history (the Council of Nicaea, most important of all the general councils, was summoned by the Emperor). A bad pope could be disciplined by a council. 'I will not endure', wrote Luther, 'that men shall establish new articles of faith and judge all Christians in the world as heretics, schismatics and unbelievers, only because they are not under the

Pope.' He attacked not only the Pope's authority but his pomp and luxury, and urged the German states to refuse to pay papal taxes and exactions, to abolish all rights of the papacy to interfere in German ecclesiastical and temporal affairs and to expel papal legates from their territories.

Other reforms included a simplifying of church life by an abolition of many of the processions, annual festivals, saints' days and masses for the dead. No one was to enter a monastery before the age of thirty. The Bible was to be taught in schools and the universities to be reformed. Begging, especially ecclesiastical begging, was to be abolished, and the genuine poor in each town were to be looked after by the civic authorities.

Luther's writings, circulated through Germany and other countries by the printing press, caused a tremendous stir. The Pope realized that he had a much more serious opponent than a mere recalcitrant monk. On 15 June 1520, a papal bull condemned forty-one Lutheran errors, ordered the burning of the books that contained them and summoned the heretic to recant within sixty days. On 10 December, much more the birthday of the Reformation than 31 October 1517, the day of the posting of the theses against indulgences, Luther publicly burned the bull–and his bridges–at Wittenberg, together with the Decretals, other papal documents and some of his opponents' writings, before an audience of teachers, students and the general populace. The next day he warned his hearers to separate from the Pope, who in turn demanded that he should be placed under the ban of the Empire and sent to Rome for trial.

The heretic was saved from what seemed inevitable death at the stake by political considerations. German public opinion, including that of some of the princes, was with him, and Charles V, newly elected Holy Roman Emperor, though an ardent Catholic, was suspected by the Pope because of his influence in Italy. Frederick, Elector of Saxony, summoned Luther before the Diet of Worms, where a dramatic confrontation resulted in his refusal to recant unless convicted by Scripture and plain reason, for, since the authority of popes and councils contradicted each other, he could not accept them. 'Here I stand', he is reported to have concluded, 'I can no other.' The clash was one of two irreconcilable principles, without one of which the Christian Church would not have come into being at all, while without the other it would not have survived. When Peter and his fellows before the Sanhedrin in the earliest days of the faith said, when forbidden to preach, 'We must obey God rather than men', they were asserting the principle that a man conscientiously believing himself to have received truth from God must assert his conviction if necessary against those of the whole Church and the whole of society. Luther did the same. Yet if the opposite principle is not upheld, that an individual submit to the judgement and authority of the collective Christian body, the result is anarchy. The multitude of fringe sects within Protestantism shows what happens when private judgement is allowed to have its way.

In May 1521, Charles V decreed Luther to be 'a limb cut off from the Church of God, an obstinate schismatic and manifest heretic' and placed him under the ban of the Empire, which made him outlaw. He was saved for the next nine months by being taken prisoner by friends to Wartburg Castle. There he wrote nearly a dozen books and translated first the entire New Testament from Greek to German, and later the Old Testament, both of which he continued to revise until his death. His translations had much the same effect, if not more, on the German language as the Authorized Version had on the English.

In his absence his followers carried on the Reformation, centred at Wittenberg, too radically for comfort, and when Luther returned in March 1522, at considerable risk to his life, he urged moderation. Combining radicalism with conservatism, he preserved from the past what was not contrary to Scripture, keeping such aids to worship as candles and crucifixes but denying them special veneration. He compiled services of mass and baptism, wrote many stirring hymns, and emphasized the importance of preaching. He stimulated education and upheld the value of family life, himself giving an example by his happy 'parsonage life' marriage to the ex-nun Katherine von Bora, with their several children. Although he believed that God alone knew who the redeemed were and that the true Church could not therefore be identified with any man-made institution, he realized that there must be organization, especially as the more radical reformers tended towards anarchism. At his prompting the lay princes became responsible for ecclesiastical order. So, in Luther's native Saxony, the Elector divided his state into districts, each under a superintendent responsible to him who had power over the parish clergy and some control over worship so as to bring it uniformity. Luther believed in toleration, but also that the majority faith in any state should be the faith of that state, and those who differed should go to a district where their co-believers were in a majority.

The weakness of Lutheran Protestantism was that it had no hierarchical unity of its own with which to oppose the unity of the Roman Church. Luther himself was too opposed to the constraint of other men's consciences to wish to enforce unity even if he had had the power. The result was separation between him and others who could have been his allies. He broke with Erasmus over the latter's contention in his *On the Freedom of the Will* that man could of himself fulfil the conditions which God had ordained for salvation;

and the two men were incompatible in that Erasmus was a scholar, a moderate and a man of peace who feared Luther's violence and a breach in Christendom. The only Humanist of note to remain at Luther's side was Philip Melanchthon. The reformer lost the support of the peasants by his fierce pamphlet *Against the Murderous and Thieving Hordes of Peasants*, written during the Peasants' War (caused by taxes, injustice and oppression, but for which Luther was blamed by many), resulting in the virtual loss of southern Germany for Protestantism. He rejected as fanatics the Anabaptists and agreed to the banishment of their leaders, Carlstadt and Müntzer, from Saxony, later reluctantly agreeing to the death penalty for their followers, who were accused of sedition and murder. An attempt at a union with Zwingli and Bucer failed, partly because of fundamental differences over the theology of the Eucharist (although a compromise might have been reached on this point), and partly because of Melanchthon's fear that a movement by Luther towards Zwingli's position might make reconciliation with Catholicism impossible.

Fortunately for Luther, still under the ban of the Empire, which was to remain in force until his death, the preoccupation of Charles V with wars against France and Italy gave the new religion time in which to get rooted. The northern German states for the most part sided with Luther, the southern with Rome—the Catholic princes had united in the League of Ratisbon in 1524 to enforce the Edict of Worms, to which the Protestant princes replied in 1526 with the Alliance of Torgau. In the latter year a diet at Speier refused to accede to the Emperor's demand that the Edict of Worms be enforced, decreeing that, until a national council decided the question, each prince was to follow his conscience. A second diet at Speier in 1529, with a Roman Catholic majority, demanded religious liberty for Catholics in Lutheran territories while refusing it to Lutherans in Catholic states, an injustice that drew from the heretic princes a formal protest which is the origin of the name 'Protestant', at first applied to Lutherans and used in this chapter as a synonym for them. Calvinists received the name of 'Reformed'. Later, Protestant came to be used loosely of all movements in western Europe which broke with Rome.

In the year following a conference at Marburg in 1529, in which Luther and Zwingli failed to agree, a diet was held at Augsburg, at which Charles tried to restore religious unity by asking where the Lutheran beliefs differed from the Catholic. Melanchthon produced the Augsburg Confession, based on earlier Lutheran definitions of faith agreed on at Schwabach the previous year, a frank but irenic document which might have brought about reconciliation but for the opposition of the more extreme Lutherans and the intransigency of Campeggio, the papal legate. The Swiss reformers, following Zwingli, and the Strasburgers refused to assent to the Confession, presenting documents of their own.

The Roman Catholic majority at the Augsburg diet declared that the Protestants had been rejected, and Charles gave them until April 1531 to submit. The Lutheran princes formed the defensive Schmalkalden League, named after the town in which they met and made political allies with France and other powers hostile to the Emperor. Pressure of external events led in 1532 to the religious truce of Nuremberg between Emperor and League, renewed in 1534, but further attempts to reunite Catholics and Protestants at conferences in 1540 and 1541 failed. Charles, temporarily freed from external embarrassments, called for a general council (the Council of Trent, 1545–63) to be convened by the Pope, and determined to stamp out Protestantism by fomenting the obvious disunity among the non-Catholics and, if necessary, by war.

His policy of division was helped by an incident which reflected little credit on Luther. Philip of Hesse, a leader of the Schmalkalden League, was married. However, troubled by his innate sexual promiscuity which his conversion to Lutheranism could not cure, he felt impelled to marry again, believing that a second wife might help him to continence. His bigamous marriage was approved not only by his first wife but by his second wife's mother, and Luther and Melanchthon both knew of it. Luther, who was opposed to divorce, believed monogamy to have been endorsed by Christ but saw a precedent for polygamy in the Old Testament. Since polygamy was, however, against German law, he advised that the second marriage be kept secret, and, when the news inevitably leaked out, that it be denied with 'a good strong lie'. Philip and the girl's mother would not agree. The incident shocked Catholics and Protestants alike, and gave Charles a tool with which to prise apart the Protestant union.

The year after Luther's death (1546), Philip of Hesse and the Elector John Frederick of Saxony were defeated and imprisoned. In 1548 Charles conceded communion in both kinds in an edict called the Augsburg Interim, but it upheld Roman Catholic doctrine in too many other respects to satisfy the Protestants. After some setbacks they renewed the war against Charles with the aid of France (it is strange how political considerations always overcome religious ones) and the defeat of the Emperor, in 1552, led first to the Peace of Passau, by which Charles conceded religious liberty to the Protestants, then to that of Augsburg in 1555. By the latter the principle was established by which each lay prince was to determine the religion of his own state – *cuius regio, eius religio*. Lutheranism was to be the only form of Protestantism permitted; Catholics and Protestants were to be allowed to sell their property and migrate, if they wished; Protestant princes were to retain ecclesiastical properties in their possession before 1552; and in the imperial free cities both religions were permitted. The Lutherans demanded toleration for Protestants living under Roman Catholic princes, promised verbally but not written into the treaty, and refused to be bound by a provision which said that if a Catholic bishop were to turn Lutheran he might not retain the property and income of his see.

After Luther, Melanchthon remained the most prominent Protestant until his death in 1560. Although the territorial expansion of Lutheranism in Germany continued, reaching a maximum in about 1566, weaknesses were apparent long before that date. Minorities working for compromise were always to be found within both Catholicism and Protestantism, but the former did not weaken their church whereas the latter did. An inner reformation among the Catholics won back lost ground. Some Lutherans returned to Catholicism, others fell away at the other extreme to Calvinism, especially in southern Germany. Protestant princes and theologians developed rivalries and differences. Luther's justification by faith, which meant originally a response and commitment of the whole personality to God, became fossilized into intellectual assent to standards of belief which contained little of his spirit.

Melanchthon himself was involved in two dissensions, the Adiaphoristic Controversy and Philippism. When the Elector Maurice of Saxony introduced certain Roman Catholic practices into his state as a gesture of peace towards Charles V, Melanchthon accepted them, though reluctantly, as adiaphora, things indifferent. They were, however, regarded with horror by some Lutherans, especially as they were used in Wittenberg itself, the very city from which the true faith had started. Philippism was the name given to Melanchthon's views of the Lord's Supper, too near those of the Reformed Church, for which he was regarded as a crypto-Calvinist. He was also accused of synergism, the doctrine that man and God work together to effect the man's salvation. This was because he preached that good works are essential as evidence of salvation though they do not earn it. He was opposed by Osiander (1498–1552), who taught that justification does not arise from the righteousness of Christ imputed to believers through his cross, but by a positive righteousness resulting from a continual outpouring of Christ's divine nature. One of Melanchthon's opponents even declared that good works hinder the Christian life, and others insisted that man had no more free will than a stone or a dead body. In 1580, these and other differences were reconciled in the Formula of Concord, signed by all but a few Lutheran princes and cities, yet these few were enough to show the world a disunited front.

Although Lutheranism receded after a time in Germany it

completely captured Scandinavia. In Denmark the Catholic Church was powerful, wealthy, corrupt and worldly. Early in the sixteenth century Paul Helgesen urged reform, attacking indulgences (although he was opposed to Luther). Erasmus's works began to be read, and Martin Reinhard, a German priest who had studied at Wittenberg, became court chaplain and preached some Lutheran ideas. Other preachers such as Hans Tausen, professor of theology at the University of Copenhagen, publicized the new teachings, while Danish royal weddings with Lutheran princely families gave the reform protection. Under Frederick, a convinced Protestant who had seen and admired Luther's stand at the Diet of Worms and who as Christian III ruled Denmark from 1534 to 1559, the country became fully Lutheran. Its Catholic bishops were arrested, their property was confiscated, seven Lutheran bishops were consecrated (but out of the Apostolic Succession), a liturgy was compiled, the Bible was translated into Danish–a literary masterpiece by Christiern Pedersen–and the monasteries were eventually abolished. Christian III, genuinely religious, became the administrative head of the Church in his realm, the former Catholic Church property giving him wealth which enabled Denmark to prosper financially and intellectually.

By the Union of Kalmar Christian III was also monarch of Norway and Sweden. Norway did not look for church reformation, which came about piecemeal. Catholic churches and the cathedral at Bergen were destroyed by Christian's officials and Lutherans took over others. The Archbishop of Trondhjem opposed the King but was forced to flee when the country went over to Christian, his departure leaving the Catholics leaderless. All but two of the bishops, who turned Lutheran, were expelled from their sees, but the Lutherans who came into the country quarrelled over tithes and could not speak the language of the people. See and parish were neglected. Many of the Catholic clergy remained at their posts till death and were replaced only after delay. It took nearly a century for conditions to improve.

In Sweden Lutheranism advanced step by step with a successful revolt against Christian II of Denmark in which Gustavus Vasa fought his way to the Swedish throne. Its leading preacher was Olavus Petri (Olaf Petersson, 1493–1552), who had been a student at Wittenberg when Luther nailed up his theses against indulgences, but he had left before the break with Rome. Olaf worked for moderate reform only, but Gustavus broke with Rome in November 1523, over a matter of a papal refusal to confirm the election of four bishops without payment of annates (sums equal to the first year's income from a bishopric). These, Gustavus claimed, the land was too poor to pay. The bishops were, however, consecrated in the Apostolic Succession by two bishops who had themselves been regularly consecrated.

In 1527 the King confiscated most of the Church's property, established control of the Church and abolished compulsory confession. Succeeding measures allowed clergy and religious to marry, a tradition of teaching was nurtured among the clergy, and a Swedish translation was made of the Bible. A Swedish communion service was produced which became standard. Monasticism and clerical celibacy disappeared. Swedish Lutheranism ran an individual course, inspired by but not slavishly following German, and when a Church Manual was given official sanction in 1571 it retained confession, excommunication and public penance.

Vasa clashed with the clergy, being a much more extreme Protestant than most of them and wishing to subordinate the Church completely to the royal authority. But after his death in 1560 the Church recovered partial autonomy. Of the kings that followed, the first tried to introduce Calvinism, the second to make a rapprochement with Rome, the third, a devout Roman Catholic, was thwarted by the Swedish Church's adoption of the Augsburg Confession unmodified, and the fourth had Calvinist leanings. In spite of all these, Sweden remained Lutheran.

Through Sweden Lutheranism reached the eastern Baltic where it flourished among the Germans and Scandinavians who had settled there and won Finland. Gustavus Vasa introduced it, but it was not until a hundred years later that any real reformation took place. Then Isaac Rothovius, Bishop of Åbo (1627–52), printed a Finnish translation of the Bible, improved education at all levels, including the founding of a university, and raised the quality of both clergy and laity, enforcing church attendance.

Iceland, also under the rule of Denmark, went through a period of plague and distress in the fourteenth century followed by a religious awakening before 1540. Then, Lutheranism was beginning to become known through German merchants and Icelanders who had studied abroad. Deposition of bishops and seizure of their property by Christian III occurred in spite of a nationalist resistance under a native bishop and his two sons. The Bible and some of Luther's writings were translated into the old Norse tongue by Gudbrand Thorlaksson, Lutheran bishop for no fewer than fifty-seven years. Although the island became Lutheran, largely owing to his efforts, the Catholic features of auricular confession and reverence for those saints connected with Iceland remained.

In Bohemia, although Hus and Luther differed in their theology of the Eucharist, Lutheranism captured parts of the country through Bohemian Hussite students who had studied at Wittenberg. The Germans in Bohemia usually followed Luther and the Slavs Calvin,

but the two were later united by a common confession of faith agains
a Roman Catholic ruler and an aggressive Roman Catholic counter
attack led by the Jesuits. By 1600 nine-tenths of the country is sai
to have been Protestant.

Further east, reformed doctrines spread similarly along nationa
lines. Hungarian and Transylvanian German and Slav people
inclined to Lutheranism, Magyars to Calvinism, except west of th
Danube where German-Slav influence swayed the Magyars t
Lutheranism. Several factors helped the reformers. There was th
usual Catholic corruption among clerics and laity. Hussite an
perhaps Waldensian influence prepared the way. Hungaria
students, like so many others, returned home with the doctrines c
Luther and Melanchthon. A Hungarian translation of the Bible wa
made. Humanism, popular particularly in aristocratic circle:
inspired a demand for reform. The disaster of Mohács Field (1526)
in which many prominent Roman Catholics were among thos
slain by the Turks, deprived the Church of leadership at a tim
when it was vitally needed to resist the Reformation. On th
Protestant side, on the contrary, leadership was found in th
'Hungarian Luther', the great preacher Matthias Biró of Deva, an
the theologian Stephen Kis of Szeged University. The Turk:
occupying a large part of the country, favoured Protestants rathe
than Catholics who might rally to a crusade of deliverance by th
Pope and Catholic rulers. Not only did the two major reformin
movements gain adherents, but Anabaptists and Unitarians did als(
and in 1568 and 1571 measures by the Prince and Transylvania
diet gave equal rights to Catholics, Calvinists, Lutherans an
Unitarians.

Luther's writings became widely known throughout the rest (
Europe, although in the Low Countries the Protestants followe
Calvin rather than Luther. England developed its own *via medi*
much in the spirit of the reformer but moving in its own directio
of Anglicanism. The writings had a limited circulation in Italy, an
Erasmus's call for internal reform of the Roman Church rathe
than a breach with it appealed more strongly in Spain.

By 1600 Lutheranism had reached and declined from a peak (
territorial expansion in Europe. Not only was the Catholic Churcl
by setting its own house in order, enabled to counter-attack wit
considerable success, but other reforming doctrines, particular)
Calvinism, gave Protestants a choice between them and Lutheranism

CHAPTER 13

The Reformed Churches to 1600

Huldreich Zwingli, born in 1484 in a prosperous Swiss peasant home, had no spiritual awakening like Luther's yet possessed an independent spirit, deep moral earnestness, quick intelligence, an admiration for humanism and a bent for democracy. He was ordained priest but was forced to leave an early charge of the parish of Glarus because he aroused the hostility of the French by expressing his dislike of the use of the Swiss as mercenaries. After three years as People's Priest at the pilgrimage centre of Einsiedeln he took a similar position at Zürich Great Minster. His fame as a preacher spread from there, and he was granted a papal pension which he resigned in 1520 for conscience' sake. He was already preaching reform, mostly advocating the abolition of the mercenary system and pensions, and in a course of sermons on the New Testament he broke away from accepted teaching. He gladly received and circulated Luther's writings, like him stressing the authority of Scripture and, more radically, rejecting everything in the Roman Church which found no support in the Bible.

In 1520 the Zürich civil authorities decreed that priests should freely preach anything that conformed with Scripture (though freedom in its interpretation was allowed); in 1521 an indulgence-seller was expelled from Swiss territory, largely at Zwingli's instigation; in 1522 the civil authorities, by making rules for fasting in Lent, virtually usurped the Bishop of Constance's prerogative; and in 1523 Zwingli declared against monastic vows, clerical celibacy, the intercession of saints, the existence of Purgatory, the sacrificial aspect of the mass and the attainment of salvation by good works. Supported by the town authorities, he proclaimed salvation by faith. In the same year the Pope sent a nuncio to offer Zwingli 'anything but the Papal chair' in return for his submission. But the reformer was not to be bribed. Like many other released priests and nuns he married, in his case a widow with whom he had been living previously. By Easter 1525, Zürich churches were empty of images, relics and organs; mass was replaced by a simple German service centring on the sermon; and the property of dissolved monasteries was given to schools. A theocratic system was set up by which authority in Church and State was wielded largely by the Church authorities, who based their actions on the Bible.

The conference in 1529 with Luther at Marburg and its failure have already been mentioned. Luther believed that the words in the communion service, 'This is my body', indicated a real but inexplicable presence of Christ, a view which seemed a Romish superstition to Zwingli who saw the Lord's Supper as a memorial—had not Christ said, 'Do this as a *memorial* of me' (Luke 22:30)? Christ was present, not in the bread and wine, but spiritually among worshippers bound to him in common loyalty. The Marburg Articles, however, declared the points on which the two reformers agreed, notably that salvation is by faith alone, though Luther's faith was the response of the whole man to God, and Zwingli's trust in God through Christ.

Zwingli formed a Protestant Alliance to compel the five Roman Catholic cantons to stop persecuting Protestants and perhaps to accept evangelizing missions by reforming preachers. An attempt to form a league of all Protestant territories failed because of the differences between Luther and Zwingli. The canton of Schwyz had kidnapped and burned a Zürich preacher, and in spite of Berne's objection that 'Faith is not implanted by spears and halberds' Zwingli went to war. His death at the Battle of Kappel, in 1531, was a waste in that nothing changed, Protestant cantons remaining Protestant and Catholic Catholic. But his views had some success in south Germany which, for political and geographical reasons, favoured Zwinglianism rather than Lutheranism, and there were others left to carry on his work.

At Basle John Hussgen (Heusgen, or Hauschein), known as Oecolampadius (1482-1531), had done notable work, and while he died at the same time as Zwingli, there were others still to come: Martin Bucer (1491-1551), Henry Bullinger (1504-75), Guillaume Farel (1489-1565) and, the greatest of them all, John Calvin (1509-64). Bucer, with influence in Strasburg and, through the preachers he trained and sent out, in central Europe, held a middle view between Luther and Zwingli but could not heal the breach. Bullinger was nearer the Lutheran view of the Lord's Supper. Because of this variety of views held by different reformed communities, the First Helvetic Confession, issued in 1536, was conciliatory, but failed to win the Lutherans. The Second (1562-6) also failed, but at least it drew the Reformed churches together.

Farel, educated by men who wished to reform the Catholic Church from within, was modest, scholarly, chivalrous, deeply religious, influenced by humanism, fearless and impetuous. Driven from France because of his outspokenness, he flamed through the French-speaking Swiss cantons into the Waldensian Alpine valleys, where he won some of the inhabitants to the Reformed cause. Like Bucer, he trained and sent out young preachers. In 1532 he was expelled from Geneva, but he returned in 1533, the city officially adopting the Reformed religion in 1535, partly for political reasons, trying to rid itself of the control of its bishop and of the Duke of Savoy. It was Farel who forged the connection of Calvin with Geneva, which lasted but for three years until the latter's death.

Calvin, born in 1509 at Noyon in Picardy and reared in the manner of an aristocrat, went to the University of Paris where he was named the Accusative Case because of his condemnation of his laxer fellows. In his early twenties he experienced a religious conversion of which no details are known, and at the age of twenty-six published *The Institutes of the Christian Religion*, first in Latin, then in French, revising and enlarging it four times before his death.

The *Institutes* contains Calvin's idea of the teaching of the Christian Church before it was corrupted by the Roman Catholics. It is a clear, logical, systematic and comprehensive work, strongly influenced by Augustine's thought, and based on the Scriptures as the record of God's dealings with man in the matters of creation, sin and redemption. Its four books, planned to follow the articles of the Apostles' Creed, deal with: God the Father; redemption through Christ; the Holy Spirit; and the Church and its relation to the State.

Knowledge of God, the true end of man's existence, said Calvin, comes through natural religion arising from observation of the universe, and revealed religion to be found in Scripture. Calvin was strongly trinitarian. God concerns himself with every individual. He is free from all evil, man being fully responsible for evil done even at the decree of God. Calvin made no attempt to explain this paradox but urged its acceptance on Bible authority.

Man's immortal soul was created in the image of God, but Adam's revolt against God's authority handed on 'original sin' to all the human race, resulting in 'total depravity'. This so impairs the will that men can do no good work without the special grace that God gives to the Elect, chosen to be saved as he has chosen others to be damned. This double predestination is a mystery, for we must not judge God's justice by human standards. We cannot know that we are among the Elect, but the tests are a profession of faith, an upright life and participation in the sacraments.

The Law was given to keep alive the hope of salvation until the coming of Christ, who is wholly God and fully Man. By his resurrection not only from physical death but the spiritual death of one irretrievably lost ('he descended into hell'), Christ satisfied the righteous judgement of God and conquered both deaths.

Only through the Holy Spirit's working does faith come, when heart joins with mind in accepting the truth. It leads to repentance which is the forsaking of self and the turning to God, producing the fruits of love towards God, charity towards men and a sanctified character expressing itself in good works. God gives to each man his vocation in life. The Christian has liberty and obeys the will of God voluntarily.

The Church is not identical with any visible institution but includes all the Elect, alive and dead. It is universal, indivisible, invisible, known only to God, one body with Christ as its head. But Christians must be loyal to the visible institution, even if imperfect and containing many hypocrites. Like the Elect, the Church is not perfect, but is daily improving.

There are two sacraments, baptism and the Lord's Supper. In the latter 'the bread and wine are visible signs, which represent to us the body and blood . . . they are, as it were, instruments by which the Lord distributes them to us'.

Calvin laid down a structure for the visible Church as he saw it, thus counterbalancing the Catholic hierarchy with a Protestant constitution. Bishop, elder, pastor, minister, are different names for the one office of minister, inwardly called by God, to be ordained by the laying-on of hands and chosen by the people. Deacons are lay officers who administer alms and look after the business side of congregational affairs. Church and State are parts of the same holy community. The latter is responsible for providing for the material needs of its citizens and for law and order, for ensuring a public form of religion and preventing offences against it. Capital punishment and some wars are lawful, and nations may enact any legislation provided it is in accordance with the law of love.

In 1536 Calvin and Farel began work in Geneva to make of it a model Church-State unity as pictured in the *Institutes*. In 1538 the city authorities expelled them for their objection to the former's interference in church affairs, and Calvin spent the next three years in Strasburg where he made friends with Bucer and Melanchthon, married, and, as pastor of French refugees in the city, devised a liturgy which became a model for the Reformed churches. Recalled to Geneva in 1541, he remained there until his death in 1564, the real power in the city although he never held any office other than that of a church minister. Under the theocracy he set up Geneva prospered, for Calvin developed commerce, investment and education, as well as controlling community morals, discipline being administered every Thursday morning by a consistory of ministers and lay elders which dealt with heresy, among other crimes. Some of the punishments meted out for what would be regarded today as trivial offences were horrifying, but there was beneficence shown as well, and allowance must be made for the climate of belief and opinion so different from the modern outlook. Calvin was as intolerant of heresy as any inquisitor. He dismissed the humanist Protestant scholar, Sebastian Castellio (1515–63), from his teaching post for questioning the inspiration of the Song of Songs and disagreeing with Calvin's interpretation of Christ's descent into hell. The incident of Michael Servetus (1511–53) has rightfully blackened Calvin's name, even though the case was a test of strength between Calvin and his opponents. Servetus, a deeply religious Spanish scholar and scientist, Unitarian, Anabaptist, a rejector of predestination and a believer in the imminent millennial reign of Christ, condemned for heresy in Vienne, a Roman Catholic city, was recognized passing through Geneva and arrested, in spite of possessing a safe-conduct. He was tried for heresy, Calvin's enemies supporting him to such an extent that, had Servetus, who counter-charged Calvin with false accusation and heresy, been acquitted, the latter's power in Geneva would have been at an end. Servetus was condemned and burned at the stake, the one mitigating factor in Calvin's favour being his plea for a more merciful death.

Meanwhile, by the Consensus Tigurinus of 1549, the Zwinglians and Calvinists had agreed upon their doctrine of the Lord's Supper, repudiating any kind of local presence but asserting that Christ is spiritually present to the faith of the recipients and feeds them with the Holy Spirit. Calvin died, worn out, on 27 May 1564, in the arms of Theodore Beza (1519–1605), who succeeded him. An aristocratic Frenchman like Calvin, Beza was converted during an illness, became a Reformer working on behalf of the Waldenses and Lutheran-Calvinist unity, in 1559 was appointed rector of the school of theology in the Academy (later the University) of Geneva, continued Calvin's policy in the city and became the leading Reformed theologian of the next generation.

As Lutheranism captured considerable tracts of Germany and other lands, so Calvinism spread into many countries, capturing parts of Germany which had previously fallen to Luther. Many Strasburgers, already influenced by the sojourn in their city of Calvin and Bucer, were driven to the Reformed Church by the obstinacy of uncompromising Lutherans. The Palatinate, ruled by Frederick III, 'The Pious' (1515–76), a zealous Calvinist, became officially Reformed and persecuted not only Catholics but Lutherans. In 1563 the Heidelberg Catechism was issued, a more moderate document than most in those days, and this had wide influence in

the Dutch, German, Scottish and American Reformed Churches
In the years before 1600, Calvinism gained ground in Brandenburg
Bremen, Hesse and Nassau.

The Bohemian Brethren (United Hussites) were driven from their
native land in 1548 and, seven years later, united with the Calvinist
in Poland, the country to which they had fled.

To the west Lutheranism had made an early impact on the
Netherlands, together with other heretic movements such as the
Anabaptists, and both provided victims for the flames. Heresy was
encouraged by translations of the Bible and New Testament, of which
more than one a year into Dutch, Flemish and French appeared in
the eighteen years following 1513. Charles V's vigorous efforts to
eradicate heresy failed. As in parts of Germany, so in the Netherlands
Calvinism partly replaced Lutheranism. In 1561 Guy de Bray,
Walloon who had studied at Geneva, produced the Calvinistic 'Belgic
Confession', which remained standard in the Dutch Reformed
Church for some time. Meanwhile, Charles V's abdication in 155
made way for the no less Catholic Philip II. He left the Netherlands
in 1559 for Spain, but his tyranny from afar, including measures
for the repression of heresy, aroused opposition, notably from the
'Beggars', a movement led by nobles belonging to all three faiths
Calvinist, Catholic and Lutheran, who demanded a change in Philip'
policy and an end to the Inquisition.

The behaviour of the more extreme reformers in their destruction
of images and pictures in churches did not endear them to Philip
He sent more troops, which brought William of Orange, the Roman
Catholic son of Protestant parents, to head the revolt against him
In 1573 William, from conviction, joined the Reformed Church
which, in spite of the troublous times, had held its first general
synod two years earlier, and led the United Provinces of the seven
Protestant northern Netherlands districts against Philip until he was
murdered in 1584. William's efforts were not in vain and a quarter
of a century later, in 1609, the Provinces finally gained their freedom

Meanwhile, the Dutch Reformed Church evolved, growing
stronger as the war progressed, and adopting a Prebyterian form
of church government, the Heidelberg Catechism and the Belgic
Confession. After 1609 a degree of freedom was given to Anabaptists
and Roman Catholics.

In France there were no Protestant districts as in the Netherlands
although the reformers were far stronger in the south and south-west
where the spirit of the old Cathari lingered on than in the rest of the
country. The Huguenots, as they came to be called (possibly from
Hugues, a political leader in Geneva, and Eidgenot, Swiss variant
of German Eidgenoss, a confederate), formed a minority, never more
than an estimated one-ninth of the population, living in a sea of

Catholics. However, their discipline, puritan morality and higher thinking afforded them an influence in the national life out of all proportion to their numbers. Their life was never easy in the sixteenth century, in spite of the fact that they drew some of their inspiration from that Humanism which appealed to aristocratic thought, and they were not unfavoured by some in high places.

Jacques Le Fèvre d'Etaples has already been mentioned as a leading humanist. An even more influential thinker was Guillaume Briçonnet (1492–1549), the reforming Bishop of Meaux, spiritual director of Margaret, sister of Francis I, King of France, and grandmother of the Protestant leader, Henry of Navarre. Impressed by Luther and Calvin and influenced by mysticism, she disagreed with many things in the Roman Church but never left it. Her brother persecuted or tolerated Protestants according to the veering of the winds of politics. But for the most part the reformers were not tolerated. The Sorbonne refuted and prohibited their books. The French Parlement proscribed them, wiping out their villages and burning a number of the Meaux group. In 1535 an alleged affront to the Host was avenged by the burning of six heretics at each of six stations during a solemn procession of the consecrated element. The royal power in the person of Henri II (1519–59) fully supported repressive measures, but in spite of them the reforming movement spread, largely from Geneva, Lausanne and Strasburg, whence French-speaking Calvinist missionaries carried the message of the Frenchman whose clarity of mind appealed to the logical habits of thought of his countrymen. In 1559 a national synod at Paris framed a confession of faith, and two years later the French government, trying to reconcile Catholics and Protestants, granted the latter limited toleration. Over thirty years of religious wars followed, bedevilled by politics, family feuds and personal rivalries and ambitions, and marked by the Massacre of St Bartholomew, in 1572, in which the Catholics almost annihilated the Huguenot leadership in a night of murder. They were ended by the 'conversion' of the Protestant Henry of Navarre, who decided that Paris was 'worth a mass', his coronation in 1594, and the issue in 1598 of the Edict of Nantes. This gave the Huguenots rights of worship in a large number of cities, districts and castles, full civil rights, admission to public office of every kind, entry to the universities, and other safeguards.

Lollardy and Lutheranism had a little influence at the beginning of the sixteenth century on Scotland, a country torn with strife and dissension at that time. In 1528 Patrick Hamilton, who had studied at Wittenberg, was burned at St Andrews for Lutheran opinions, his heresy including denial of the freedom of the will. Edicts against heresy and other burnings followed, including that in

1546 of George Wishart who had imbibed Calvinism at Geneva and suffered as an early Presbyterian. Partly in revenge for his death Cardinal Beaton, who was responsible for it, was murdered a few weeks later. Wishart's disciple, John Knox (1505–72), who could have suffered with his master, escaped with nineteen months as a galley-slave, but was released to return to England where he became a chaplain to the reforming Edward VI. On Catholic Mary's accession he fled to Geneva, became an ardent disciple of Calvin and returned to Scotland for a few months in 1555 and 1556, where he gave considerable impetus to an already fast-growing reformation movement. The following year a number of Scottish nobles formed themselves into the 'Lords of the Congregation', and they were to put teeth into the reforming side in the civil war of 1559. Knox returned permanently to Scotland in that year. The regent of the kingdom forbade reformed preaching but was defeated by the Calvinists in the war that resulted, and during 1560 and 1561 the Reformed faith became the official form of Scottish Christianity.

A Calvinistic confession of faith was adopted, the Pope's jurisdiction was abolished, and mass forbidden. By *The First Book of Discipline* Knox ordered the administration of church finance and wealth, the ordination of the clergy, education and poor relief. One rank only of minister was acknowledged, for 'superintendents', roughly corresponding to the former bishops, were given the same status as the parish clerics and differed from them only in administrative functions. Because some nobles opposed the book, Parliament did not officially approve it, and this led to a partial separation of Church and State in Scotland. A little later, in 1564, *The Book of Common Order*, popularly known as 'Knox's Liturgy' was adopted by the General Assembly of the Scottish Church, a democratic organization in which the laity had a considerable voice and influence. This governed public worship.

In 1561 the widowed and ardently Roman Catholic Mary, Queen of Scots, returned to Scotland from France. She and Knox, antagonists in every way and with none of the attractions opposites are supposed to have, clashed violently from the first. In the struggle that followed, Knox and the Reformation temporarily lost ground, but Mary's intrigues backfired against her, leaving Knox and his cause triumphant, as they remained until his death in 1572.

Knox was succeeded by other able men, of whom the most influential was Andrew Melville (1545–1622), who gave the Scottish Church a thoroughly Presbyterian organization in *The Second Book of Discipline* of 1577.

So the sixteenth century ended with Protestantism of one kind or another established as the official religion of many lands. Where in

1500 to have been anything but a Roman Catholic in any country of western Europe would have marked a man as an undoubted heretic, in 1600 it was the Roman who was the heretic in the whole of Scandinavia, large parts of Germany, many cantons of Switzerland, the United Provinces and Scotland.

And that is not the end of the story.

CHAPTER 14

Anglicanism to 1600

If refusal to acknowledge the supremacy of the Pope was heresy, then many English, otherwise orthodox, were heretics long before the Reformation. England had never accepted the Hildebrandine doctrine that the Pope was the source of all spiritual and secular authority, and from time to time the English monarchs had passed laws which ran counter to papal claims. The country was as ready for the Reformation when it came as any on the continent and the movement took fire almost simultaneously with, although its course was erratic and its outcome different from, that of both Lutheranism and Calvinism. Its importance, comparatively insignificant at the time, seen as the breakaway from Rome of a small island on the western boundary of Europe, later became considerable, Anglicanism spreading to many countries which later were to become part of the British Empire and then the Commonwealth.

Scorn for the shortcomings of the Church was a feature of English life long before the Reformation, and indeed it has never ceased to be so, and in pre-Reformation times it was often savage. Chaucer's ironic sketches in *The Canterbury Tales*, though the comments of a tolerant, sophisticated townsman, are revealing in their implied criticism rather than explicit statement; while Langland's long poem *Piers Plowman*, a work contemporary with Chaucer's, attacks the abuses of Church and clergy, among others, with satiric savagery that is unsurpassed.

Matters did not improve in the fifteenth century. Concubinage among the clergy, simony, absentee clerics living soft lives on the revenues of benefices or livings, the idleness and ignorance of monks, nuns and friars, the preoccupation of the higher clergy with affairs of state, all weakened the Church in the eyes of a laity whose devoutness was admired by foreign visitors. The climate of intellectual opinion was changing with the encroachment on

feudalism and the old social order, weakened to disappearing-
point by the Wars of the Roses, of the ideas of the modern age
which, historians say, began in England approximately with the
Tudor dynasty. Growing nationalism, which was part of the modern
age, resented papal interference in English affairs, and still more
papal financial exactions levied to pay for luxurious living of the
princes of the Church in Rome. The work of Luther did not go
unnoticed in England, and stirred to small flames here and there the
embers of Lollardy. At the universities Erasmus's version of the Greek
New Testament and its Latin translation were studied by English
scholars.

One of these from Cambridge, Thomas Bilney, teacher of Hugh
Latimer, was moved to heresy by the writings of Luther and burned
in 1531. Another English heretic, William Tyndale (c. 1494–1536), a
priest educated at Oxford, made it his life's work to translate first
the New Testament into English, then a large part of the Old
Testament, these being printed with heretical notes on the text and
circulated in England in spite of all efforts to suppress them. Tyndale
was executed by strangling in the Netherlands for adopting the
Lutheran doctrine of justification by faith and his body burned. An
assistant of Tyndale was Miles Coverdale (1488–1568), for a time
Bishop of Exeter, who issued a translation of the Bible of his own
in 1535 and was responsible for other translations later.

It is likely that all these factors – corruption of the Church,
the atmosphere of reform, the circulation of vernacular Scriptures,
nationalism and the blood of Protestant martyrs – would slowly have
moved the conservative English to reformation. This could easily
have been a reformation from within rather than a break with Rome.
The direct cause of the breach was the affair of Henry VIII's
first marriage.

In 1501 Henry's elder brother, Arthur, aged fourteen, married
Catherine of Aragon, but died the following year. Henry VII,
unwilling to lose the alliance with Spain and Catherine's dowry,
obtained a dispensation from the Pope allowing his younger son to
marry his deceased brother's widow, against the law of the Church,
arguing that Arthur had been too young to consummate the marriage.
Henry VIII has often been accused of hypocrisy on the pretext of
invalidity of the marriage, which he later used to divorce Catherine.
But it is worth noting that there was doubt at the time as to whether
the Pope had the right to set aside what was regarded as the law of
Christ, and Warham, Archbishop of Canterbury, had misgivings
about the marriage, which he nevertheless conducted in 1509. When
after some twenty years Catherine had failed to provide him with
the male heir Henry regarded as essential to safeguard his throne,
it may have been a genuinely troubled conscience as well as the

witchery of Anne Bullen which caused him to seek a divorce. Wolsey's failure to serve his master's will, due to Campeggio's, the papal legate's, playing for time and to the reluctance of the Pope to offend Charles V, Catherine's nephew, more powerful, more threatening and closer than Henry, brought to the fore the architect of the Reformation in England. It was Thomas Cranmer (1489–1556) who in 1529 suggested that Henry's cause should be put to the universities of Europe; and even though the suggestion did not obtain the unanimous result Henry desired, most replies were favourable to him.

The following year Henry blackmailed the clergy by indicting them as a body under the ancient statute of Praemunire, enacted in 1353, which sought to prevent lawsuits being taken out of England to papal courts, basing his charge on their acceptance of Wolsey as papal legate. Convocation, the clerical parliament of the province of Canterbury, voted a large sum of money to the King and recognized him as the supreme head of the Church in England 'as far as is permitted by the law of Christ'. In 1532 Parliament transferred the payment of annates from the Pope to the King, and, Warham dying in that year, Cranmer was consecrated Archbishop in his place. In 1533 Henry bigamously and secretly married the pregnant Anne Bullen, and, when Parliament, less than three months after the marriage, declared that the Church of England could decide its own cases without reference to Rome, Cranmer's court pronounced Henry divorced and his second marriage valid. The Pope excommunicated the King, declaring his marriage with Catherine a true one. Parliament retaliated in 1534 by cutting off 'Peter's Pence', a papal tax levied on every householder for the building of St Peter's at Rome, and in the same year declared the King 'supreme head of the Church' in England, strengthened the following year into 'supreme head on earth of the English Church'. All references to the Pope were removed from English service books and the break with Rome rendered temporarily complete.

It is perhaps worth noting that Forest, an Observant friar, was subsequently executed for heresy and treason because he declared that the Pope should be obeyed in spiritual matters. This was the only occasion on which denial of the King's supremacy was held to be heresy. Two birds were killed with one stone when Forest was executed, for a great wooden idol, called Darvell Gathern, which had been venerated in Wales and brought to London to be destroyed, was set fire to under the wretched man while he hung alive in chains above it.

The Pope replied by placing England under an interdict, a punishment which would at one time have brought any Christian king to his knees. In the England of the sixteenth century it passed almost unregarded.

Nevertheless, Henry regarded himself as a loyal and orthodox son of the Catholic Church, attending mass daily (often more than once) and observing all the usages of the faith. No mean theologian, he had written a book against Luther (or at least affixed his name to it), for which the Pope gave him the title of Defensor Fidei, Defender of the Faith, a title somewhat illogically kept by every English monarch since. But Protestants complained that though the King had broken with the Pope, he had kept the papacy, and had good cause for the complaint. He personally sat in judgement over one John Nicholson, for example, who denied the Real Presence and held the Lutheran doctrine of consubstantiation. For five hours the King and some of his bishops, a total of ten opponents, debated theology with their unaided victim who was eventually silenced and, after throwing himself upon the King's mercy, was burned.

Yet Henry's actions not only brought about a permanent breach with Rome, but they unwittingly made inevitable the triumph of Protestantism. In 1536 Thomas Cromwell, the King's vicar-general in ecclesiastical matters, caused a Latin and an English Bible to be set up in every church so that the laity could read it, thus enabling the ordinary literate man to search in vain for scriptural authority for many teachings and usages of the Roman Catholic Church. The need for an authorized English translation of the Scriptures purged from heretical teaching led to the publication of the Great Bible, or Cranmer's Bible, derived from Matthew's Bible which, in turn, derived from Tyndale's and Coverdale's translation. By 1540 a savage blow of demolition was delivered against the Catholic edifice in England when the monasteries, small and large, were dissolved and the pilgrimage centres were abolished and their treasuries pillaged. The monastic movement throughout Europe had long lost its original impetus, but however strong the arguments against or for the monasteries in Henry VIII's England (and they have had notable and scholarly apologists defending them), their removal meant putting forward the clock of history in such a way that it could never be put back. Not only were their lands and possessions irretrievably lost to them, but they were plundered by or sold to so many local men, who received them at give-away prices from the King – who needed cash on the barrelhead – that they could never be recovered.

It was not long before the physical break with Rome was followed by a spiritual one, for the Church in England (it is not correct to call it the Church of England until after the Elizabethan settlement) began to issue articles of belief. In 1536 the Ten Articles appeared, mostly Catholic but tinged with Lutheranism. They mentioned three sacraments, the Eucharist, baptism and penance, and that Christ is physically present in the first; that masses for the dead, the invocation of saints and the use of images, confession, absolution, good works, are all desirable practices; but that justification is by faith as well as by the last three of these, and that Christian people should be taught the Bible and the Apostles', Nicene and Athanasian Creeds. In 1539 the Six Articles, much more Catholic, was issued to abolish 'diversity in opinions'. Punishments decreed for the disobeying of it were so severe that the historian Froude called it 'the whip with six strings'. It dogmatically asserted the Real Presence, rejected outright the administering of communion in both kinds to the laity, enforced the celibacy of the clergy, and upheld private masses and auricular confession. Those who denied the Real Presence were to be burned as heretics; any who violated the other five articles were to be executed as felons. Cranmer (who had married) opposed the Six Articles, but unsuccessfully, the result being that he had to conceal his wife. A comparatively few Lutherans and Zwinglians were burned, three at one time in 1543 (three other 'felons' being hanged on the same day for denying the King's ecclesiastical supremacy), and an estimated twenty-eight in the whole of Henry's reign.

A further step towards reformation was taken near the close of the reign when Cranmer began to prepare forms of worship in the tongue 'understanded by the people'. These were to find full expression in the short reign of Henry's son, Edward VI (1547–53).

Edward, strongly Protestant, intelligent, religious and determined in spite of the frustrations that his chronic ill-health and extreme youth imposed upon him–he was only nine when he came to the throne and died before his sixteenth birthday–was in the hands of regents whose intrigues he could not control. But Somerset, his uncle and first Lord Protector, was also sincerely Protestant and Dudley, Earl of Warwick, later Duke of Northumberland, who replaced him, was Protestant for political motives. In the six years of the reign, therefore, England moved rapidly away from Catholicism. The first act of the new government, hiding the nakedness of its greed under a cloak of Protestant reform, was the abolition of the chantries on the excuse that 'the doctrine and vain opinion of purgatory and masses were upholden by the abuse of trentals and chantries'. Chantries not only provided priests to say masses for dead benefactors but maintained schoolmasters throughout the country. Under the Act there were also given to the Crown all colleges, free chapels, rents and annuities for the payment of stipendiary priests and all guilds and fraternities–in short, the sixteenth-century equivalents of educational and welfare services in the entire country. The excuse of the Act was not only the abolition of superstition but the setting up of educational and charitable institutions. Its effect was the enrichment of the Crown and a shock to English society in the destruction of educational facilities from which it did not recover until the twentieth century.

Happier reforms were the repeal of the Bill of Six Articles and the abolition of the laws against heresy. The Scriptures were to be freely printed and circulated. A decree of the government that images should be removed from churches was followed by a violent iconoclastic movement in some localities. The marriage of priests was allowed. English reformers, who had fled abroad to escape the lashes of the whip with six strings, returned, some ardently inspired by the reforms they had seen in Geneva and elsewhere. They were accompanied by notable foreign Protestants such as Bucer who were given positions of influence by the government.

In 1549 an Act of Uniformity was passed, enforcing the use of a Book of Common Prayer by all clergy. This was a Catholic rather than a Protestant book, claiming to be a return to primitive usage. Cranmer was the genius behind its compilation, though he was restrained from advancing as far as he would like to have gone by the more conservative members of his commission. He used many old sources for his new book, combining wide knowledge, religious sincerity, sensibility and a fine command of English in its compilation. In some doctrinal matters he had to compromise: there was no outright rejection of Transubstantiation such as he would have liked, but expressions suggesting it, together with invocation of the saints and any mention of purgatory were omitted, although the commemoration of the faithful departed was retained. The book omitted the chrism in baptism, the oil in confirmation, the carrying of palms on Palm Sunday, the kissing of the Pax, the elevation of the Host in the mass; made more use of the Bible; and presented worshippers with a simplified system of services. The compromise pleased neither conservative Catholics nor radical reformers, but the book was sufficiently Catholic for such staunch upholders of the old faith as Bonner and Gardiner to accept it. But there was a revolt against its use in Cornwall, resulting in the execution of eight priests. They were executed not for heresy but for rebellion – yet heresy, whatever it is called, has been seen in most cases to be revolt against the local Establishment.

In 1552 the more Protestant Second Prayer Book of Edward VI was imposed upon the nation by a second Act of Uniformity, the work of Cranmer, Ridley and the continentals, Bucer and Peter Martyr. The priest became a minister, his vestments were limited to the surplice, exorcism and anointing were omitted, and the altar became a table (though no Anglican bride has yet been led to the table). But the word 'Protestant' was and is not to be found in any Anglican Book of Common Prayer, and the Catholic Church is the only one mentioned.

The Crown had moved too fast for popular support in Edward's reign, and when Mary (1553–8) came to the throne, the majority of the country was at first willing to support her in her attempt to return to the old faith. Prominent Protestants fled to the continent while the going was good. Catholic bishops were restored. Mary's first parliament in 1553 repealed all ecclesiastical legislation, returning to the position held at Henry VIII's death, although refusing to restore papal supremacy or stolen church property and lands. Mary bowed to the latter refusal, realizing that there were too many vested interests for her to oppose, but reversed the former in 1554 when Cardinal Pole, the papal legate, received the wandering English sheep back into the Roman fold. (Pole, desiring the reform of the Roman Catholic Church, had been both denounced to the Inquisition for heresy and almost elected pope.) In January 1555, special commissions were set up and sent throughout the kingdom for trying heretics.

Mary's third parliament revived the heresy laws. In all, 282 victims passed through the flames to the Moloch of persecution. Between 1510 and 1527 there were four executions for heresy in the diocese of London. Under Mary there were more than a hundred in four years. Of the total number of 282, one in three were clerics, one in five women, and two in three in London and the south-east of England. Archbishop Cranmer and Bishops Latimer and Ridley were among the victims.

The position of Elizabeth I (1558–1603) at her accession was difficult. Catholics had seen that the royal supremacy could be as oppressive as the Pope's and that Protestantism could easily lead to danger to their property and lives. Protestants returning from exile, on the other hand, were more extreme, wanting to eradicate as far as possible the whole development of the Christian Church in the centuries between the first generations of believers and the present, and to start again on a purely scriptural basis. Mary's persecution had aroused anti-Catholic feelings among the ordinary folk who had lived through it. Elizabeth was faced with three choices: to revert to Rome, which would have aroused opposition strong enough to topple her from her throne; to throw in her lot with the Geneva Protestants, which would also prove utterly distasteful to very large numbers of her subjects; or to take a middle course, offending extremes on both wings, but carrying the mass of her people with her.

She chose the middle way. In 1559 an Act of Supremacy denied the authority of the Pope and any payments and appeals to him but, with a subtle change in the wording from Henry VIII's, made her the 'Supreme Governor', not 'Supreme Head', of England 'as well in all spiritual or ecclesiastical things or causes as temporal'. In the same year the use of the Second Prayer Book of Edward VI, so revised in a Catholic direction that the Pope is said to have been willing to confirm it if the Queen would acknowledge its receipt from him, was imposed upon the country by yet another Act of Uniformity and all subjects of the Queen were required to attend church on Sundays and holy days. Marriage of the clergy was permitted, simony forbidden, and all pictures, relics and superstitious objects removed. New bishops were appointed to replace the Marian bishops, thus giving rise to a Roman Catholic charge, denied by Anglicans but confirmed by the Pope in 1896, that Church of England orders, not having been received in the line of Apostolic Succession, are invalid. If the charge were true (the arguments against it seem far stronger to an objective student of history than those for it), it would put every bishop and priest in the Anglican Church since Elizabeth's time outside the Catholic Church and make them in that sense heretic.

The Forty-Two Articles of Edward VI were modified in 1571 into the Thirty-Nine to which Church of England clergy still assent today. As a statement of the Anglican view on points of doctrine then in controversy, with specific statements against the tenets of certain contemporary sects, they are a compromise, containing Catholic, Lutheran and Calvinist elements. They are orthodox in their Trinitarianism and Christological doctrine. Their view of Scripture is a Lutheran one 'that whatsoever is not read therein nor may be proved thereby, is not to be required of any man, that it should be believed as an article of the Faith, or be thought requisite or necessary to salvation'. They were specifically anti-Pelagian, Augustinian in their doctrine that man cannot turn to God without his prevenient grace, Lutheran in their assertion of justification by faith. Good works cannot put away sins but are the fruits of faith; those before faith are useless as a source of merit and even 'have the nature of sin' (a statement which must be taken in the context of the medieval doctrine of a reserve of merit earned by the saints and of indulgences). Works of supererogation do not exist. Christians may sin after baptism, repent and be forgiven – baptism neither eradicates the tendency to sin nor is a sinning Christian to despair of committing unpardonable sin. Predestination *to life* is emphasized, the possibility of God's *sentence* of Predestination being mentioned as a warning to 'curious and carnal persons'. The visible Church is defined as a congregation of faithful men practising the ministry of the Word and Sacraments; but individual churches, including that of Rome, have erred in practice and doctrine. The Church may organize its worship and be authoritative in matters of faith, provided that these do not contradict Scripture, of which she is 'a witness and a keeper'. General councils 'may not be gathered together without the commandment and will of Princes' and both can err and have erred. Their decrees must be tested by Scripture. Purgatory, pardons, veneration of images and relics, invocation of saints, masses for the dead, are all condemned. Ministers must be properly authorized and services must be in the vernacular. There are two sacraments, baptism and the Lord's Supper. The unworthiness of ministers does not hinder the effect of the sacraments. Infant baptism is to be retained. Transubstantiation is 'repugnant to the plain words of Scripture', Christ's body is received spiritually by the faithful. The sacrament is not 'to be reserved, carried about, lifted up, or worshipped'. Communion is to be in both kinds for all Christians. Clergy may marry. Traditions and ceremonies may differ from place to place and time to time, provided that they are not against Scripture, but men may not purposely break any of these through private judgement, and national churches may change or abolish any ceremony or rite 'ordained only by man's authority'. The validity of Anglican consecration and ordination is upheld. The monarch has 'chief government of all estates of this realm, whether they be Ecclesiastical or Civil', which are therefore subject to no foreign jurisdiction. This does not mean that the 'godly Prince' acts as a cleric, but that he rules through a prerogative given by God himself. The Bishop of Rome has no jurisdiction in England. Capital punishment, the fighting of wars, the possession of private property and the taking of oaths in court are lawful.

The Thirty-Nine Articles and their spirit were supported by writers, notably Richard Hooker in his *Laws of Ecclesiastical Polity*, which is still considered by some scholars to be the best statement of the Church of England's position against Roman Catholicism and Protestant sectarianism. Together all these measures taken by Elizabeth and her parliaments satisfied the great central mass of her subjects, and it was possible for moderate Catholics and Protestants reasonably tinged with Lutheranism and Calvinism to worship within the one national church. Those outside it became the heretics. For the modern man, accustomed to churches and sects of a hundred kinds and a very large number of non-worshippers of any kind, it is difficult to visualize a climate of thought that could conceive of only one national church to which every loyal subject was expected to belong. For Elizabethans, such ecclesiastical totalitarianism was essential for the safety of the realm. Those who rebelled against it were, first traitors, second heretics, and it was for treason that they who were executed died. In a proclamation of 1591, in reference to the 187 victims executed in the forty-five years of her reign, Elizabeth stated this categorically.

No compromise can wholly satisfy and Elizabeth suffered all her life from attacks by extremists. The obdurate Roman Catholics, known as Recusants (from the Latin *recuso* = I refuse), who refused to conform, led by William Allen (1532-94), a former Canon of

York, organized the English College at Douai which sent back hand-picked trained priests ready to die martyrs' deaths for the Pope's cause. Jesuits also came, and of Elizabeth's 187 victims 123 were priests or Jesuits. Yet the first priest was not executed until after 1570 when the Pope's excommunication of the Queen released her subjects from their allegiance to her and put her in mortal danger. The many plots and intrigues against her, in which religion and politics were inextricably mixed, need not be detailed here. Suffice it to say that so far as the conspirators were Roman Catholics, they were considered as much heretics in England as an Anglican conspirator against the pope would have been considered a heretic in Rome.

The Puritans (so called because they wished to 'purify' the Church) were in a stronger position in the Church of England than the Catholics, partly because of their numbers, and partly because the Anglican Church had moved towards them and away from Rome; and they believed that it could be pulled further towards what they regarded as a truly reformed community. Believing in the priesthood of all believers, they attacked vestments, in what became known as the Vestiarian Controversy, because these were not ordered in the Bible and had been used in the pre-Reformation Church. They condemned mere Bible-reading without an explanatory sermon following, and despised the Anglican practice of the bare reading of psalms, lessons, and 'patches and pieces of epistles and gospels'. They wanted equality of all ministers and a Presbyterian style of church government. The services in the continental and Scottish Reformed churches they thought better than the English. They objected to private communion and baptism, the hindering of free preaching by insistence on licences, kneeling at the Lord's Supper, tantamount in their eyes to adoration of the elements, and special orders of service for saints' days.

Throughout Elizabeth's reign they were an 'everlasting argument'. In 1570/1 Thomas Cartwright, Lady Margaret professor of divinity at Cambridge, was dismissed for advocating the replacement of episcopacy by Presbyterianism, thereafter leading a wandering and persecuted life. In 1572 and 1573 the Puritans issued two Admonitions to Parliament and in 1584 a petition calling for further reform in a Presbyterian direction. There was to be rigid Sabbath observance and severe punishment for blasphemers, swearers, perjurers, drunkards and fornicators, while adulterers were to be punished by death 'without redemption'. Parliament, always markedly Puritan in temper, was favourable to their demands and greatly offended the Queen by its attempted action in their favour. But she held rigidly to her *via media*, loyally supported by her Archbishops of Canterbury, notably Whitgift (1530–1604), a believer in iron discipline and censorship of the press, who vigorously controlled the Puritans by means of a Commission for Causes Ecclesiastical and was most violently attacked himself in the anonymous Martin Marprelate tracts. Parliament was compelled in 1593 to pass anti-Puritan acts and to order all who refused to come to church 'to hear divine service' to leave England.

The Puritans wished to cleanse the Anglican Church by working from within. The Separatists or Independents, like the continental Anabaptists, believed that the Church in any locality consisted of those who were true Christians called out from the world and forming small pockets within the mass of unbelievers and worldlings, among whom they included Christians who belonged to any church other than theirs. Each local community was an autonomous congregation whose members were united with each other and with Christ by a covenant, appointing its own priests and officers, with no authority over other congregations and submitting to none over itself. They were the ancestors of the modern Congregationalists.

The Brownists, or Barrowists, were followers of Robert Browne. He considered any kind of ordination an abomination and the whole church system mistaken, but after a stormy career he submitted to the Archbishop of Canterbury. He was succeeded by Barrow, who was executed in 1594 with two followers for alleged involvement in the Martin Marprelate tracts, two others having been put to death in 1583 at Bury St Edmunds for publishing Browne's works. All five were condemned under a Libel Act of 1581.

There existed also Anabaptist sects, forerunners of the Quakers, and some extremist groups. The Libertines taught that whoever had God's Spirit could not sin. Others claimed that an extraordinary inspiration of the Holy Spirit made the believer independent of any corporate faith or dogma.

It is debatable whether Elizabeth was more troubled with Ireland or Ireland with her. Henry VIII had been declared head of the Church in Ireland in 1536, but the Archbishop of Armagh cursed any who should acknowledge the King's headship, declaring that 'this isle belongs to none but the Bishop of Rome who gave it to the King's ancestors'. From then on there were two bishops for every diocese, as the bishops needed replacement – one nominated by the King, the other by the Pope. As in England, so in Ireland the monasteries were dissolved; but there the destruction was a far greater catastrophe than in England, for they were the only means of education, the only inns and the only relief for the poor and sick and aged. The destruction of images, shrines and relics caused horror in 'holy Ireland'. Mary's accession was welcomed with the utmost rejoicing, but under Elizabeth the Act of Uniformity imposed the English prayer-book which, for the Irish, meant grappling with an unfamiliar language, accustomed as they were to Latin. No attempt was made to win the Irish to the new faith, and they were treated with that arrogance and lack of sensitivity which seems always to have bedevilled English dealings with Ireland. The Anglican bishops and clergy behaved as they would not have dared in England. Unashamed pluralism was rife, the Archbishop of Cashel at the end of the century holding four bishoprics and twenty-seven livings. There were not enough Irish clergy and those who came across from England were either ignorant or escaping from a country too hot for them to remain in. Their language was different and they were altogether foreign. The Jesuits penetrated into Ireland from 1542 and the loyal Catholics formed a league not to attend church and to provide education, which met with considerable success.

In short, the Reformation failed utterly in Ireland, and the presence of a base for Catholic political activity on her western flank posed a serious threat for Elizabeth throughout her reign.

Elizabeth died in 1603, Whitgift in 1604. By that time, in spite of the temporary upsets that were to come, the Anglican settlement had taken shape in England, and it was later to become a force in world Christianity. Whitgift saw it as distinct both from Romanism and from Calvinism and in many essentials unlike Lutheranism though, like it, a middle way. Loyal English churchmen see it stretching back, often marred but unbroken, to the days before the Synod of Whitby, when Britain had been evangelized by missionaries from the Celtic Church—it was the Roman Church whose development had deviated from the true. To an equally loyal Roman Catholic the Church of England went astray under Henry VIII and Elizabeth I and, though it contains much of the truth in its Christology and episcopal organization, must remain heretical as long as it denies the infallibility of the Pope.

CHAPTER 15

Other Movements in the Sixteenth Century

Once main breaches had been made in the sea-walls of orthodoxy, there followed trickles that widened into streams of various strengths and intensity. Both Lutheranism and Calvinism tried to replace a church which governed the whole of society by another which did the same; but there were some movements which differed from them in giving up society altogether. They disagreed with each other as well, although they had many principles in common. They agreed in discarding anything that was not expressly authorized by Scripture, but disagreed on what was authorized. They wished to return to the primitive Christianity of the first century, but differed as to what that was. They liked simple forms of worship and church government but did not always like each other's. They believed that the 'saved' should be gathered into groups of the faithful who would inevitably be a minority in a majority of 'worldlings', the 'world' including the official churches, for these were either wholly corrupted or contained at best only part of the truth. The 'world' could never be converted, but one day would have to hear in answer to their 'Lord, we didn't know' the judgement reply, 'Well, you know now', while the small company of elect would be tucked up cosily in their undercrowded heaven. This led to an introversion, a withdrawing from the world, which was encouraged by persecution. Many of them rejected infant baptism as unscriptural, believing only in the validity of conscious adult believers' baptism, and were thus known as Anabaptists or Rebaptists.

Some refused co-operation with the State entirely; others believed that they should render to Caesar the things that were Caesar's. Some believed in community of goods, others that private property and prosperity were God's reward for virtue. Many were pacifist, many others believing that they should resist persecution, while yet others believed that Christ would return to lead them in a holy war against the wicked. Some were Unitarian, others Trinitarian. Some believed in the revival of prophetic gifts, like the modern Pentecostalists. Some were strongly Adventist, accepting the almost immediate return of Christ, others were Millennialists, looking for a rule of the saints (themselves) over a world subjugated by Christ ruling from an earthly throne.

Many were individualists, almost impossible to classify. The mystics tended to slide into pantheism, holding that 'there is only one sole Spirit of God which is and exists in all creatures'. The Humanists inclined to Rationalism and Unitarianism, substituting a high ethical and moral code for the life of faith. Most were filled with missionary zeal; some made no effort to convert, giving up society as lost. Nearly all were puritan in morality, temperate in food and drink, modest in dress, careful in speech, honest, peaceable, humble, hard-working in useful trades and enemies to amusements which they regarded as worldly – and often that meant all amusements. They were persecuted because they opposed the existing order whether it were Catholic, Protestant or Reformed. Often they had no beginnings that can be certainly traced and yet they had always been there from the time that the Montanists tried to return to a primitive charismatic Christianity. The Reformation gave them opportunity for organization and the expression of separate identity. They have been with society ever since in a thousand shapes – Quakers, Shakers, Independents, Separatists, Baptists, Seventh Day Adventists, Plymouth Brethren, Pentecostalists and many others. Many have disappeared, some have become 'respectable', and a few, forces of considerable importance in world Christianity.

Their complications are difficult to unravel. They may conveniently be classified as Anabaptists, Socinians (Unitarians), Erastians, Arminians, and mystics and individualists, provided that it is realized that this is an over-simplified classification and that members of one group often showed some of the characteristics of others. There was a great deal of cross-fertilization of ideas.

Anabaptists

Menno Simons (1496–1561), a Catholic priest, was influenced by the death of an Anabaptist martyr to study his Bible and reject infant baptism. He became an Anabaptist minister and wandering missionary, persecuted by Catholics and Lutherans alike, but eventually found a refuge under the protection of a Holstein nobleman. From this base he made perilous forays into Germany and the Netherlands, and by his preaching and writing organized Mennonite churches in those countries. The movement spread to Switzerland; the Swiss Mennonites were, however, driven to the

Palatinate in the seventeenth century, thence to Russia, and thence to the Americas, especially the United States. There they found other exiled Anabaptist communities, notably the Amish, founded by Jacob Ammann, and Taufers, both of German origin. The former, so strictly primitive that they wear clothes without the worldly adornment of buttons (hooks and eyes are fortunately permitted to prevent their reversion to the ultimate primitiveness of Adam and Eve) and use no machinery, can be seen to this day in their black clothes and horse buggies, a peaceful anachronism among the automobiles of twentieth-century Pennsylvania. The Taufers, or Church of the Brethren, founded by Alexander Mack in 1708, began with a group of eight men and women. Making the New Testament their only guide, these were baptized by total immersion in the River Eder and were later compelled by persecution to flee abroad.

Conrad Grebel (c. 1498–1526), a former Humanist and Zwinglian and Feliz Manz (?–1526) founded the Swiss Brethren. They believed that the Church should be independent of the civil authorities. For this and other radical opinions the Zürich city council ordered them to disband the Brethren, but they continued to baptize in alliance with another former Zwinglian, Balthasar Hubmaier of Waldshut. These all followed adult baptism with a simple Lord's Supper, Hubmaier adding a ceremony of foot-washing. Grebel and Manz were sentenced to life imprisonment by the Zürich authorities for their disobedience. They escaped, Grebel dying of natural causes almost at once and Manz, recaptured, being executed by drowning. Hubmaier was released after imprisonment and torture at Zürich and went to Moravia, where he preached with revivalist fervour and baptized thousands. He was burned at Vienna in 1528.

During the years following, hundreds of Anabaptists were drowned burned or beheaded, Calvinists, Catholics and Lutherans alike persecuting them. Thomas Müntzer, called an Anabaptist perhaps inaccurately, fomented the Peasants' Revolt in Saxony, and from 1533 to 1535 John of Leiden confirmed the worst fears of the opponents of the radicals by his reign at Münster in Westphalia. The city revolted against its Bishop-ruler, became Protestant and joined the Schmalkaldic League. When Bernard Rothmann, an ex-Catholic priest, advocated adult baptism in a public debate in the town against Catholics and Lutherans and won the day, Münster became a refuge for Anabaptists. It was prophesied that the city was to be Christ's capital from which he would reign millennially, and an Anabaptist society was imposed upon it. Horrifying stories were circulated about this, most of them untrue. All property, it was said, was held in common, polygamy was rife, opponents were ruthlessly exterminated. So extreme were the feelings raised by these tales that Lutherans helped the Catholic Bishop to reimpose his rule on the city; the leaders were executed, and another attempt at government by saints came to an untimely end.

The Hutterites, or Hutterian Brethren, another Anabaptist sect, founded by Jacob Hutter, who was executed in 1536, did practise community of goods. They were strong in Moravia but suffered hideously in the Thirty Years War, the remnants fleeing to Hungary. Late in the eighteenth century they migrated to south Russia, where their thrift and industry made them acceptable to the government. They attracted one notable individual, Bernardo Ochino (1487–1564), a Sienese, formerly head of the Capuchin order. Given papal permission to study Protestant books in order to refute them, he was instead converted by them. He became a Calvinist, was then attracted to the Schwenkfelders, helped with the Reformation in England under Edward VI, and was forced to flee to Zürich at Mary's accession. There he clashed with the Zwinglians. He moved to Poland and thence to Moravia where he died in communion with the Hutterites.

Anabaptism, surprisingly, proved temporarily strong in Venice. As so often, religion was influenced by politics, the Venetians wishing to maintain their independence against the power of the papacy and, in particular, from the machinations of the Inquisition. Many Venetian Anabaptists became Unitarian, owing to Servetus's writings. In 1550 they produced a statement of belief. Christ, born of Joseph and Mary, is not God but man, though he was filled with the powers of God. The Elect are not justified by anything that Christ was or did but by God's everlasting love. All that Christ's death did was to reveal God's mercy and goodness. The Venetians did not long desert their natural Catholicism and soon the Anabaptist congregations in the city were persecuted and scattered abroad.

Attempts were made to find a confession of faith upon which all Anabaptists could agree. In 1527, Michael Sattler, a former monk, drew up articles which laid down that churches should be independent local congregations of adult baptized believers, each choosing its ministers and independent of all others. Their only link was to be a particular method of celebrating the Lord's Supper. After Sattler's revoltingly cruel execution, six further attempts to draw up a confession of faith were made between 1577 and 1627, and a union of the Anabaptist churches was attempted in the Dortrecht Confession of 1632. Mutually exclusive doctrines held by different sects within the movement, however, made permanent union impossible.

Socinianism

This drew its name from the Sozinis, uncle and nephew, Lelio Sozini, or Suzzini, better known by his Latin name of Laelius

Socinus, born about 1525, was a Sienese lawyer. Through reading the Bible, Laelius, a deeply religious Humanist of attractive character and irreproachable life, who valued reason as well as the scriptures as a guide to faith, developed anti-Trinitarian views. He was a friend of Bullinger and acquainted with Calvin, but deplored the burning of Servetus and was consequently suspected by the Reformed Church. He died at Zürich in 1562 after a life of wide travel in a number of places from Venice to the Grisons, then an independent republic between Italy and Switzerland. The little country had been a centre of anti-Trinitarian activity since 1526, when it gave religious liberty to Catholic and Reformed alike. It was thus an acceptable spiritual home for Socinus who was but one of many Unitarian Italians driven from Italy by fear of the Inquisition.

Far more outstanding an anti-Trinitarian was Laelius's nephew Fausto, or Faustus, born in 1539. Originally a Catholic, he went to Basle in about 1574 and became a Calvinist. He expressed his Unitarian views in *De Jesu Christi Salvatore*, basing his doctrine on his reading of Scripture. He maintained that the miracles and especially the resurrection of Christ proved the truth of Christianity. Christ did not pay the penalty for man's sins, thus appeasing the wrath of a righteous God. He was a real man, though not an ordinary one, being at once prophet, priest and king, and existed to bring mankind the knowledge of God which would show them how to come to him. This knowledge and the imitation of Christ's life bring about salvation. Baptism is the outward act by which converts acknowledge Christ as their master, an acknowledgement infants are not able to make. The Church consists outwardly of the adult baptized, inwardly of those who adhere to the saving doctrine and allow the Holy Spirit to be a power in their lives. The Lord's Supper is commemorative only. Christians are known by their renunciation of the world, their endurance of tribulation and persecution, their prayer, thanksgiving and joy, their obedience to lawful magistrates, their modest wealth and their use of any superfluity for the relief of the poor.

After a time in Transylvania, where the creed was strong and the name 'Unitarian' was first officially used in 1600, Faustus spent twenty-five years in Poland, dying there in 1604. The Socinians were active in the Ukraine, made contact with the Dutch Mennonites and with the Arminians and all but won Poland. Rakow, their headquarters there, produced a catechism as a statement of Christian belief, but it was not accepted by all and passed through several revisions. Faustus's followers disagreed over pacifism. They became increasingly rationalist, accepting Jesus as 'the best of men'. They stood for religious liberty, seeking neither to force their views on others nor suffer force themselves.

Their wishes were thwarted by the brothers Sigismund III (1566–1632) and John Casimir (1609–72), a Jesuit priest and Cardinal, who between them ruled Poland for sixty-six years. Sigismund persecuted the Socinians and Casimir expelled them. Some went to Transylvania, others to Germany and Holland. They had a considerable influence on Christian Humanists, Calvinists, English Presbyterians and New England Puritans, and are today strong throughout the United States.

They suffered a number of setbacks, however. The Reformed Church tried hard to impose Trinitarianism on its members. In 1533 the Grisons outlawed Unitarianism by adopting the Rhaetian Confession, which incorporated the Apostles', Nicene and Athanasian Creeds. By 1575 it had all but disappeared in Switzerland.

The reasons for its continuing appeal to men of various types, however, are not far to seek. Its high ethical standards attract those who believe that right belief should result in moral living. Its view that man does not need to be converted but can, with God's help, live the good life by his own efforts, appeals to the type of self-reliant character which often emerges in pioneer, frontier and capitalist societies. Its rationalism and anti-mysticism attract the sophisticated believer, hence the strong Unitarian streak in the Deist movement later.

Erastianism

Thomas Erastus (1524–83), a Swiss doctor of medicine, gave his name to the heresy of Erastianism. He asserted that a Christian ruler should have authority over the Church and that excommunication was never permissible. 'The Christian magistrate', he wrote, 'possesses ... the authority to settle religion according to the directions given in Holy Scripture and to arrange the ministries and offices there' but 'ought to consult, where doctrine is concerned, those who have particularly studied it'. The Church of England is regarded as heretical by the Roman partly because it is Erastian, whereas Catholics and Calvinists both claimed, in their different ways, the control of secular affairs by spiritual leaders. Modern Erastians see Church and State as separate entities and believe that the latter should control the former.

Arminianism

Jacob Arminius (1560–1609), professor of theology in the University of Leiden, asserted the power of man's free will against a rigid predestinarianism and became an early champion of toleration for heretics. The occasion of his heresy was a dispute in the Dutch

Reformed Church between Supralapsarians, those who believed that God had decreed who should be saved and who damned before he created the world, and Infralapsarians, who held that God made his decision after Adam's fall—not that so academic a dispute would have mattered a damn to the damned. Arminius led those who remonstrated against both views and were thus known as Remonstrants. They also rejected 'limited atonement' (the doctrine that Christ died only for the Elect), irresistible grace and the perseverance of the Elect. They almost rejected Calvinism. Christ, they said, died for all men, believers are saved, salvation being by faith alone, rejecters of God's grace are damned and, while God foresees, he does not ordain the loss of the sinner.

An international Calvinist synod held at Dort in 1618–19 condemned Arminianism in forthright Calvinistic terms—no idle censure, for it was followed by the beheading of a leading Remonstrant a few days later and the imprisonment of another, who was lucky enough to escape. Nevertheless Arminianism did not disappear. In Holland, the Remonstrants broke away to form their own church, and rigid Calvinism nearly always results in the reappearance of Arminianism as a reaction.

Mystics and Individualists

Caspar Schwenkfeld (1487–1541) wished to free Christianity from dogma, believing that a formal church organization was superfluous. Originally a Lutheran, he came to reject sacraments and to believe in an inner experience of God expressing itself in righteous living. He opposed coercion of conscience. He was not an anarchist and was willing to impose and accept a stricter discipline than the Lutheran. His followers, whose tenets were not unlike those of the Quakers, formed societies of 'Confessors of the Glory of Christ'. They were popularly known as Schwenkfelders and eventually found their way to Pennsylvania in the eighteenth century.

Like Schwenkfeld was his friend Sebastian Franck (1499–c. 1542), a Catholic priest who reacted against the authority of the written word and all external observances, church machinery and organization. He was a pacifist and abhorred persecution for differences in religion. He taught that in every man there is an element of the divine which is the source of all religious life, that the Spirit of Christ turns men towards such living and that the Church consists of all those who have received the grace of God. He gloried in the great original thinkers throughout the ages, heretics and orthodox alike, realizing that men of such great soul as Paul and Jesus himself were heretics to their contemporaries.

Influenced by the Spanish Catholic mystic Juan de Valdes, Pietro

Martire Vermigli (1500–62), already mentioned under his better known name of Peter Martyr, was also a Catholic priest and abbot of an Augustinian monastery. He read the works of Bucer and Zwingli, became suspected of unsoundness and fled to Strasburg where he met Bucer. Invited by Cranmer to England, he became regius professor of divinity at Oxford, fled at Mary's accession and died at Zürich as professor of Hebrew there. By his lectures he influenced the Piedmontese Humanist and professor Celio Secundo Curione (1563–69) who became an early Independent, an individualist who fitted into no Protestant community and who advocated religious toleration for all men.

Similar to Curione in his individualism was Pierpaulo Vergerio, a former papal nuncio and Bishop of Capodistria. He urged the reform of morals and doctrine, refused to answer charges of heresy at Rome and was denounced by the Inquisition. He fled north and became a wanderer, never conforming to any school of Protestant thought.

John à Lasko or John Laski (1499–1560), an ex-Catholic priest of good family and a friend of Erasmus, was an individualist of another kind. Instead of fitting into no denomination, he tried to unite all the varieties of Protestantism in Poland into one church. He failed because of Protestant squabbles and the overwhelming resources open to the Jesuits under a Catholic monarch. These enabled them to recover completely a country which could at one time have become entirely Protestant.

These are but some of the more notable of the scores of religious radicals who preached throughout Europe in the sixteenth century. An exhaustive study of them all would need a volume.

The sixteenth century was the age of another reformation, the Catholic, which was much more a positive setting of the Catholic house in order than a negative counter to Protestantism. Since any realist church historian must recognize Roman Catholicism as the standard of orthodoxy in western Europe and any deviation from its doctrine as heterodox even if not heretical, the Catholic Reformation has no place in a history of heresy except insofar as it affected non-Catholics or gave rise to heretical teachings within its own ranks in its efforts to reform. Seven factors may be listed as composing the Reformation: the Council of Trent (1545–63); the founding of new orders, of which the Society of Jesus was incomparably the most important for countering Protestantism; inner reforms of the Church itself; reforming bishops; the capture by the reforming spirit of the papacy; the emergence of gifted individuals and mystics; and scholarly writings against Protestantism.

The Council of Trent was a battleground between conservative reformers within the Catholic Church who wished to cleanse it but keep the old dogmas, and progressives who wanted to come to terms with the Protestants. This is an over-simplification, for there were many undercurrents of rivalries and differences of opinion within these principal divisions. The conservatives won, establishing as orthodox a number of doctrines which have been accepted Catholic faith since and making heretical differing Protestant dogmas. These may be summarized as follows, with the general Protestant view in brackets, where it is practicable to include this in note form.

1. Holy Scripture consists of the Old Testament, including the Apocrypha, and the New Testament (Protestants on the whole reject the Apocrypha as part of the 'inspired' word of God). The old Vulgate text is alone authoritative and authentic (scholarship sees many errors in it). The unwritten traditions received by the Apostles from Christ and preserved in the Roman Church are of equal authority with the Bible, since they have God as their author and were dictated by the Holy Spirit (many of the traditions are unwarranted, obviously man-made assumptions which at best cannot be proved). No one was to interpret the Bible contrary to the sense authorized by the Church (God's Word in Scripture is the touchstone by which the Church's doctrine and practice must be judged, not the other way round).

2. Original sin exists in man and is taken away only by the form of baptism used by the Church, applicable to adults and infants alike. (One Protestant view is that all baptisms are valid, because believers are baptized into the Church, not into a denomination; the Baptists, Pentecostalists and some others insist on adult baptism.)

3. Christ died for all, but only those receive the benefit to whom the merit of his passion is communicated. Men cannot move without God's grace first inspiring them to approach him, but they can accept or reject it, for man's free will was not extinguished by Adam's sin. Justification comes through a new birth in baptism or the desire for it, and although it is through faith it is not through faith alone. A justified believer *can* keep the commands of God and the Church and by doing so can advance and gain further justification and merit earned by good works. Good works done before justification are not sins, nor are only the Elect justified and the rest predestined to evil.

4. Purgatory does exist.

5. The priesthood of all believers does not.

6. There are seven sacraments (Protestants admit two, sometimes three, sometimes – as with the Quakers – none). In communion the doctrine of Transubstantiation and the Real Presence becomes a required dogma, that of Consubstantiation is condemned. Since

Christ is in both bread and wine, it is unnecessary for the laity to receive the chalice.

7. Only bishops and priests can forgive or retain sins (only God has this power, independent of anything any priest may say).

8. Invocation of saints, veneration of relics, sacred images and pictures, and indulgences are acceptable practices to be retained.

The supremacy of Rome was recognized (after a struggle and with reservations).

Of the new orders the Society of Jesus was founded by Ignatius Loyola (c. 1491–1556), who emerged from the same kind of spiritual conflict as Luther as an intensely loyal Roman Catholic. Yet even he was suspected by the Inquisition at one time of being a heretic. He formed his society in 1534, and this body vowed to do whatever the Pope commanded and go wherever he sent them, including 'the lands of the heretics'. It received authorization from the Roman see in 1540. By Loyola's death over a thousand Jesuits were operating in almost every western European country, and it was largely owing to them that the Reformation was checked and rolled back and parts of Germany, Bohemia, Moravia and Poland recovered for Rome. Their success may be measured by the hatred and fear which they aroused among Protestants.

Reforming bishops such as St Charles Borromeo, Archbishop of Milan (1560–84), fought heresy with energy. He visited those Alpine districts of his diocese particularly affected and, backed by the Inquisition, won many converts. Parish priests were ordered to report suspects and were warned specially 'to smell the words and deeds of each single one' of those who came from a heretical district. Secular rulers were required as far as possible to stop all trade and intercourse with heretical countries and to assist and enrich the Inquisition in every way. Prohibited books were to be entirely abolished. Doctors were forbidden to visit sick people who had not made their confession by the third day after they had become ill. In 1583 Borromeo burned eleven old women and the Rector of Rovedo in the Alps for sorcery.

St Francis de Sales (1567–1622), Bishop of Geneva for the last twenty years of his life, is claimed to have converted 72,000 heretics from among the Calvinists of the Chablais. He never resorted to force until persuasion failed. But even he, after two years, was compelled by the 'invincible obstinacy' of the Calvinists to appeal to the Duke of Savoy to expel their ministers, deprive Calvinists of places of honour and dignity and return their churches to the Catholics. Francis shed no blood and did not use the Inquisition, but he was adamant in rooting out Calvinism, maintaining that it had neither ministry nor sacraments. Energetic propaganda coupled with expulsion banished heresy from the Chablais, though de Sales's cathedral city of Geneva remained firmly in Calvinist hands, and in 1610 the Bishop was able to go to Paris to help Henry IV to suppress heresy in parts of his kingdom.

By the end of the sixteenth century there came a subtle change in the nature of heresy. In retrospect, there is not one, well-defined river of Christian doctrine from which heretics can be clearly seen to differ. Rather the stream divided into a delta of three or four principal divisions, of which the original stream was still the strongest and could still be distinguished; but its parallel branches are different in kind from the brooks and rills of unorthodoxy and heresy which ran off from the river in former times. They had a strength and sufficiency of their own which made the term 'heresy', though still technically applicable, inappropriate. They could be termed local orthodoxies. This is, indeed, an idea conformable with the Anglican position which recognizes that all churches, including the Church of England, have erred from the whole truth. It conflicts with the Roman Catholic claim that they alone are the one true church, in the same way that some Protestant fringe sects claim that they alone have the 'full Gospel'. To a Christian observer trying to be objective, there seem to be truth and error in all denominations.

Two more changes may be seen. First, Catholicism and Protestantism become much more entwined with politics, the former being associated with Latin Europe, the latter with the Anglo-Saxon part of the continent. Men in those days were Catholic and Protestant, as much belonging to a type of political outlook as adhering to doctrinal positions. Cromwell's Ironsides, for example, allied their staunch Puritanism with a tendency to republicanism, while to Charles's Cavaliers high church principles and loyalty to the King went hand in glove. Students of philosophies might differ in their estimates of the strength and importance of this change, but it cannot be denied that it was there.

The other change was the gradual development of more tolerant attitudes. This was partly brought about by the strength of heretics – even the Inquisition could scarcely have found the fuel to burn every Englishman and Scandinavian, and Protestant and Catholic nations had to learn to coexist. There was the strange sight of a prince of the Roman Church like Cardinal Richelieu allying with a Protestant nation against another Catholic country for the aggrandisement of his own Catholic France. And with the gradual growth of the modern outlook there came a slow but sure increase of tolerance among individuals. As men grew more sceptical, so they came to regard 'superstition' as contemptible rather than criminal. Heretics – and the gullible orthodox, for that matter – were to be pitied by the intelligent rather than sent to the stake.

CHAPTER 16

The Seventeenth Century

By 1600 the outlines of divided European Christendom had been drawn. Protestant churches throughout the states of Italy had been suppressed, their pastors escaping abroad or submitting, their flocks fleeing or conforming. In Spain they had scarcely existed and disappeared like mist in the Catholic sun. Southern Germany had returned to the papal fold, the southern Netherlands (now Belgium) were Catholic, as was France except for a temporarily legally recognized Huguenot minority. Northern Germany, Scandinavia, the British Isles (save for Ireland), and the northern Netherlands (Holland) were Protestant. Outside Europe, Catholic powers took their religion via missionaries to South America, large parts of North America and the Far East. To wherever Protestant countries sent settlers or had influence, Protestantism was understandably exported.

The history of heresy may be presented in two ways. It can be put forward as a story of ideas, heretical thesis and antithesis often settling into orthodox synthesis. Or the historian may record a series of events built around personalities. Both methods must be used if a complete picture is to be painted. In the present work ideas will be dealt with first, followed by a very brief summary of the political background against which orthodoxy and heresies played their considerable roles.

Cornelius Jansen (1585–1638), Catholic Bishop of Ypres from 1635, founded a heresy of major importance in the seventeenth century in the shape of a genuinely religious movement which demanded strictness in living and morals at a time of general laxity. It arose from his book, *Augustinus*, a commentary on the works of St Augustine published posthumously in 1640. Jansen wrote that the full Christian life was possible only in the Roman Catholic Church and rejected justification by faith, but he emphasized personal religious experience and the direct contact of a man with God in sudden conversion. His book was alleged to contain five heretical propositions (Calvinistic in their emphasis on the predestination to salvation of the Elect), which were condemned by the Pope and the Inquisition in 1653. These were as follows:

1. Some of God's commands are impossible for just men wanting and struggling to keep them, considering the powers human beings actually possess. The grace by which these commandments can be kept may also be withheld.

2. In the state of fallen nature, interior grace once granted is irresistible.

3. In the state of fallen nature, to merit or deserve punishment men need not be free from interior necessity but only from exterior constraint.

4. The semi-Pelagians, though admitting a necessity of interior preventing (i.e. prevenient or initiated by God) grace for all acts, even the beginning of faith, fall into heresy in saying that this grace may be either followed or resisted.

5. To say that Christ died for all men is semi-Pelagian.

In simple language, Jansenism asserted the power and majesty of God, the insignificance of man and the necessity of grace as against the Jesuits who, in the view of Jansenists, allowed free will and works to play too big a part in the scheme of salvation. Pascal, whose *Provincial Letters* was written to defend the Jansenists, wrote in his *Pensées* that 'we understand nothing of the works of God, if we do not take it as our starting-point that he willed to blind some, to enlighten others' (iii. 6). It also stressed the need for a more rigid, puritanical morality, disapproving of the Jesuits' laxity in demanding too little penance from their penitents. Jansenist churches lacked flowers, decoration and music, and all other things in life were considered trivia compared with the facts of the corruption of man, the reality and awfulness of God and man's redemption by Christ. Like some moderate Protestants, the 'heresy' upheld the authority of Scripture and of the early ecumenical councils against later developments in the Church, and it emphasized the importance of education. It was condemned for wanting to return to a primitive purity and discipline which differed from the accepted doctrines and practices of its day and which, Catholic critics allege, could have been dangerous in the conditions of the seventeenth century. It is not cynical to say, too, that its high ideals and standards troubled the consciences of, and consequently exasperated, its opponents.

The heresy was supported by Port-Royal, near Paris, a community of Cistercian nuns and solitaries governed by Mère Angélique Arnauld. When the five propositions were condemned in 1653, Dr Antoine Arnauld, a relative of Mère Angelique, denied that they appeared in the *Augustinus* at all, and later went further in asserting that, although the Pope can define a doctrine and condemn a heresy opposing it, he cannot infallibly declare such heresy to be contained in any individual book. The controversy was intensified by political enemies of the French government and the Jesuits, who used the movement as a stick with which to beat their opponents.

The papal condemnation was renewed in 1661 and a general assembly of French clergy endorsed an anti-Jansenist formula, which all clergy were required to sign. Four years later the Pope published a similar formula. Under it four bishops were excommunicated, but the other bishops rallied to them and a compromise was reached. Meanwhile some of the supporters of Jansenism were affected by a curious hysteria. Upon the death of a Jansenist cleric, François, Archdeacon of Paris, his tomb in St Médard's Cemetery became a centre of pilgrimage and alleged miracles. Excesses broke out among the Convulsionnaires, as they came to be known. Among them were gently nurtured young ladies who witnessed to the glory of God and the justice of the Jansenist cause by eating excreta, allowing paving-stones to be broken on their stomachs and speaking in tongues. Encouraged, perhaps, by such devotion, the nuns of Port-Royal persisted in their refusal to sign the papal formulary and were much persecuted as a result. Louis XIV, urged on by the Jesuits, asked the Pope for an unequivocal pronouncement on Jansenism. In 1705, therefore, a papal bull condemned Jansenism for the third time in terms which left no doubt that it was heretical. The nuns still refusing to submit, Port-Royal was closed, its buildings destroyed and its graveyard ploughed up.

This ended the matter for a few years. In 1713, however, a book by Quesnel, *Moral Reflections on the New Testament*, was swiftly condemned by a papal bull, *Unigenitus*, for 101 Jansenist propositions contained in it. The Parlement of Paris was a strong supporter of Jansenism and the French Church resented the bull as an interference with its internal affairs. Nevertheless, there was persecution and some Jansenists fled to the Netherlands, where several thousands of Catholics, both clerics and laymen, broke with Rome and helped to form the Dutch Old Catholic Church. This came into existence as follows.

Since Jansenism had originated in Holland, the Dutch bishops were suspect; and in 1670 the Archbishop of Utrecht was summoned to Rome to answer a charge of heresy. He returned uncondemned, but in 1710 the Archbishop-elect, selected by the chapter, was excommunicated for protesting against a summons to appear before a papal nuncio at Cologne. After thirteen years' limbo, however, on 15 October 1724, Cornelius Steenoven was consecrated

Archbishop, in due line of apostolic succession, by the Bishop of Babylon, whereupon the Old Catholic Church of Holland began a separate existence, one which still continues. Jansenism also survived in France but almost entirely politically and without its original idealism. The conflict it caused has, in fact, led to the accusation that it fomented the spirit of atheism and anti-religion which helped to bring about the French Revolution.

Mysticism continued to manifest itself in various forms. Miguel de Molinos (d. 1697), a Spaniard, spiritual descendant of those visionary Illuminés who believed that they had been chosen by God to reform the Church, founded Quietism. He advocated a passive, receptive attitude in religion, and taught interior annihilation as a means of obtaining the purification of the soul, a state of perfect contemplation and inner peace. It was permissible to indulge in sins of the flesh because they were committed only by man's lower nature and did not touch the soul. He expressed these views in *Il Guida Spirituale* (The Spiritual Guide), a work published in 1675 which proved extremely popular and won many adherents, especially in Naples, where he had an estimated twenty thousand followers. In 1687 Molinos was condemned for his heresy to life imprisonment clad as a penitent and died in prison.

Another mystic, in France, was Madame Guyon (1648–1717). She has been described as an energetic, charming but neurotic woman who claimed she could preach with ease in words given her from above, write without thinking because an excellent Penman guided her hand, perform miracles, read the minds of others and have absolute power over their wills and bodies. Partly as a natural psychic, as her claims seem to show her to have been, partly under the influence of a Barnabite spiritual director, she developed a kind of mysticism which made her a protégée of Fénelon (1651–1715), Bishop of Cambrai. He modified her ideas into a Neoplatonic Christianity which aroused the condemnation of a famous preacher, Bossuet (1627–1704). The affair caused a temporary flurry of partisanship on both sides. Fénelon appealed to Rome, but papal condemnation of some of his views caused his instant submission and retirement to his diocese, where he remained with the taint of heresy hanging about him for many years. Madame Guyon was imprisoned until her death.

Not unlike Quietism in spirit, although more orthodox, was the Lutheran Pietist movement. This sprang up in Germany in reaction to the arid, rationalist theology which was one result of the devastation of the Thirty Years War. It is not easy to say what is heretical in the Pietist view unless it be that over-emphasis which is so often the cause of heresy. It is true that Dr Müller (1631–75), an early Pietist, seemed to condemn preaching, baptism, communion and confession as 'idols', but he defended himself successfully by saying that he rejected only the *opus operatum* as a means of grace (i.e. the view that grace resides in the mere exercise of a sacrament or sermon and that its administration alone is sufficient to convey it to the individual, who needs make no positive preparation). Philip Spener (1673–1705), who has been described as the John Wesley of the German Pietists, was a puritan, eschewing dancing, the theatre and cards. He republished earlier devotional works by such men as Tauler and à Kempis as well as writing his own *Pious Desires*, and he tried to establish in each church devotional gatherings for prayer, Bible study, confession and mutual encouragement, not unlike the later Methodists.

Augustus Francke (1663–1727) founded the Collegium Philobiblicum for the devotional study of the Bible at Leipzig University with such success that many students spent all their time studying the Scriptures. Other schools in the university were almost deserted, opposition was aroused, the name 'Pietist' coined in derision and Francke expelled from Leipzig. At Halle, whither he went in 1691 to teach Oriental languages, he founded an orphanage, student hostel and almshouses, held weekly conferences for divinity students and inspired the first missionary enterprise outside the Catholic Church to non-Christian nations. The Pietist movement was an attempt to revive the initial enthusiasm of the Reformation.

The above heresies may be called theological. There were others that arose out of the growing scientific, rationalist spirit which was partly the result of the Protestant exaltation of private judgement, and partly of observation and discoveries which the inquiring mind of man inevitably came to make. Galileo (1564–1642) was condemned by the Inquisition and compelled to recant the heresy that the earth went round the sun, thus earning the distinction of being perhaps the first victim of the war of science versus religion. The denial of scientific fact in the name of religion was at least a new kind of orthodoxy and one to be repeated to their shame by Christians many times in the centuries that were to come. And unlike previous heresies which could only oppose unprovable speculation by speculation equally unprovable, in these denials orthodoxy could in time be shown to be wrong.

A number of thinkers, however, used reason to vindicate their religious ideas. Sir Francis Bacon (1561–1626) was the father of the scientific inductive method of discovering general laws from the observation of particular phenomena, which was to cause difficulties later for conservative theologians. William Chillingworth (1602–44) fought for the place of reason in religion, offending both Catholics and Presbyterians by his views. He denied the infallibility of the Pope and of the Church. Somewhat ahead of his time – for the eighteenth century rather than the seventeenth was the Age of Reason – his complete works, moderately read before, ran through five editions between 1704 and 1742. Lord Herbert of Cherbury (1583–1648) believed in natural religion and rejected all revelation. He founded the study of comparative religion, rejecting Christianity as the sole source of the knowledge of God. Thomas Hobbes (1588–1671), author of *The Leviathan*, was an Erastian, maintaining that the monarch or civil power was the supreme pastor in every Christian commonwealth, all other priests and ministers receiving their authority from him. He was an early biblical critic, denying the Mosaic authorship of the Pentateuch. Yet he recognized the authority of Scripture, and of reason as supplying all rules and precepts necessary to salvation.

The other heterodoxies of the seventeenth century are best dealt with within the history of individual countries – beginning with Germany, the home of the Reformation, and her neighbours in middle Europe.

In 1604 Stephen Bocskay led the Protestants of Upper Hungary in a revolt against government persecution and made himself prince of the country and of Transylvania. In 1606 Emperor Rudolf II granted freedom of worship to Hungary, but the shadow of war was beginning to loom. In 1608 a Protestant Union of German states was created for defence, and the following year the Holy League of Catholic states was formed to face it. Like many treaties, the Peace of Augsburg had not been kept. The Lutherans had seized Catholic Church property to which the Peace had not entitled them. The Catholics reacted increasingly sharply. The Calvinists, who had no place in the treaty, being tolerated by neither side, were indifferent to war or peace. There needed only an excuse for war to be welcomed by Catholic and Protestant alike.

It came in 1618 when Ferdinand of Habsburg, elected Emperor and rightful ruler of Bohemia, rescued it from the Protestant prince whom the Bohemians had placed on the throne. The Lutheran Danes went to the aid of the German Protestants and were thrashed. The Emperor, in an Edict of Restitution, demanded the return of all properties seized unlawfully by the Protestants. Gustavus Vasa of Sweden intervened successfully on the Protestant side, though he lost his life doing so. The details of this particularly horrible, bloody and destructive war are not the concern of this book except that it was in essence religious. By the Treaty of Westphalia, in 1648, which brought it to an end, it was recognized that Protestantism and Calvinism had the right to exist equally with Lutheranism. In short, heresy was now officially respectable in the comity of nations in this life, whatever the fate of heretics in the next. But the treaty did not end religious troubles. In 1651 Frederick

William, Elector of Brandenburg, had to invade Berg to secure liberty of conscience for persecuted Protestants, and in 1673 Leopold I harassed his Protestant subjects in Hungary.

The Swiss Confederation was granted independence from Germany by the Treaty of Westphalia, but continued to have trouble in religious matters. In 1618 Nicholas Rusca, Archpriest of Sondrio, leader of the Catholics in Valtellina, had been tortured to death and his body burned. He was avenged by a well-organized massacre of Protestants in the district two years later—only five, for example, escaping from the village of Tirano. However, in 1654 the Protestant Swiss were powerful enough to have influence with Cromwell and to bring pressure to bear elsewhere to help the Waldenses. Zürich and Geneva continued to be a refuge for Protestants from the Catholic parts of Switzerland, and although the Swiss Catholics beat their Protestant compatriots in the first Villmergen War in 1656, the individual sovereignty of each member of the confederation in religious matters was confirmed. In 1668 French Protestants fled in thousands to Switzerland and greatly strengthened their co-religionists in manpower and skills.

Religious troubles in France lasted throughout the century. In 1621 the Huguenots published a declaration of independence at La Rochelle, which was followed by various attempts at peace and further wars until, in 1628, Richelieu took the city. The Peace of Alais in the following year fatally weakened the Huguenots by depriving them of the towns they had been granted under the Edict of Nantes. Richelieu also used bribery with great success, and through taxation, suppression and the closing of professions to them, Calvinists in France suffered grievous losses. The Cardinal's Catholicism did not prevent his supplying the English Covenanters with money in 1639; nor did Cardinal Mazarin's stop him from allying with Cromwell in 1657; nor did France's restrain her from humiliating the Pope in 1664 or check her Gallicanism (the doctrine, regarded as heretical by some Catholics, of restricting papal authority over the French Catholic Church) in 1682; nor did it prevent her from quarrelling with His Holiness again in 1687.

The Huguenots had caused little trouble since the loss of their towns and Richelieu's restrictions and, sober and industrious as they were, and peaceful, too, in order not to draw upon themselves the resentment of the overwhelming Catholic majority among whom they lived, they contributed much to the trade and financial well-being of France. But Louis XIV could not abide any hint of a state within a state; France must be one and France must be Catholic. In 1680 Huguenot religious liberties began to be curtailed. Two years later French Protestants began to flee abroad. Those who remained were exposed to forcible conversion by missionaries assisted by dragoons, considered to be the cruellest and most licentious troops in the French army – in 1684, sixty thousand Huguenots are said to have become Catholics in three days. The following year the Edict of Nantes was revoked and more Protestants fled, all freedom of religion now being denied to them. But in the Cevennes the revocation of the edict resulted in a Judas Maccabaeus type of epic struggle in which three thousand peasant Camisards, so called from the white shirts they wore as uniforms, for a time victoriously resisted sixty thousand royalist troops. They were encouraged by strange phenomena – hallucinations and 'Little Prophets', aged from the early teens down to babyhood, speaking in tongues and preaching exhortatory sermons in excellent French.

Spain continued on her Catholic way, burning eighty-five heretics and Jews in a single day in 1680. England persecuted her minorities with lesser punishments and, by the end of the century, had moved into a position almost modern in its general acceptance of a number of different philosophies. The seventeenth century began for England with a continuation of the struggle between the Puritan and Anglican strains within the national church. The Hampton Court Conference in 1604 was a victory for the latter, but James I, faced with a Puritan Parliament which claimed jurisdiction over both Church and State, appeased it by persecuting Catholics. The 1605 Gunpowder Plot of Catholics enabled Parliament to increase the severity of the laws against them, and, on the other flank, the Court of High Commission under the inspiration of Abbot, Archbishop of Canterbury, became more severe against Puritan nonconformists in the Anglican Church.

Relations between James and his increasingly Puritan subjects worsened as the reign went on, and these sowed some of the seeds of the trouble his son, Charles I, was to harvest. In 1625 politics once more overpowered religion when English Protestant ships were lent to Catholic Richelieu to reduce Huguenot La Rochelle, although in 1627, at the outbreak of war between England and France, an English fleet sailed to the city's aid. The war is said by some historians to have been a pre-emptive stroke by England against an alliance between France and Spain, partly inspired by Pope Urban VII. The Pope complained to the French that Charles had broken his promise that Henrietta Maria, his French wife, should bring up their children as Catholics. Louis XIII, then on the French throne should compel him to keep his word or wrest the crown from the heretic king.

In England the Church was dividing more and more sharply into Arminian and Calvinist sections, with their different views on free will and predestination. The former was high church, supporting the divine right of kings; the latter low church, strong in Parliament. To each side the other was heretical, and the Puritans were no more restrained in their language (bishops being 'satanical lords', 'ravening wolves', 'servants of the devil', 'promoters of superstition, popery and impiety') than the high churchmen in their punishments (Puritan preachers and writers being fined, pilloried, publicly whipped, branded on the cheeks with 'SS'–'spreader of sedition'–and having their ears cropped and their nostrils slit). One of its last acts before the Civil War was the impeachment by Parliament of the bishops in 1641 following a bill to root out episcopacy 'root and branch'.

Parliament's victory in the Civil War, which resulted n Charles I's beheading in 1648, meant the apparently complete triumph of Presbyterianism in the English Church. The Westminster Assembly of Divines in 1647, which produced the Calvinist Westminster Confession, had, it seemed, seen to that. But the blanket name 'Puritan', often used to cover all opponents of the Royalists as if they were in complete agreement, included a variety of very different sects. Some of the more extreme thought that there was little to choose between bishops and presbyters. The Independents or Congregationalists, half-way between Presbyterians and Brownists, emphasized the personal inspiration at the expense of Scripture, tradition and church discipline. All congregations should be autonomous and equal, their only supremacy being the seniority of sisters. The State had no right to interfere in church affairs, and the Independents were theoretically in favour of toleration.

Close to them were the Anabaptists, who added the dogma of adult baptism. These English Baptists originated with John Smyth, a Cambridge man, who baptized himself and other adults in exile in Amsterdam and, in London in 1611, formed the first Baptist Church in England. Other believers in the 'Inner Light' were the Quakers, whose apostle was George Fox, an unlettered man who believed that the Spirit could dwell within individual men, influencing their hearts through the love of God. Fox, a pacifist, believed that God wanted every man to be reconciled to himself, and that this could be achieved without sacraments, priests and any outward show or music. He laid less emphasis on the Bible than other Protestants. The early Quakers, as their name indicates, shook and trembled in the ecstasy of their worship, though nothing could be more restrained or decorous than the Society of Friends, their modern descendants. As many as 3,170 Quakers are said to have suffered punishment under the Commonwealth.

Close in belief to the Quakers but more violent were the Ranters, who set up 'the light of Nature under the name of Christ' and decried the Church, Scriptures, ordination and regulations of any sort. Their anarchy led to charges of libertinism against them – resulting from their belief that God took no notice of men's outward actions but only of their hearts. Also close to the Quakers were the Behmenites, followers of Jacob Behmen. Fewer in number and of greater meekness than other dissenters, they too accepted 'the sufficiency of the Light of Nature' and depended on the revelations they received through it. The Levellers, religious and political democrats, among other principles advocated religious toleration. The Fifth Monarchy Men were Millennialists who believed that King Jesus would return to set up the kingdom of God on earth as the fifth empire mentioned in the Book of Daniel. And there were other sects, too numerous to be mentioned.

The Independents quickly replaced the Presbyterians as the religious authority in England, but, by their very nature, could scarcely act as an authority. At the Restoration the Church of England and episcopacy were re-established and action taken against recalcitrant dissenters – John Bunyan, author of *Pilgrim's Progress*, was jailed for twelve years from 1660 for 'upholding unlawful conventicles'. By an Act of Uniformity the 1662 prayer-book, a revision of the 1552 book of Elizabeth I, was made compulsory and one result was 'Black Bartholomew', St Bartholomew's Day on which between twelve hundred and two thousand ministers were compelled to secede from the Anglican Church. Charles II's strong Catholic tendencies made him favour toleration, but Parliament, although high church, were prepared to tolerate neither Catholics nor Puritans. A series of severe acts was aimed against the latter and the Test Act in 1673 disqualified all Roman Catholics from holding public office. Hysteria against the Catholics was whipped up for political reasons through fear of the accession to the throne of Catholic James, Charles II's brother, resulting in the invention by Titus Oates of the Popish Plot and the execution of leading Roman Catholics.

The worst fears of Protestants seemed justified from the moment James came to the throne. His Declaration of Indulgence, plainly intended to favour Catholics, together with other pro-Catholic actions, compelled his expulsion from the throne in 1688, and he was succeeded by William III and Mary, who safeguarded the Church of England. William was more tolerant than Parliament, and by the Toleration Act of 1689 Baptists, Congregationalists, Presbyterians and Quakers were granted the right to independent worship. Only Catholics and Unitarians were excluded, and the century was closed with a severe act against Roman Catholics. Not all his subjects, however, were opposed to William's toleration. In the Anglican centre were the Latitudinarians, opposed to popish superstitions on the one hand and dissenting 'enthusiasm' on the other. They emphasized reason in religion and were tolerant of those outside the Church of England and those who differed from them within it, and although they favoured the episcopal form of ecclesiastical government and ritual, they did not regard it as divinely inspired.

It is significant that the two parties in English politics in 1700 called their opponents Whigs, a contemptuous name for Scottish Presbyterian covenanters, and Tories, an equally contemptuous name for Irish popish outlaws. Men are no longer heretics in England; they are political opponents whose religious and political opinions are lumped together under a single jeering nickname.

By the seventeenth century, the American colonies had grown sufficiently civilized to persecute those who did not agree with the majority, even though the majority had themselves once been a minority suffering persecution. English Congregationalists originally from Scrooby, Nottinghamshire, who had fled to Holland, formed the Pilgrim Fathers who, in 1620, sailed for Plymouth, Massachusetts. During the next decade or so many outposts of Congregationalism sprang up all over New England, of which Boston was the chief. It is true that a minority of the settlers had been Anglicans, but the very nature of frontier churches, far from all authority, meant that Congregational principles prevailed. The theocracy set up by Congregationalism meant short shrift to any who refused to conform. In 1631 the Massachusetts franchise was limited to Congregationalists, and in 1650 a colonial law required the consent of the government for the admittance of any other form of Christianity. Even those believers who, like themselves, obeyed the principle of the lawfulness of dissent, were punished. Roger Williams, an Anabaptist minister who differed from them only in his insistence on adult baptism and an attitude of tolerance, was banished for declaring that the union of Church and State was unjustifiable. In 1637 Ann Hutchinson, who trusted to Holy Ghost revelations via the Inner Light, was likewise banished after a formal trial on a charge of Antinomianism. Her real crime seems to have been criticism of a Boston minister. But this rigorousness broke down with the second generation, more interested in material fortune-making than church membership. A Halfway Covenant, much opposed by the diehards, was passed in spite of them, admitting to baptism the children of those who were not full members. By the end of the century, owing to the intervention of the English government, the colony was forced to widen its franchise, and Baptist and Episcopal churches were opened in Boston.

Roger Williams, expelled from Boston, founded a Baptist church at Providence, Rhode Island, instituting the separation between Church and State which was his ideal. Rhode Island became a haven for Baptists of various kinds, some Calvinist, some Arminian, some stranger than these, like the Seventh Day Baptists, who observed Saturday instead of Sunday as their holy day, the Six Principle Baptists, who advocated the laying-on of hands in baptism, and some Fifth Monarchy Men. The Baptists slowly established themselves in other parts of America in spite of much opposition – imprisonment and the whip were their lot in Massachusetts – and by the War of Independence were a recognized church.

The Quakers, believed to be anarchists rejecting all civil authority, were most hardly treated. In 1656 Massachusetts decreed that every ship-master landing a Quaker on American soil was to be fined £100, and every Quaker landed was to be severely whipped and imprisoned. In 1657 anyone entertaining a Quaker was to be fined £2 for every hour's entertainment, and male Quakers were to have their ears cropped and female Quakers to be whipped. Three, one a woman, were even hanged in 1659. The Quakers of those days were provocative and offensive but, when reformed by William Penn and settled in Pennsylvania, they became more like the philanthropic, idealistic social workers that they are today, with an influence out of all proportion to their numbers.

Pennsylvania opened its borders to many sectaries. Mennonites from Holland, Dunkards (Baptists) from Germany, Calvinists, Lutherans, German Moravians, Amish, all made their homes there. Elsewhere, as in New York, Episcopalianism existed and Maryland was a refuge for English Roman Catholics. The south was mainly Anglican, though, its population not being religious refugees, they were not earnest worshippers. Dissenting preachers were, however, disapproved of and punished. In the Carolinas there were Episcopalians, Baptists, Dutch Calvinists, French Huguenots, Moravians, Presbyterians and Quakers, and in Georgia Anglicans and Moravians.

In such a conglomeration who can judge today who were heretics and who orthodox? Only members of a church who have the temerity to say that they have the whole truth and that what they believe is orthodoxy and every deviation from it heterodox. The New World turned out to be like the Old – crossing the Atlantic did not change human nature. So individual districts and states began by setting up state religions, to deviate from which was heresy. Those few which practised tolerance did so not by any native virtue peculiar to America, but because tolerance had begun to be recognized as desirable by individuals in many lands and even by a very few societies in the old lands across the sea.

CHAPTER 17

The Eighteenth Century

The increasing awareness of the futility of religious persecution, the growing emphasis on reason and the study of natural science continued the process of toleration that had begun in the seventeenth century. It can be said with some truth that there were no new heresies to be found from 1700 onwards, but merely permutations of old ones. These were, and are, to be found in the plethora of sects which appear increasingly in Christianity as the centuries pass. The Enlightenment, which lasted for most of the eighteenth century, made it respectable for sophisticated scholars and members of all strata of society to reject irrational beliefs. An increasing number of them discarded all religion and cannot be classed as heretics because, as was stated in the first chapter, those who accept no religion at all are no more heretics than those who belong to another.

There were negative and positive reasons for the development of the Age of Enlightenment. Reaction against mysticism and against the unreasonableness of Pietism in Germany was one cause, impatience with the everlasting squabbles of the religious another. More positive were the writings of scientists and philosophers. Descartes, Leibnitz, Spinoza and Hobbes all played their part in stimulating men's minds. The founding of the Royal Society in England in 1662 spurred on scientific research. The mathematical universe of Isaac Newton (1642–1727), while not ruling out God, removed him from immediate juggling with his creation. Voltaire (François Marie Arouet, 1694–1778), 'Enlightenment Man' as Leonardo da Vinci was 'Renaissance Man', blasted the monstrous cruelty of the Church against those who questioned its dogmas. He described the beginnings of religion by naming the first divine as being 'the first rogue who met the first fool' while the Encyclopedist, Denis Diderot (1713–84), foresaw its end together with the death of tyranny as occurring when 'the last king is strangled with the entrails of the last priest'. The Encyclopedists, so called from their contributions to the French Grand Encyclopedia which did much to circulate the new ideas through the country, also included Jean d'Alembert (1717–83), who expected one day the universal enlightenment of the common man.

Other thinkers contributed in other countries. Wolff (1679–1754), a professor of mathematics at Halle, although an orthodox Lutheran, was expelled from Prussia for holding that the truths of religion could be given demonstrative proofs like mathematical problems. He was recalled by Frederick the Great, a Deist who despised all varieties of Christianity equally and who declared for the toleration of all religions. Gotthold Lessing (1729–81) urged toleration, since no religion had a monopoly of truth. He published the *Wolfenbuttel Fragments* in 1774, under the name of Reimarus, a supposed Hamburg schoolmaster, attacking Christianity on historical grounds as a deliberate imposture, while his own *Nathan the Wise* (1779) urged toleration because members of other religions could show as much nobility of character as the Christian, as well as possessing their own validity. Nicolai began in 1765 to publish the *Universal German Library* discrediting religion. Basedow, a pioneer in Germany of modern education, tended to replace Christianity in education with a religion of philanthropy. First in Switzerland, then in France, Jean Jacques Rousseau (1712–78) put forward his plea that man should follow his emotions and return to nature, noble savagery and egalitarianism, conceptions romanticized out of all relation to reality but none the less popular and acceptable. He would have reformed, not destroyed, the Church, believing that religions had helped to serve mankind and that civil government should preserve what doctrines were worthy of belief. David Hume (1711–76), the philosopher, by a scepticism which denied the competence of reason itself, first upheld the Age of Enlightenment, then, when his thought was taken to its logical end, helped to kill it. Another philosopher who eventually killed the rationalistic arguments against theism and undermined rationalism was Immanuel Kant (1724–1804), who concluded that religion was outside the province of reason. His conception of the 'categorical imperative' convinced him by practical reasoning of man's moral nature, freedom and immortality.

Within religion writers were weakening the old certainties. Haller's poem, written in 1729, 'Thoughts Concerning Reason, Superstition and Unbelief', Wettstein's revised text of the Greek Testament of 1751, Ernesti's biblical criticism, and Semler's (1725–91) *The Free Investigation of the Canon* all raised questions. Semler would have excluded the Song of Songs and the Apocalypse. And among religious people, still exposed to intolerance and disqualifications if they did not conform to their local form of worship, the theory of accommodation began to be held, by which a man could assent to one idea of religion in public while holding another in private.

The 'theology' of the Age of Enlightenment may be summarized under four headings:

1. Reason is the only infallible guide to knowledge and wisdom.

2. Since science has shown that the universe is subject to inflexible laws, miracles cannot happen.

3. The simplest and most natural form of society is best; to be a 'noble savage' is better than to suffer the tyranny of priests and rulers.

4. There is no such thing as original sin. Man in society would become perfect if he were left to follow his own interests governed by reason.

Deism, which had already raised its head to some extent in the seventeenth century, was a suitable creed for wide adoption during the Enlightenment. It revived with John Toland's *Christianity Not Mysterious*, published in 1696, a book which made reason the only test of faith, Collins's *Discourse of Freethinking*, which gave the Deists the name of Freethinkers, and Mathew Tyndal's *Christianity as Old as Creation*, which maintained that only those parts of Christianity were true which honoured God and served man. Deism could be either a Christian heresy or a creed with nothing of Christianity in it, for in many respects it was similar to the Modernism of the present century. All Deists would agree that one God exists who created the universe and the natural laws that control it; that he does not capriciously interfere with human affairs by miracles; that religious observances are for the most part at best symbolic acts and at worst mumbo-jumbo; that man can by exercising his will choose good and reject evil, and that his choice in this life will determine his rewards and punishments in the next. Christian Deists would find a place for Jesus in their scheme as a revealer, perhaps a unique one, of God, but discount the miraculous element recorded in his life as so many wonder stories.

Alexander Pope, Lord Bolingbroke and Lord Shaftesbury were effective English Deists and Thomas Paine, Benjamin Franklin and Thomas Jefferson spread the creed in America where French influence was also strong. The movement was effectively answered by Bishop Joseph Butler (1692–1752) who, in his *Analogy of Reason*, argued that if nature is from God, as the Deists held, there is no good reason for doubting that Scripture, morality and revelation also derive from him. Deism lacked constructive ideas. It did not solve the problem of evil, nor had it anything to offer to supply the loss of a loving divine Providence and a God personally concerned with men.

Another radical sect of the eighteenth century were the Universalists, who came into existence about 1750 and were organized into a distinctive communion in Gloucester, Massachusetts, in about 1780. They rejected Trinitarian doctrine, denied the Fall and asserted that all men would be finally saved.

There was also a revival of Arianism at the turn of the seventeenth century (John Milton is said to have turned Arian at the end of his life). Samuel Clarke (1675–1729), vicar of St James's, Westminster, was the most celebrated eighteenth-century Arian, justly considered heterodox for his *Scripture Doctrine of the Trinity*, answered by Waterland's book, *Vindication of Christ's Divinity*, published in 1719. Clarke was not regarded as a Christian by some of his contemporaries. The mantle of the Arians later fell upon the Unitarians, where it rests to this day.

The Christology of the Moravian Brethren was directly opposite that of the Arians, for they identified God and Jesus Christ in an unsophisticated modalism. Spiritually descended from the Hussites, they formed a colony called Herrnhut (the Watch of the Lord) in Saxony under Count Zinzendorf (1700–60) on an estate he provided for them. His ideal was a philadelphian community which should unite Christians of different traditions without taking them from their own communions. The Herrnhut was organized under Zinzendorf as superintendent and a council of twelve elders, in which the Apostolic Succession was traced to the consecration of one of their predecessors by a Waldensian bishop. The brotherhood was closely organized on a co-operative trade basis. It revived the love-feasts and foot-washing ceremonial of the early Church, and from 1731 organized the sending of missionaries to the West Indies, Greenland and Georgia. In the 1730s the Herrnhut became an independent church in spite of Zinzendorf's ideal of a united Christian community, and in 1736 the Count, accused of heresy and schism, was banished from Saxony to Wetterau in western Germany. He eventually resigned from the community, of whose independence he disapproved.

In 1745 the Brethren stated that they had no doctrine of their own but consisted of three 'tropes', Lutheran, Calvinist and Bohemian. In 1747 they adopted the Augsburg Confession, and in 1749 were accepted as a Lutheran, Episcopal church with bishops, priests and deacons, commonly known as Moravians. After a period of charismatic 'enthusiasm' they settled down under Zinzendorf's sober, practical successor, Spangenberg (1704–92), and councils in 1764, 1769 and 1775 settled their polity and doctrine, though they acknowledged no doctrinal statement as of binding authority. The Scriptures were their sole guide. Their central doctrine was the atonement through the blood of Jesus. They believed in the total depravity of man, the love of God towards fallen humanity, the divine and human natures in Christ, justification, sanctification and the Second Coming. Their worship was simple, in a 'hall' not a church, and included purely liturgical services, love-feasts ending in Holy Communion and special liturgies on great feast-days. They always celebrated communion in the evening. They had an influence out of all proportion to their numbers. Their attempt to rise above differences of faith somewhat influenced later revivalist movements in a non-denominational direction.

Emanuel Swedenborg (1688–1772) was a mystical Sabellian. After a distinguished public career he had a series of visions, beginning in London in 1745, and devoted the rest of his life to theosophical speculations. He rejected orthodox Trinitarian doctrine because it prevented the worship of Christ as Almighty and Father. The Council of Nicaea, said Swedenborg, had perverted the true faith, for Father and Son were a single Person revealed in different ways. He gave new meanings to theological words like mediation and atonement, and censured all the major Christian churches of his time, rejecting Catholicism for its veneration of the Pope and concealment of truths in Scripture, Lutheranism for its preaching of justification by faith, and Calvinism for its doctrine of predestination. The Bible, interpreted in a Neoplatonic sense, that every phenomenon in the material world has its counterpart in a spiritual reality, was the source of Swedenborg's doctrine, except that only the Gospels and Revelation are fully inspired in the New Testament, and Job and the Song of Songs lack full authority in the Old.

Swedenborg himself did not found a new church, but after his death his followers, in 1778, issued a Short Confession of Faith which embodied his Trinitarian doctrine, and authorized liturgies for the New Church, the Church of the New Jerusalem or the Swedenborgians, as their communion is variously known. Some English Swedenborgians use a revised form of the Anglican prayer-book, America has a Book of Worship, Baptism and Holy Communion are observed and there is a church hierarchy – ordaining ministers, ministers and ordained leaders in England, and general pastors and pastors in America.

A Moravian, Peter Böhler, was the agent responsible for John Wesley's spiritual breakthrough. Wesley (1703–91), brought up in a pious home, and a member with his brother Charles of 'The Holy Club' or 'Methodists' at Oxford University, as their fellows mockingly named them, obeying rules of fasting and regular communion, was ordained in the Church of England, then went as a missionary to the new American colony of Georgia, from which he returned to London a failed and dispirited man. He met on shipboard a party of Moravians who impressed him. Feeling his heart 'strangely warmed' at a subsequent Moravian mission meeting in London, he began a revival campaign in the Church of England. This alarmed the clergy who, in a rationalistic age, disliked irrational 'enthusiasm'.

Wesley was joined by George Whitefield (1714–70), another Anglican priest, John Wesley becoming the organizer of the movement, Whitefield its most powerful preacher, and Charles Wesley its hymn-writer.

Often denied the churches, the Methodists preached in the open air with enormous effect, for they appealed to the unlettered masses of the early Industrial Revolution with whom the parochial system of the Church of England was quite unable to cope. Wesley effectively followed up preaching by forming Class Meetings for the converted, which gave them a simple rule of life and supplied them with a society which held them together. He was not afraid to use lay preachers, and although he died an Anglican and wanted his reform to exist within the Church of England and not apart from it, by his genius for organization he prepared everything necessary for a separate church. He was heterodox in that he ordained priests himself, seeing no essential difference between the episcopate and presbyterate. In 1795, four years after Wesley's death, Methodism became a denomination on its own (in Ireland the break did not come till 1870), not standing for any distinctive doctrine but temperamentally out of tune with Anglicanism.

Methodism had several offshoots and schisms within itself. In 1784 Wesley appointed Dr Coke, an Anglican priest, Superintendent of Methodist Societies in America, and two preachers as 'Elders'. Dr Coke acted as bishop without the title and was the founder of the Methodist Episcopal Church of America. Whitefield, a Calvinist, broke with Wesley in 1741 over the doctrines of predestination and sinless perfection, accepting the former and rejecting the latter. He was welcomed by Selina, Countess of Huntingdon, a godly woman who had invited high society to her 'spiritual routs' where her preachers tried to convert them. She left the Church of England because the law would not allow her to open a chapel in Clerkenwell, her chaplain left her, she set up a seminary for the instruction of lay preachers at Trevecca in south Wales, dismissed the staff there for holding Arminian views, and with Whitefield founded the Countess of Huntingdon's Connection, which still exists in a congregational form. An offshoot of this was the Welsh Calvinist Methodist Church, created in 1742–3, which became numerically the biggest denomination in the principality.

In 1796 a certain Kilham, wishing laymen to attend the annual conference of Methodists, was expelled, whereupon he formed the Methodist New Connection. By 1800 Methodists were respectably worshipping in chapels, and an enthusiast, Hugh Bourne, wanted to revive the old open-air evangelistic campaigns. He therefore founded the Primitive Methodists, or Ranters, and in 1815 yet another group of dissidents for much the same reason formed the 'Bible Christians' in Devon. Both the Primitive Methodists and Bible Christians admitted women as itinerant preachers.

The further history of the Methodists is that in 1857 the United Methodist Free Churches gave the laity rights which the more conservative members were unwilling to concede. In 1907 three principal Methodist churches in England combined to form the United Methodist Church, and in 1932 all but very small minorities combined to form the Methodist Church. A similar reunion took place in America in 1939, and it would seem only a matter of time before Methodist and Anglican Churches reunite in England. An attempt at reunion in recent years failed only narrowly.

Methodism was particularly suitable to the frontier society of the United States, for, by its emphasis on the obtaining of salvation by the 'heart-experience' of individuals in direct conscious touch with God, it bypassed bishops, priests, sacraments and ritual. Its demands for self-discipline also appealed to a society where discipline in daily life might mean the difference between life and death, and its puritanism gave standards to small communities far from authority other than the morality they imposed on themselves. So it renounced worldliness, supported the Temperance movement and demanded abstinence from tobacco of newly ordained ministers in the United States, while the Moravian influence could be seen in its emphasis on communal life. The Methodist circuit riders in America were the principal early agents of both the establishment and revival of religion, beating the Baptists into second place and the Calvinists, handicapped by their doctrine of predestination, into a poor third.

Methodist doctrine may be judged heretical by its opponents in several details. It is Lutheran in its belief in justification by faith and Arminian in its doctrine of grace. The believer is assured of salvation by experience as well as by faith, and he can achieve the entire sanctification of Christian perfection in this world, not in the sense of being completely sinless but of reaching a development where God's laws are never consciously broken. Christ died for all men. The sacraments are spiritualized, for baptism, while neither affecting nor effecting salvation, is a sign of the new birth, and in the Eucharist Christ is received really but spiritually. The Bible, without the Apocrypha is the sole rule for faith and living, and other standards of doctrine, including the historic creeds, are more or less accepted. But Wesley omitted the Athanasian Creed and the Psalms (as unsuitable for Christians) from his prayer-book, based on the Anglican, and his Twenty-Five Articles, a revision of the Anglican Thirty-Nine, are at once less Calvinist and less Catholic. Purgatory and conversion after death are rejected, and in America Methodists omit 'He descended into Hell' from the Apostles' Creed, and neither use nor reject the Nicene Creed in the communion service, whereas British Methodists repeat it. Great importance is attached by Methodists in all countries to church organization and discipline both on the local and national levels.

Belief in Christ's Second Coming is an orthodox Christian tenet, but the Adventist movement is heterodox in its insistence that prophecy proves that mankind is now living in the last days. Down the Christian ages there have been fanatics who have even given dates for an event which Christ plainly said was not within man's province to know. An Adventist sect which appeared in the 1760s was the United Society of Believers in Christ's Second Coming, or Shakers, as they were popularly known. They gathered at Manchester under the leadership of Ann Lee, who was convinced that the greatest evil in the world was sex. Much influenced by the charismatic side of the French Camisards, their fondness for speaking in tongues and shakings led to persecution, which in 1774 drove nine Shakers to America. They were Millennialists, regarding themselves as children of the millennium in advance, as it were, who were both saved and resurrected through their confession of, repentance for and abandonment of sin, especially sex. The Shakers were by no means anarchists or introversionist. Their worship was well organized, with a pattern of routine dancing of men and women in different groups following an initial 'shaking in the Spirit'. Their belief included contact with the spirit world and they may be said to have been the first Christian Spiritualists. Their well-organized colonies were evangelistic, philanthropic and inventive, and they were among the few whites who attempted to befriend and help the Indians. Their leaders were always women, and one of them later put forward the novel doctrine that Christ at the Second Coming would return as a woman.

Meanwhile, even in Catholic Europe changes were slowly taking place. Italy expelled the Jesuits in 1767 and abolished the Inquisition in 1782. An attempt was made to curb its power in Spain in 1713, but it failed in the face of clerical resentment, and sixty more years were to pass before it was robbed of most of its power. In both Spain and Portugal the Jesuits had been suppressed and expelled. In 1784 the Inquisition in Spain was forbidden to proceed against grandees and officials without the approval of the king, though in all other respects the country remained totally Catholic without a flicker of tolerance of any Protestant sect within its borders.

The eighteenth century was eventful for France. There was a flurry of Camisard trouble in 1702 until their suppression in 1704, and Jansenism proved troublesome until the middle of the century. French Gallicanism led to Febronianism which arose from a book written in 1763 by Febronius (van Hontheim, Coadjutor Bishop of Trèves) entitled *De Statu Ecclesiae et Legitima Potestate Romani Pontificis* (The Condition of the Church and the Lawful Power of the Pope of Rome). The Bishop maintained that a general council was superior to the Pope and could depose him, that it might be summoned in spite of him, that its authority came directly from Christ, that in a general council bishops are co-judges with the Pope and that appeals from a pope to a general council are legitimate. The true holders of power were the bishops. The Church was not a state and was not monarchical. Febronius also asserted the rights of the national churches to summon national councils to carry out reforms, and although he was forced to retract in 1778, his heresy survived for a while. The Emperor Joseph II adopted Febronianism in the Articles of Ems in 1786, as did Da Ricci, a Tuscan bishop, but both these attempts eventually failed and Febronianism died.

Gallicanism itself died at the end of the century. After the French Revolution had temporarily established the worship of the Goddess of Reason in Notre Dame, Napoleon by a concordat with the Pope in 1801 arranged for the First Consul to nominate the French Bishops and for the Pope to institute them. The Organic Articles of 1802 agreed that no papal decrees should be published without the consent of the French government, and this agreement killed Gallicanism by removing its cause. The process was completed in 1905 when, after considerable anti-clericalism, the Church in France separated from the State.

Anti-clericalism, fanned by the Ultramontanism always emanating from Rome (that is, the policy of that party in the Catholic Church favouring the increase of the power and authority of the Pope over national Catholic churches) was not confined to France. It was to be found in many European countries throughout the eighteenth, nineteenth and twentieth centuries, and to an enthusiastic Ultramontanist always had the seeds of heresy in it, for it belittled the power of the Holy Father and, if carried to its logical conclusion, could even question his infallibility. It was particularly to be found in the Catholic districts of the Netherlands, especially as they had moved in the eighteenth century to a position of toleration. In 1731–2, for example, religious disputes were settled, at least in the public and legal sense, sectaries were tolerated and the Jesuits expelled.

Germany also moved erratically towards a policy of religious live and let live. In 1781 a Tolerance Act in Austria granted liberty of worship to Protestant and Orthodox Christians, though it was withdrawn in 1790. In 1788 a Prussian edict restrained liberty of preaching. These measures, although seemingly one-step-forward, one-step-back, gradually prepared the states for the greater toleration of the nineteenth century. The beginning of the eighteenth century in

Switzerland saw further armed struggles between Catholic and Protestant, but towards its close the contests became more political – the liberals and progressives against the conservatism of the Catholics.

England established the Protestant succession to the throne in 1702, accompanying it with further actions against Roman Catholics. But again by the end of the century there was an advance towards greater toleration, and in 1791, 1792 and 1793 there were Acts of Parliament removing some disabilities from Catholics in England, Ireland and Scotland successively. Such intolerance as was shown was directed against Protestant dissenters, as in riots in Birmingham in 1791. But by 1800 the Age of Enlightenment had done its work in Europe, for all its naïveté and limitations. It had dissipated much superstition, done away with legal restraints which had been inspired largely through fear in past centuries, weakened political tyrannies, made the ideal of religious freedom a common-place instead of a rarity among civilized men, enhanced humanitarianism, destroyed many archaisms which had outlived their usefulness, developed individualism and, above all, established a new climate and new habits of thought. In 1600 men burned each other for disagreeing with them; in 1800 most cultured men would at least outwardly have agreed with Voltaire's famous dictum, 'I do not agree with a word you say, but I will defend to the death your right to say it'.

America also advanced towards toleration. In 1785 a law recognizing the principle of religious liberty was passed, and after the winning of independence the Constitution declared that 'Congress should make no law for an establishment of religion nor prevent its free exercise'. This did not mean that every individual state followed suit – it was not, for example, until 1833 that Massachusetts gave the same legal standing to all denominations. The significance of independence was that it destroyed heresy in the United States, for where no system of belief has precedence over any other, there is no legal or recognized orthodoxy and therefore no heterodoxy.

Independence also broke the line of historical succession, destroyed the pattern of Christianity enshrined in a church national or supra-national (except, possibly, for Roman Catholics, and even their loyalty to their faith was different from that of European Catholics), and removed the barriers between clerics and laymen, who enjoyed the same privileges and suffered the same disabilities of American citizenship in absolute equality before the law. The democracy of America produced denominationalism with such strongly divergent tendencies that splinter group after splinter group cracked off from their parent communions, resulting in a multiplicity of sects, some numerous, many insignificant (it has been estimated that the Protestant sects in America alone number over six hundred).

Equally unprivileged at law, every denomination in the United States had to depend on self-help and was responsible for its own organizing and financing. American religious history may be summed up by saying that until independence the New World imported religions from the Old; after independence it created its own versions of these which it exported with the same generosity, energy, enthusiasm and expertise that it brought to its commercial ventures.

CHAPTER 18

The Nineteenth Century

While the modern age began in a sense with the Renaissance, the nineteenth century may be regarded as a bridge between a way of life still simple, agricultural, national and, in some ways, feudal, and the industrial, international, accelerating complexity of the modern age. Religious life, too, became more complex, for the removal of the sanctions of imprisonment, torture and the stake, with the growth of tolerance and variety in thought, led to agnosticism becoming respectable and a proliferation of sects which continues today. For the first time the Christian religion as a whole was thrown on the defensive in the face of scientific discoveries which could not be permanently resisted; and in Europe even those who were nominally orthodox Christians began to lose their overwhelming majority. The nineteenth century was also the age of the greatest expansion in missionary activity since the first. Since Christianity became identified with Europe and most missionaries were of European origin, this was to lead in time to unforeseen results. As native churches mature, weaning themselves from the Christianity of the white imperialists, so they are developing their own thought and expression of worship—and their own forms of heterodoxy.

Even in the Latin countries toleration grew, though slowly, Protestants still remaining rare and understandably shy creatures. In Spain the Inquisition, resurrected in 1814, was abolished in 1820. In an 1868 revolt the rebels proclaimed toleration and Protestant services were held in Barcelona and Madrid. But religious liberty was abolished in 1875 and only a minimum allowed under the new constitution of 1876. Yet in 1894 toleration had sufficiently advanced for the first bishop of the Spanish Reformed Church to receive consecration.

In Switzerland struggles between the Liberals and Catholics continued, and in 1835 monasteries were suppressed in Argau.

However, in 1902 a decree by the federal council for suppressing religious congregations and orders was not recognized by law, and in 1907 Calvin must have turned in his grave when the people of Geneva, his old theocracy, voted for the separation of Church and State.

In Prussia the Lutheran and Calvinist Churches combined to form the Evangelical Church in 1817. Nonconforming conservative Lutherans were treated with great harshness, many who ministered to the Separatists being imprisoned. In 1873 a Prussian law demanded secular university training for the clergy and punished Catholic resisters.

Where Prussia was harsh, England was liberal. In 1828 the Tests and Corporation Acts, handicapping Roman Catholics and Protestant dissenters, were repealed, and in 1829, after considerable struggle, the Catholic Relief Bill was passed. In the same year abuses were removed in the Church of England. In 1843 the Free Church of Scotland (the Wee Frees) was established, and in 1850 Roman Catholic bishops were consecrated in England and English Catholic dioceses established. The movement towards Catholicism within the Anglican Church itself was checked, however, by the Public Worship Regulation Act.

A quite different kind of toleration was granted in Bulgaria in 1856 when the Turks granted civil and religious liberty to their Christian subjects.

For the rest, the religious and heretical history of the nineteenth century is the history of modes of thought and of sects. Deism moved via Jeremy Bentham (1748–1832) and John Stuart Mill (1806–73) and the Utilitarians (believing in the greatest good of the greatest number and that education and progress would provide everything necessary for the welfare of mankind – a kind of secular millennialism) to Modernism, which had a number of tributaries feeding its main stream and was to be found in different forms. Modernism minimizes the importance of tradition and authority, refusing to be bound by the words of Scripture, the opinions expressed therein, the tradition of the early Church or the decisions of popes or councils. It emphasizes the need for restating traditional teaching in the interests of contemporary requirements and in the light of the latest findings of the best religious and scientific opinions. The great dogmatic definitions, if needed at all, must be made afresh for each generation.

The Germans did much for the cause of Modernism. Schleiermacher (1768–1834) inclined to Sabellianism, rejected the Virgin Birth and Ascension and advocated a rationalism which should 'create a new dogmatic rather than revivify the old'. F. C. Bauer (1792–1860), founder of the Tübingen school of radical theological thought and criticism, rejected all New Testament writings except

Romans, Corinthians, Galatians and Revelation. The rest were second-century forgeries, fruits of a struggle between Pauline and Petrine factions in the Church. David Strauss (1808–74), in his *Life of Jesus* (1835), proposed the myth doctrine–that enough time elapsed between the events of Jesus's life and the record of them in the Gospels for the free development of legend. Miracles need not be accepted as historical facts, the Resurrection was a series of visions and St John's Gospel a second-century document. A. Ritschl (1822–89) tried to reconcile the conclusions of biblical criticism with faith in the Gospel. Religion was not to be tested by its intrinsic truth but by its effect on the believer. If Christ has the value of God, and his death has the value of an atonement for the believer, that is enough. Harnack (1851–1930) in *What is Christianity* rejected the divinity of Christ. Jesus revealed not himself but certain truths: the kingdom of God and its cause, the rule of God in the soul; the Fatherhood of God and the infinite value of the human soul; and the higher righteousness and the commandment of love. 'The Gospel as Jesus proclaimed it has to do with the Father only and not with the Son.' German modernistic theological thought found its culmination, perhaps, in *The Quest for the Historical Jesus* by the saintly Alsatian Albert Schweitzer (1875–1965), who saw Jesus as a man who expected the manifestation of the kingdom before the return of his disciples from their preaching and died a crushed and disappointed victim of the inscrutable divine will.

In France Ernest Renan's *Life of Jesus*, sentimental-Modernist, caused a temporary stir in 1863, but the real struggle there reflected one within the Roman Curia itself. One party wished the Catholic Church to be the pioneer of political and intellectual freedom; the other, the conservatives, wanted it to secure its own position and then utterly resist change. In 1864 Rome issued a 'Syllabus of Errors' which included condemnation of toleration and 'progress, liberalism and civilization as lately introduced'. In 1870 the dogma of Papal Infallibility became *de fide*, causing much heart-burning among many Catholics, and in 1878 the Catholic Institute of Paris was founded. Among its professors was the independent thinker Louis Duchesne, whose pupil was Alfred Loisy. By the time Duchesne and Loisy appeared on the scene, the publication by Charles Darwin (1809–82) of *The Origin of Species* (1859) and *The Descent of Man* (1871) had caused the battle between science and religion to be joined in real earnest, the churches being thrown back on the defensive in meeting a dogmatic authoritarianism as vigorous as and better evidenced than their own, for perhaps the first time in their history. Duchesne and Loisy believed that scientific study should be used in their own disciplines and that truth should be followed whether this agreed with held opinions or not. Duchesne's *Liber Pontificalis* was put on the Index because he rejected on critical grounds the tradition that the Church of Chartres had been founded by Christ's disciples. Loisy, seeing contradictions between scientific teaching and Genesis, asked how a church with an infallible head could admit mistakes. The two scholars solved the difficulty by postulating that what was not strictly true in history might yet be suitable material for faith and edification, a view which aroused much opposition. Duchesne was suspended for a year, and Leo XIII (1878–1903) appointed a commission to define what was permissible in biblical criticism. Its reply in brief was 'Nothing'.

In 1892 another scholar, d'Hulst, in an article on 'Inspiration', allowed that the Bible might contain scientific and historical errors. This drew a papal encyclical which condemned 'disquieting tendencies' in biblical interpretation which could 'destroy the inspired and supernatural character of the Bible' and stated that 'Divine inspiration by its very nature excludes all error'. Pius X, on the papal throne in 1903, was a reactionary who refused to admit a tittle of Roman tradition untrue or imperfect. In his book *The Gospel and the Church* (1905), Loisy defended the Catholic position against Harnack. He compared Christianity to a living, growing seed clothing itself with a body suitable to its environment, adopting an organized form and creed to enable men to understand and appropriate its essence–'To blame the Catholic Church for having developed its constitution is to blame it for having lived'. But Loisy undermined traditional beliefs such as the Virgin Birth and the authenticity of John's Gospel, and his opponents complained that his general thesis could justify any change, a perversion as well as a true development. Pius X, not prepared to submit the New Testament or Catholic Church history to candid examination, excommunicated Loisy and banned his books. George Tyrrell, a Jesuit, was also excommunicated in 1906 for defending Modernist views in *The Much Abused Church*. The Pope went over to the attack against Modernism in 1907 in an encyclical *Pascendi Gregis*, in which he also assaulted the heresy of 'Americanism'.

'Americanism' was a form of Modernism which had arisen from the American spirit upholding democracy, human progress, education uncontrolled by the Church, unfettered human reason, and the natural virtues of honour, courage and trustfulness. The heresy had been promulgated by Father Hecker (1819–83), a Humanist converted to Catholicism who made it his life's work to win Protestants. A *Life of Father Hecker* was popular among French Catholics with Modernist views, running into six editions by 1898. It caused much controversy and was attacked by the Jesuits in 1899, and in a papal encyclical of Leo XIII before Pius X had his say.

The Catholic Church, besides maintaining its right of intolerance to differences within its own ranks, rendered itself more heretical to Protestants by the declaration of two new dogmas. The first, issued by Pius IX on his sole authority in 1854, was the Definition of the Immaculate Conception of the Virgin Mary, welcomed by the Archbishop of Trani because it made her 'the complement of the Trinity and above all our co-redemptress'. No Protestant could accept such blatant Mariolatry. In 1870 the Decree of Papal Infallibility declared that when the Roman pontiff in the discharge of his office as supreme pastor of all Christians defines *ex cathedra* doctrine in faith and morals, he speaks infallibly. His decrees cannot be changed and do not need the consent of the Church. Such a dogma makes reunion impossible unless all other churches surrender unconditionally to Rome.

Anglicanism also had its Modernists in the Noetics, or Neologians, with headquarters at Oriel College, Oxford. Led by Thomas Arnold, Whately and Hampden, they were dissatisfied with current theology and opposed to accepted views. Arnold's pupil, A. P. Stanley (1815–81), with Benjamin Jowett, Master of Balliol College, kept up Neologianism and by 1850 were known as Broad Churchmen. King's College, London, also produced a Modernist in F. D. Maurice, professor of theology, who was expelled in 1853 for asserting that 'eternity had nothing to do with time or duration' and that Eternal Death was the refusal to participate in Eternal Life, which was sharing in the Eternal Life of God. Maurice, who combined a liberal theology with faithfulness to the creeds and sacraments, claimed that his opinions were to be found in every creed of the Catholic Church.

In 1860 a collection of *Essays and Reviews* by Broad Churchmen caused a storm of controversy and hostility. Where Scripture disagreed with science, it argued, the former must be rejected. Jowett declared that the Bible should be critically interpreted like any other book, Powell that miracles were a main difficulty of Christianity. Two of the essayists were prosecuted in the ecclesiastical Court of Arches, one for denying the inspiration of Holy Scripture, the other the eternity of future punishment, and were eventually acquitted. Wildly indignant at this, 11,000 clergy and 137,000 laymen presented the Archbishop of Canterbury with a petition upholding both doctrines.

At about the same time John William Colenso (1814–83), Bishop of Natal, published the first three volumes of a critical work on the Pentateuch, denying its Mosaic authorship, saying that Joshua was mythical, that there were two incompatible accounts of the Creation and Flood and that much of it was unhistorical and uninspired. Colenso also suggested that God's punishments were not eternal, leading at last to universal salvation. Forty-one bishops meeting at Lambeth asked him to resign his see, and on his refusal he was tried for heresy by Bishop Grey of South Africa, condemned, excommunicated, deprived, but acquitted on appeal to the Privy Council. The incident led to the formation of an autonomous South African Church in communion with Canterbury, in which Colenso continued to minister until his death. The schism was not completely healed till the mid-twentieth century.

Queen Victoria favoured Broad Churchmen against both Ritualists and Evangelicals. Arthur Stanley, Dean of Westminster in 1864, tried to reconcile people of all opinions, even admitting a known Socinian to Holy Communion. In the same year an Act of Parliament decreed that the clergy were not bound by every word of the Thirty-Nine Articles but should assent to their general tone and meaning. In 1889 *Lux Mundi*, another collection of essays, spoke for those who held the traditional body of faith and believed in a liberal approach to it. Science and faith were compatible. Accretions that had overlaid the original deposit, such as belief in verbal inspiration, might have to be given up. Bishop Gore's essay in the collection asserted that the Bible recorded a progressive revelation of God which was not necessarily accurate in every detail. In 1898 the Churchmen's Union affirmed that a continuous, progressive revelation was given by the Holy Spirit and that the Church of England had a right and duty to restate its doctrines from time to time in accordance with this revelation.

In Scotland, in 1876, Robertson Smith, professor in the Free Church College at Aberdeen, wrote two articles for the *Encyclopaedia Britannica* on the subjects 'Angel' and 'Bible'. These led to his trial for heresy by the General Assembly which, after three years, acquitted him in 1881 but dismissed him, illegally, from his post. Instead of appealing, Smith went to Cambridge as professor of Arabic in 1894.

In England and Scotland Modernists claim liberty of restatement of the orthodox faith without repudiating it. French and German Modernists tend to throw out the baby of faith with the bath-water of orthodoxy.

A movement of an almost opposite kind to Modernism was the Holiness movement, which began with Wesley's preaching of holiness of heart and an entirely sanctified life that men could attain through their experience of salvation. This sanctification was a 'second blessing' after the first of conversion, and became a somewhat heterodox doctrine in the evangelistic preaching of many famous, mainly American, missioners who carried on revival campaigns in most English-speaking countries. Charles G. Finney and Asa Mahon in the 1830s, Dwight L. Moody and Ira Sankey, his hymn-writer, and Pearsall Smith all made an impact, resulting in annual international Holiness conventions such as those at Keswick in Cumberland, and the creation of many tiny independent Holiness missions. These sometimes had minimal creeds and dissociated themselves from faith-healing, Adventists and charismatic movements and, while not setting up independent churches, aimed to bring people together for prayer, conversion and sanctification. Sometimes splinter churches were set up in which 'Holiness' mingled with one or all of these elements. The movement was the first in Christianity to give women power and influence on a large scale.

Both the nineteenth and twentieth centuries have also been prolific in sects and an account of the most important of these must now be given, in chronological order of their foundation. Many dozens of sects have to be omitted for reasons of space; those described below are typical in that they contain most of the important heterodox dogmas and doctrines which are to be found variously in the others.

Adventism has appeared already in these pages. J. G. Bengel (1687–1752) prophesied Christ's return for 1836, and William Miller (1782–1849), a New England Baptist farmer, in about 1818 named dates between March 1843 and October 1844, calculated from Daniel and Revelation. After the return would come the first resurrection of believers and the millennium, followed by the general resurrection and judgement. When the dates passed, Miller admitted his mistake, but nevertheless he was excommunicated by the Baptists. Some of his followers, however, tried to rationalize the failure by mystical interpretations. The Adventists set up their own church, combining Congregational, Baptist and extreme Puritan elements. The Millerites divided into several groups, of which the Seventh Day Adventists are probably the best known. Established in 1860 under the leadership of James and Ellen White, they are orthodox in their Trinitarianism and Christology but hold many unusual beliefs, including the keeping of Saturday as their holy day, dietic taboos based on Old Testament food laws, conditional immortality and a somewhat materialistic eternal existence for the saved on a renewed earth. Catholics and Protestants are identified with figures in the apocryphal books as enemies of God.

The Rappites took their name from George Rapp, a late eighteenth-century 'prophet', converted from Lutheranism to a more pious way of life. They were concerned with inward communication with God, inward baptism and the inner guidance of the Holy Spirit, expecting an almost immediate Second Coming and end of the world. While not opposed to civil government, they rejected military service. In 1804 they settled in the United States as the Harmony Society, standing for a communitarian ordered way of life of prodigious hard work with minimal rules and a tendency to celibacy, in spite of which marriage increased their numbers. They became 'the wonder of the West', their order, security, good living, civilization and hard work benefiting American frontier life out of all proportion to their numbers.

For the Rappites God and holiness were to be found in the community. By 1824 celibacy had become almost a law, the Rappites regarding themselves as a bride awaiting the Bridegroom, Christ, whose advent was rapidly approaching. False Christs caused them to become increasingly withdrawn and introvert, and they dwindled out of existence, their property being divided among their few descendants in the early twentieth century.

The Campbellites, Disciples of Christ, Churches of Christ or Christian Church, were founded by Alexander Campbell (1788–1866) and his father, the Reverend Thomas Campbell, who were originally Irish Presbyterians. In 1807 they emigrated to America where, in 1811, they founded their first independent congregation, associated with the Baptists. They broke away in 1833, although adhering to Baptist principles, joining the Stoneites, followers of Barton W. Stone, an evangelistic preacher who sought freedom from all denominations. The Campbellites became a denomination against the will of their founders who had a strong belief in the organic unity of the Church and had from the beginning strong ecumenical ideals. They reject all creeds, making a distinction between faith and opinion and thus admitting the holding of widely divergent views. The Bible is their authority for faith and practice. They believe in adult believers' baptism by immersion and weekly open communion. Their membership is confined to baptized believers, and their churches, organized on the Congregationalist principle, are staffed by a hierarchy of ministers, elders and deacons. Their social ethic is rigidly Puritan, and the conversion of sinners their overriding aim.

The Plymouth Brethren began in the late 1820s in Dublin, taking their name from outsiders who were the object of the Plymouth branch's evangelism in 1830. Their ideal was of a simple, informal brotherhood united in purity of worship and a common Christian life without doctrinal tests, organized membership, priests and ritual –the very antithesis of the Catholic and Anglican Churches. The Bible interpreted literally is their sole rule of faith. Baptism is normally not practised, or is restricted to adults after confession of faith, and there is a 'breaking of bread' service. The normal form of worship is like that of the Friends, silent communal meditation unless and until a member is moved by the Spirit to read the Bible, speak, pray, or lead an unaccompanied hymn.

John Nelson Darby, a former Anglican cleric, wished to bring together believers of all denominations to await Christ's return, but succeeded only in leading a schism of 'Exclusive Brethren' as opposed to 'Open'. These separated in 1840 and became known in

Europe as Darbisten. Darby believed in 'dispensationalism', the theory that God's promises were made to the Jews, not the Church, and that the earth would be offered to them after the saints had been caught up to be with Christ in heaven. Christ saves men objectively, but only in the Brethren is the Spirit free to act and only there can the believer be aware of salvation.

The Exclusives now have no association with unbelievers or other Christians, an 'Exclusive' husband even refusing to eat at the same table as a non-Exclusive wife. The 'Open' Brethren welcome any convinced Christian to 'break bread' in fellowship, and non-members are admitted to some services, but deepening of the community's spiritual life is more important than evangelization. The lack of organization and authority sometimes leads to difficulties in communication between meetings in different localities under different leaders.

Joseph Smith (1805–44), who came from a poor home and was burdened by a pathological constitution, was visited in New York State in 1823 by the Angel Moroni who gave him golden plates on which were written the Book of Mormon. He also received a pair of spectacles of precious stones set in silver, that he knew to be Urim and Thummim, by which to decipher the plates, written in 'Reformed Egyptian'. After three years' work by Smith on the plates, Moroni removed them. The Book of Mormon revealed that America was originally inhabited by Jaredites, divided between Lamanites, from which the Red Indians (ten tribes of Israel) are descended, and Nephites to whom Christ revealed himself after his resurrection; for America had been the scene of Christ's past activity on earth as much as Palestine and would be again. There the true church would arise against the apostate church of Europe. The Nephites were exterminated, and their holy scriptures, recorded by Mormon and his son Moroni, buried until their revelation to Smith.

In 1829 Smith and a colleague were ordained priests by John the Baptist, whom they saw descend from heaven, baptizing each other at his command, and in 1830 the Mormon Church, or Church of Jesus Christ of Latter-day Saints, was founded. Later, Peter, James and John appeared and ordained Smith priest after the order of Melchizedek. In 1831 the Mormons, numbering about two thousand, were driven west by local hostility from their headquarters, then in Ohio, and in 1840 founded the town of Nauvoo, Illinois, where their numbers doubled in four years. Polygamy was introduced in 1843, first as a privilege for the leaders, but Joseph and his brother Hiram were arrested in 1844 and shot by a lynching mob.

Brigham Young (1801–77) became the Moses of the movement, and in 1846 he led fifteen thousand Mormons through an uncharted wilderness to the Great Salt Lake in Utah, where a colony was founded on a theocratic basis. Polygamy was officially introduced in 1852, three wives being the necessary qualification for the higher ecclesiastical offices. A Mormon belief is that children provide bodies for waiting spirits to occupy, and polygamy was well suited to a community small in comparison with a vast continent urgently needing people. Young was a despot ruling by 'blood atonement' (execution), but his community grew in numbers and wealth owing as much to its unflagging industry and self-discipline as to his rigorous rule.

In 1869 the Pacific Railway opened Utah to non-Mormons and the state was added to the United States in 1896, polygamy and 'blood atonement' being abolished. An actively evangelistic creed, Mormonism spread to Europe, missionaries being particularly active after the Second World War, where they tried to fill the void in Germany left by the disappearance of the Nazi creed.

Young, who was almost polytheistic, taught that God the Father had a body of flesh and bones as tangible as a man's, and had, in fact, been a man who had advanced himself to become God. It is the task of all men to progress in the same way. Jesus is a Saviour who will found a millennial Zion in America. Full salvation, to be found only in the Mormon Church, includes the belief that Jesus is the saviour of the world and Joseph Smith a true prophet of God; conversion, which is the observance of God's commandments and the Mormon ordinances; and baptism, which can only be administered by a Mormon priest, who confers the Holy Spirit by the laying-on of hands. Proxy baptisms and marriages are carried out for ancestors to enrol them among the saved, something like fifty million such ceremonies having now taken place. Only proven Mormons can take part in the Salt Lake City Temple ceremonies, which are mystery rituals something like Masonic rites. All young men are expected to serve as missionaries for one or two years, and, since tithes are exacted from all Mormons, worldly goods are valued.

There are four doctrinal authorities: the Bible, 'so far as it is correctly translated'; the Book of Mormon; the Book of Doctrine and Covenants (i.e. church order); and The Pearl of Great Price (a collection of oracles and imitations of Biblical texts). At the head of the Mormon hierarchy is the First President, assisted by two other presidents; then a supreme council of twelve apostles; next, a group of 'patriarchs' or 'evangelists', followed by 'high priests'; after them a group called the Seventy, though numbering many times more. These are all entitled to preach, ordain and be called 'elder', and are all Melchizedekian priests. The lower order, of Aaronic priests, is divided into bishops, priests, deacons and teachers. Nearly every Mormon male is a priest.

Mormons work like Puritans but enjoy all worldly pleasures and make use of every modern facility to ease their lives and spread their message. They number over two million, mostly in the United States.

Edward Irving, an impressively earnest and eloquent Presbyterian preacher, gained a great reputation at the Caledonian Church, Hatton Garden, in the early nineteenth century. Unfortunately for him he became associated with a school of thought inspired by a group of ministers and laymen from various denominations who met at conferences at Albury Park, Surrey, and concluded that the Second Coming was imminent and that only a special outpouring of the Holy Spirit could avert the dreadful punishments that would accompany it. Irving preached both Advent and Millennium and also welcomed an outpouring in his congregation of speaking in tongues, which made his church appear a bedlam to his many critics. He longed to speak in tongues himself but was never granted the gift; and when he was condemned by the Presbyterian Church for Christological heresy and excommunicated, he was swept along by his followers into founding with them the Catholic Apostolic Church. He died aged forty-two in 1834, a pathetic, even tragic, figure.

Before his death the 'prophets' in his congregation chose twelve 'apostles' for their prophetic utterances, ordaining the non-glossolalic Irving an 'angel' or bishop. The new church was organized with a hierarchy of apostles, prophets, angels (bishops), elders (pastors) and deacons (evangelists), all laymen. The apostles were to preach to the Pope, kings, archbishops and all church rulers that the kingdom of God was near, and that the Second Coming would happen in their lifetime. They were each assigned a different geographical area from which they were to recruit 12,000 converts, making 144,000 in all, when the end would come. The Church, though separately organized with an elaborate ceremonial and liturgy culled from Roman, Orthodox and Anglican sources, was non-sectarian, ecumenical, above parties and divisions and open to all baptized Christians, and was even joined by an Augsburg Roman Catholic priest who was not excommunicated for ten years when he was anathematized with five other priests and four hundred laymen. The Second Coming was successively dated 1835, 1838, 1842, 1855, 1866 and 1877, but in spite of serious schisms, continually disappointed hopes and the death of the last 'apostle' in 1901, since when there have been no propaganda, ordinations or confirmations, there were still some thousands of adherents throughout the western world in 1930, and a tiny minority survives in 1976.

The Church's doctrine was in the main orthodox, and after the dashing of its advent hopes, there is no reason for it to maintain a separate existence. In 1882 Geyer, a German prophet, excommunicated for secretly appointing an 'apostle' to replace one who had died, formed a neo-Apostolic Congregation, the difference being that, unlike the parent body, new apostles were allowed to be appointed to replace those who died. The new church spread rapidly in Germany, North and South America, Java and Australia. In addition to the orthodox sacraments, it included the old heretical vicarious baptism for the dead.

John Humphrey Noyes, a Congregationalist minister, conceived the idea that men could become perfect by attaining total security against sin. He founded a community at Oneida, New York State, in the late 1840s. Seeing the evils of society as selfishness engendered by devotion to property, monogamy and possessiveness of mothers over their children, Noyes advocated a communion of property and sex. He did not uphold promiscuity, but an eugenic policy of selected mating for the scientific propagation of the race, which in fact demanded considerable control. Sexual communism was practised only among the totally sanctified, the relationships being organized and disciplined. Their theological basis was that a woman was the bride of Christ and therefore could be bride of all the saints.

The community members believed that the Second Coming had happened in AD 70; that only those descended from the early saints were perfect; that they were a continuation of the primitive church; that personal sanctification was a prerequisite for social reconstruction; that saintliness meant bodily perfection, attained by faith-healing. They practised self-criticism and mutual criticism, like modern Buchmanites.

Under Noyes's skilful, authoritative leadership the community grew in numbers and stability, but in 1881 hostility from without and tensions within caused the Oneidans to abandon community of both sex and goods and they dissolved. Their industries continued as joint-stock companies.

Walter Scott, of the American branch of the Campbellites, converted Dr John Thomas, an English emigrant to America, in about 1836. Thomas gave up medicine for theology, broke with the Campbellites and founded the Christadelphians or Brothers of Christ in 1848. He claimed that his church was a reproduction of the primitive church, its founder being Christ himself. He called it Christadelphian to distinguish it from Christians whom he regarded as anti-Christian.

Thomas drew from the Bible, in which he regarded Old and New Testaments as equally authoritative and inerrant, a materialistic doctrine. God had a personal form and dwelt in some sanctified suburb of the universe. Man was created for a physical immortality on this earth which was lost at the Fall but could be recovered by faith in Christ. But sinners (with pagans, imbeciles and infants) return to dust at death as if they had never existed. Yet when Christ returned in the flesh at the Second Coming, in 1868 or (allowing for forty-two years for the subjugation of the nations) in 1910, there would be a resurrection and judgement. Christ would physically defeat his enemies at the Battle of Armageddon, setting up the kingdom of Israel in Palestine, with its capital in Jerusalem, from which the Christadelphians would rule under him. Sinners would rebel and be blotted out and the final scene would be a physical earth blissfully inhabited by immortal bodies.

Thomas rejected the incarnation and doctrine of the Trinity, though he was not Unitarian. Rebaptized himself, he required his followers to follow his example when they fully understood and accepted the Christadelphian faith. Being heirs to the Bible promises made originally to the Jews, they must become Jews themselves. This article of faith led them to help Jews. They had no professional clergy and their informal, Congregationalist type of organization resulted in many schisms. Later the Christadelphians became more devotional and more concerned about such problems as famine relief and refugees.

Thomas preached widely in Britain, Canada and the United States, demanding thorough understanding and a high ethical standard from his converts.

Thomas Lake Harris, a celibate, whose spiritual wanderings took him from the Universalist ministry to the Swedenborgian via a spiritualistic sect, founded the theo-socialist Brotherhood of the New Life at Fountain Grove, California. The sect advocated social reforms emphasizing the equality of men and their value to each other. It was spiritualistic and allowed marriage only to those who had not attained an adequate spiritual state (God was the believer's only spouse), so that in seventeen years five children only were born among Harris's followers. The Brotherhood flourished from 1860 to the 1890s until hostility forced their leader to leave California.

A curious episode took place in Italy in the 1860s when Davide Lazzaretti of Tuscany foresaw the descent of a great reformer from the mountains who would lead the Militia of the Holy Ghost to reform the government and laws and liberate the people. He organized his followers in communistic colonies. The existing dispensation, the kingdom of Grace, would be followed by the world's last age, the kingdom of Justice. When Pius IX died in 1878, Lazzaretti proclaimed himself Messiah, about to descend from Monte Amiate to set up the republic of God. He was, however, forestalled and killed by the military and his chief followers arrested, whereupon the movement evaporated.

Led by a German professor of church history, Ignaz von Döllinger (1799–1890), a group of Roman Catholic priests and theologians opposed the proclamation of Papal Infallibility on 18 July 1870. Excommunicated, they formed themselves into the old Catholic Church, claiming to be the legitimate, continuation of the Catholic Church. Being left without bishops and therefore excluded from the Apostolic Succession, they enlisted the help of the Old Catholic Church of Holland, through them consecrating their first elected bishop, Professor J. H. Reinkens (1821–96).

In 1879, the Old Catholics of Holland, Switzerland and Austria united, declaring adherence to the Catholic creeds and ecumenical council decrees. They rejected the Tridentine resolutions and all papal decrees following them. The sacrifice of the mass, conducted in the vernacular, was limited to a representation of the sacrifice of Christ, not a repetition of it. Belief in the Real Presence was maintained without the dogma of Transubstantiation. Scripture was the primary authority for faith, tradition accepted by the whole individual Church supplementing it. Clerical celibacy was abandoned. In 1931 intercommunion was established with the Church of England, complete dogmatic agreement not being required.

In 1870 a Pennsylvanian, Charles Taze Russell (1852–1916), fixed 1874 as the date of Christ's invisible return to earth. Rejected unanimously by the ministers of Pittsburgh and Alleghany in 1877, Russell became unflinchingly hostile to all existing churches. From 1878 onwards he issued a series of magazines and books, hawked zealously by his followers, and in 1881 the Zion's Watch Tower Tract Society (later the Watch Tower Bible and Tract Society), known as Jehovah's witnesses (with a small 'w') since 1931, was formed. The movement spread in 1900 to England, in 1903 to Germany and in 1904 to Australia. Russell's prophecy of 1914 as the date of the Advent set the movement back by its apparent failure, but was explained as the beginning of the heavenly kingdom of God when Christ invisibly took some of the Anointed Class of 144,000 destined to be saved. Some of them remain on earth. Russell placed himself second in a group of teachers who had taught Watch Tower truths, consisting of Paul, John, Arius, Waldo, Wyclif and Luther. He took some of his ideas from Great Pyramidism, a belief to be found in some sects maintaining that the measurements of the Great Pyramid contain the key to events until the end of the world. Russell died in 1916 and was succeeded by 'Judge' Joseph Franklyn Rutherford (1869–1942). He rejected Russell's Pyramidism and developed Watch Tower doctrine to its present form, inventing the battle-cry, 'Millions now living will never die'. His death shocked witnesses confidently expecting that he and they would live to see the millennial kingdom.

This sect proclaimed that 'Jehovah God' created heaven and earth and that Lucifer, called Satan, who rebelled against him, has increasingly controlled the world through its economic, political and religious organizations. The witnesses are God's sole representatives on earth. Christ is Jehovah's Son in the Arian sense, a creature, sometimes identified with the Archangel Michael, who became Messiah only after his baptism. The Holy Spirit is scarcely mentioned and there is no Trinitarian doctrine. The end of the world is very near, when Christ's kingdom, invisibly present in the world since 1874, will become manifest. The old order ceased in 1914, when Christ took his place on his heavenly throne beside Jehovah and Satan was cast out of heaven. Rutherford wrote in 1925 that Jesus is present, his kingdom has arrived and the resurrection of the dead will occur 'before the century has passed'. The year 1975 was expected informally to be the date of Christ's return, but such predictions have invariably proved embarrassing and there is an understandable reluctance to make formal pronouncements. Christ is judging men according to their attitude to the Watch Tower message, and his judgement will be executed at the Battle of Armageddon when, as the Avenger and Great Executioner, he will lead his angels and the witnesses in an orgy of destruction of capitalists, priests, orthodox churchmen, the United Nations, devils and demons. All Jehovah's opponents will suffer final annihilation, a new heaven, habitat of the 144,000 saved, will appear, and a millennial reign of everlasting life established on earth for those loyal to Jehovah, who will include qualified and resurrected dead. A further judgement at the end of the millennium will test the good done by those who previously had no chance to hear the message of God.

The witnesses' authority is a Bible translation favouring their exegesis and Rutherford's allegorical and allegedly unhistorical interpretation of it. The movement claims a complete doctrinal system with answers to all questions. Salvation and immortality come from complete obedience to God's will, belief in his word and adherence to the kingdom teaching. The organization consists of a nominal theocratic International Bible Students' Association, and under it an organized publishing system in which all Bible students serve as voluntary distributors, as part of God's plan. There is a hierarchy of president, board of directors, religious servants, zone servants and companies meeting in the local kingdom halls under a service director and service committee. Each company contains pioneers (full-time workers) and publishers (who give sixty spare-time hours a month selling publications from door to door). The headquarters of the movement is Beth Sharim, or Sarim (the House of Princes), in California, a house whose deeds are drawn up in the names of David, Abraham and Isaac, and in which rooms are fitted out for them when they return. In the meantime it is occupied by the president and his colleagues.

Services consist of Bible reading, prayer, addresses and catechistic sessions for training 'publishers'. Adult baptism is practised but unnecessary. Communion, purely commemorative and unsacramental, is celebrated annually at Easter, and partaken of only by the anointed class.

The Jehovah's witnesses have a bad press because of their lack of allegiance to nation states, their rejection of military service on the grounds of the priesthood of all believers, and their often-publicized refusal to accept blood transfusions for their dependants even if certain death is the result. Their social involvement is minimal, for works of charity are useless and there is no point in trying to improve a world doomed to destruction. Doctrine alone is valuable. About six thousand witnesses died in Nazi concentration camps, and prosecutions and imprisonment resulting from their refusal to perform military service have given the movement moral strength. Their ethic is puritan: they abstain from tobacco and alcohol and discourage marriage, for it is best to postpone the birth of children until the millennium. Their ideals are integrity, frugality, cleanliness of living and a spirit of sacrifice. They are estimated to have over a million 'publishers' throughout the world today.

William Booth found his New Connection Methodism too restricted and broke with it in 1861. After freelance evangelistic missions for four years, he was impressed by the inordinate wickedness of East End London and devoted his life to the poorest and most degraded. No church was able to cater adequately to the needs of his converts, so he founded his independent Christian Mission which, in 1877, became the Salvation Army. Booth, its general and a Protestant Loyola, ruled autocratically, demanding military obedience throughout all ranks. He was helped enormously by his wife who deserves remembrance for one *bon mot*: 'The Pope can claim infallibility only because he is a bachelor'. The Army's one aim was and is the conversion and sanctification of sinners, but it combines this with social services, works for social legislation, and today runs labour homes, shelters, an emigration agency, a bank and an insurance society. It made an instant impact, growing from 4,000 in 1877 to 72,000 in 1881, and spread to almost every country in the world.

The Army claimed to be interdenominational, neither a sect nor a church, but is in practice an organization on its own. The Bible is inspired and its only authority. The Army believes in the Trinity, in Jesus as true God and true man, in the fall of Adam, in atonement through the death of Christ, in the necessity of conversion and entire sanctification, and the priesthood of all believers, in the immortality of the soul, the resurrection of the body and eternal life in heaven, or eternal damnation in hell. Its ethos is rigidly puritan, eschewing worldly amusements, alcohol and tobacco, and demanding chastity, truthfulness and obedience to the Army. Sacraments were not used after 1882, but it has been said that the public confession of sins is almost a sacrament and the penitent form a real means of grace.

Mrs Mary Baker Eddy (1821–1910), thrice married, after dabbling in spiritualism and hypnosis, at the age of forty was cured of attacks of depression and hysteria by a mind-healer, Phineas P. Quimby. He believed health natural to man and disease to be the result of wrong thinking, denying the reality of evil. From this Mrs Eddy developed her own doctrine, that only subjective ideas exist – there is no objective world, and even the mind itself is unreal, carnal and mortal. In 1875 she published *Science and Health*, much changed in later editions (the early ones were destroyed wherever possible by the Christian Science organization), which had three basic axioms: God is all in all; God is good, good is mind; God's spirit being all, nothing is matter. The book sold widely, making considerable money for Mrs Eddy which she invested carefully, a fact her opponents used to discredit her. 'Error', as she called evil, and illness, especially her own, were due to the evil thoughts (M.A.M., or Malicious Animal Magnetism) of men and personal enemies.

Mrs Eddy's original Metaphysical College developed into the Church of Christ Scientist in 1879, the First Church of Christ Scientist being built at Boston in 1895. The *Christian Science Monitor*, a newspaper covering international as well as national events and religious topics, was launched in 1908.

The official summary of Christian Science belief reads as follows:

1. As adherents of truth we take the inspired Word of the Bible as our sufficient guide to eternal life.

2. We acknowledge and adore one supreme and infinite God. We acknowledge His Son, one Christ; the Holy Ghost or divine Comforter; and man in God's image and likeness.

3. We acknowledge God's forgiveness of sin in the destruction of sin and the spiritual understanding that casts out evil as unreal. But the belief in sin is punished so long as the belief lasts.

4. We acknowledge Jesus' atonement as an evidence of divine, efficacious Love, unfolding man's unity with God through Christ Jesus the Wayshower; and we acknowledge that man is saved through Christ, through Truth, Life and Love as demonstrated by the Galilean Prophet in healing the sick and overcoming sin and death.

5. We acknowledge that the crucifixion of Jesus and His resurrection served to uplift faith to understand eternal life, even the allness of Soul and Spirit and the nothingness of matter.

6. And we solemnly promise to watch and pray for that Mind to be in us which was also in Christ Jesus; to do unto others as we would have them do unto us; and be merciful, just and pure.

The fundamental error of man is to believe in the reality of matter and corporeality. Only Spirit and Mind (which are God) really exist. Evil is an illusion of the material mortal mind, the release from sin, illness, pain and death being the realization that they are illusions. Forgiveness of sin is the freedom from the illusion of it, and the work of Jesus was to bring this knowledge, reminiscent of the old secret gnosis, to men. Trinitarian doctrine is rejected and the title 'Person' never applied to God. Men are wholly spiritual, unable to suffer, be ill, sin or die, material men being illusion. The creed arose partly from Mrs Eddy's reaction against the Predestinarianism in which she had been brought up, partly from the influence of the Unitarian Universalist theology of optimism (God intends men to be healthy and happy), universal benevolence, confidence in man's progress to perfection, and partly from ideas promulgated by local sects of Spiritualists, Swedenborgians and Shakers.

Mrs Eddy proved a first-class organizer and safeguarded the truth as she saw it by suppressing all innovations, expelling deviationists and disallowing all free preaching after 1895, the same order of service with fixed readings from *Science and Health* being used throughout the world (although there are independent testimony meetings). There are no sacraments and the Bible is interpreted in an allegorical, artificial manner. The morality of Christian Science tends to puritanism, including abstinence from alcohol, tobacco, even tea and coffee for the stricter; but disciples play their full part in the world and are prominent in many walks of life.

Opponents allege that the creed can exist only in a comfortable culture and ignores the poor, oppressed and hungry. Also, if evil is mere illusion, how cruel of God as reality to allow it to continue when he could presumably sweep it away. They quote the judgement of that faith-healer of Deal, who said:

> 'Although pain isn't real,
> When I sit on a pin
> And it punctures my skin,
> I dislike what I fancy I feel.'

The interest aroused in the late nineteenth century in spiritualism and psychical research brought into existence a spectrum of spiritualistic creeds. Christian Spiritualism does not exist as a denomination but many local Spiritualist churches have a strongly Christian colouring, and there are Christians who believe that it is possible and right to communicate with the benevolent spirits of loved ones who have 'passed on'. Orthodox Christianity frowns on such beliefs, and Spiritualists and Christians are usually enemies, the former pointing out that the Anglican Church's Commission on Spiritualism never published a report, thus proving the commissioners' fear of the rival religion whose truth was only too plain to them. Christians quote the doctrine of the Communion of Saints as teaching that those who have died in Christ are at one with their family and friends, especially in the Eucharist, and that this unity in Christ is a far more vital relationship than the shadowy realm of spiritism. The neglect of the Church to preach this truth energetically has led to Spiritualism's giving the comfort needed by the bereaved – heresy always has its opportunity when the Church fails to teach its doctrine adequately.

In 1886 the Rosicrucean Society was founded in England. It claimed to be connected with an alleged German 'Brotherhood of the Rosy Cross', the origins of which went back to Christian Rosenkreuz, who lived about 1459. Its teaching, a mixture of theosophy, reincarnation theories, occultism, alchemy and esoteric knowledge, forms a modern-style Gnosticism which, like the second-century Gnostics, tries to graft its theories on to Christianity by paying lip-service to Christ. It has been described as a perversion rather than an interpretation of Christianity and is almost too far from it even to be a heresy. Societies affiliated to the English one sprang up in all parts of the world, and the present headquarters of the movement is, as might be expected, in California, the home of more modern religions than there were gods in the Greek pantheon. Theosophy, mentioned here, is still further removed from Christianity and should be regarded as another creed, accepting Christ as one teacher among many; and this is true of a number of sects which might appear Christian at first sight but in which Christ can be seen on closer examination to play only a small part.

CHAPTER 19

The Twentieth Century

The increasing complexity of modern life affects religion as it does all else. Heresies, in their original meaning of 'choices', multiply as more and more sects appear; yet, in the ecumenical movement in which all but a few Christian churches have joined, fragmentation is balanced by coalescence. Heresy as a departure from a recognized orthodoxy disappears, because such an orthodoxy has almost ceased to exist. The very word 'heresy' is not found in the indices of most histories of twentieth-century Christianity, and, if it is referred to in their texts, it is placed within inverted commas. The Bible, the creeds, the dogmas of past theologians, may still be the authorities which orthodoxy declares must be obeyed. Yet there is scarcely a Christian in any church who takes them as all literally true, much less accepting them as true in the sense of the truth they were originally intended to convey. Even in the Roman Catholic Church, the only major communion to maintain (in the words of a Catholic chaplain in the First World War) that 'We have the same Lord – you worship him in your way, and we worship him in his way', there has been a liberalization which would have been unthinkable even in 1950. At the Vatican II Ecumenical Council under Pope John XXIII, there was a revolt against tradition which questioned the centrality of Mary, the episcopal authority of the Pope and the holiness of priestly celibacy, and the one-time Rock is now more like molten lava, for all the efforts of the conservatives to cork the volcano.

It is impossible in a single chapter to do more than mention in general terms the factors affecting the choice that is heresy. If a medieval monk were transported to the modern world, he would find the greatest heresy of all to be the freedom of choice which is one of the great virtues of democracy, itself almost a religion of the western world. One may choose not only one's variety of Christianity – one can choose not to be a Christian at all. Yet in essence the monk from the Middle Ages might find matters not so altered. For him Christendom (Europe) was opposed to 'Heathenesse' beyond its borders, where adherents of pagan religions dwelt. For modern Christianity, 'western civilization', still basically Christian, is opposed to rival philosophies such as dialectical materialism, the official doctrine of vast tracts of the world's surface. The monk would have known two standards in his own world—for example, of sexual mores and of Christian love and political hate. And he would have known men like Browning's Bishop Bloughram, Gandolf and his rival, uncertain of their beliefs and rejecters of current morality at best, and, at worst, downright immoral by any standards. All that might surprise him would be the scale and openness of the breakdown of belief and morality in modern society, and he would surely be astonished that the Inquisition should stick in the craw of a century that has seen Auschwitz and Buchenwald. Yet, as he acclimatized himself to new discoveries such as the Dead Sea Scrolls, new sciences such as psychology, new scholarship such as the findings of biblical criticism, new methods of communication such as radio, and more widespread literacy than he had ever dreamed of, he would realize the inevitability of the fragmentation of Christianity and the rise of new creeds. On the other hand, he would be astonished at the resilience of a faith which has not only survived but, in the ecumenical movement, is finding a unity of spirit which may be, in the perspective of history, the hope of the world. Nor would the monk, if he knew how the Nestorian heretics had been affected by the eastern civilizations among which they settled and which regarded Byzantine civilization as an imperialist threat, have been altogether surprised at the formation of native Christian churches reacting against the forms of doctrine and worship used by their former white masters.

The twentieth century is so full of bewildering complexities, of thought and activity, that it is necessary to select and isolate certain strains to serve as examples relevant to the subject of heresy as a whole. These are arranged under seven headings.

National history

In the old Catholic stronghold of Spain, Protestantism came to be tolerated under the republic created in 1931, was suppressed rigorously under Franco in 1939, again tolerated but with severe restrictions in 1945, and then more drastically restricted in 1947. In Portugal full freedom of worship was granted in 1951, followed by a phenomenal growth of Pentecostalism (now the most numerous Protestant communion in the country), which in turn was followed, surprisingly, by the (Plymouth) Brethren.

France has seen friendly advances of Catholics and Protestants towards each other, and significant is the Taizé monastic group of Protestants who have taken vows of celibacy, community of property and obedience to their order with the aim of restoring to Protestant worship pre-Reformation liturgies of outstanding beauty and reverence.

German Christianity passed through a crisis in which a totalitarian Faith Movement of German Christians, founded by Jacob Wilhelm Hauer in 1933, included Christians who had rejected the old churches but revered Christ. The movement rejected Jews, negroes and, as full members, adherents of any other Christian church, and was open only to those of Aryan descent. In this it was supremely heretical, since in the Christian Church 'there is neither Jew nor Gentile' and the Gospel is for the whole world. It was opposed by the orthodox churches in Germany, many of whose pastors, notably Dietrich Bonhoefer, suffered martyrdom for upholding their truths.

Italy under the Fascists suppressed the growing Pentecostalism, restricted the Waldenses, and clashed politically with the Catholicism to which she paid lip-service.

Russia in the 1920s persecuted Christianity with a government-backed godless movement, but religion persisted and is said to be increasing in both the Orthodox and various Baptist communions. Because of Vatican opposition to communism, Catholicism is frowned upon.

In eastern communist countries Christianity, always numerically weak, has practically disappeared, although before China became communist there had been, in 1927, a union of Presbyterians, Congregationalists, Baptists, Methodists and the United Brethren to form the Church of Christ in China.

A still more remarkable union of churches took place when the Church of South India was formed in 1947. This was a union of Anglicans, Congregationalists, Methodists and Presbyterians, born out of a longing for unity in the mission field that found divisions in the home churches irrelevant. The final doctrinal statement declared the authority of Scripture to be 'the supreme and decisive standard of faith' by which the Church 'must always be ready to correct and reform itself'. The uniting Indian churches declared that they accepted 'the fundamental truths embodied in the Creeds [Apostles' and Nicene] as providing a sufficient basis of union; but do not intend thereby to demand the assent of individuals to every word and phrase in them, or to exclude reasonable liberty of interpretation, as to assert that those Creeds are a complete expression of the Christian faith'. The Indian Church supported the 'historic Episcopate' against the 'Priesthood of Believers', contending that although 'all share in the heavenly High Priesthood of the risen and ascended Christ ... in the church there has at all times been a special ministry'. Episcopacy was combined with a synodical organization of the church, resulting in the historical episcopate in a constitutional form. There is a lay majority in the synod.

While the United Church of South India was opposed by Anglo-Catholics, who saw it as an obstacle to a possible future reunion with Roman Catholicism, in Britain and elsewhere little reunions were taking place alongside the growing ecumenical movement. The Church of Scotland reunited with the Free Church in 1929. Methodists, Congregationalists and Presbyterians formed the United Church of Canada in 1925. Lutherans completed a process of reunion, begun in 1917 in the United States, in 1931. Methodists came together in England in 1932 and American Methodists united in 1939. And in 1941 Presbyterians, Congregationalists, Reformed, Baptists, Lutherans and Anglicans, forty-one communions in all, joined together in the Church of Christ of Japan. In 1942 almost all the Christian denominations in the British Isles joined in the British Council of Churches which, while not a reunion, at least recognized the genuineness of Christians in other denominations who, a century earlier, even though tolerated, would have been regarded as heretics.

The Ecumenical movement

The history of this movement is relevant to heresy only insofar as it has meant the diminishment of the latter on a large scale. The roots of ecumenicalism reach to the nineteenth century when challenge by secularism to Christianity emphasized the need for co-operation rather than strife between the denominations. In 1910 the World Missionary Conference initiated a series of consultations on 'Faith and Order' and 'Life and Work', resulting in the official formation of the World Council of Churches in 1948, which followed an exploratory meeting at Utrecht ten years earlier of representatives of eighty churches from thirty countries, including Anglicans, Baptists, Congregationalists, Friends (Quakers), Lutherans, the Mar Thomas Syrian Church of Malabar, Nestorians, Old Catholics, Orthodox, Presbyterians, Salvation Army and Swedenborgians. In 1957 the World Council merged with the International Missionary Council, also a child of the World Missionary Conference, uniting more Christian communions than ever before. This was a union of spirit (Christians would claim the Holy Spirit), not organizations; even so, one cannot call one's brother in the Spirit a heretic even if one disagrees with his views.

Modern theology

Theology showed a reaction to the optimism of the nineteenth century when it was believed by Christians that one needed only to see the highest to love it and by secularists that science and universal Humanist education would bring in the Golden Age. Kierkegaard, Barth and Niebuhr produced in their respective fashions a 'theology of crisis' which was a reaction in a Calvinist direction towards a statement of man's utter sinfulness and helplessness to find God for himself. The old debate which made so many heretics on both sides in the past–predestination versus free will–continues, though in perhaps more muted and intellectual terms. But theologians made little impact on the man in the pew in the past and make not much more impact today unless their theology is popularized. This has sometimes happened in the present century, as in 1963 when J. A. T. Robinson, Bishop of Woolwich, published *Honest to God*. His book ran through eight impressions in six months. It said nothing which had not been freely and openly debated in theological circles for twenty years, but said it in language which could be understood by literate laymen, and it accelerated the liberation of a generation from old theological concepts to which many men in the pew had been paying increasingly unwilling lip-service. It was a brave and timely book. Three hundred years ago its author would certainly have been burned in almost every country in Europe; and the difference in climate in twenty years may be seen in the fame achieved by *Honest to God* and the suspicion meted out to 'that Modernist' E. W. Barnes (1874–1953), Bishop of Birmingham, who in 1947 rejected the Virgin Birth, doubted the physical resurrection and ascension of Christ and whether at the Last Supper he had instituted the Eucharist. The Archbishops of both Canterbury and York dissociated themselves from his views, although one is reported as having said privately that English Modernism (the new name for the old Broad Churchmanship) had a right to be heard.

Sectarian developments

Of these, by far the most important is the Pentecostalist movement. This may be said to have been born on 1 January 1900. Tongues were spoken by a Bible School student at Topeka, Kansas. This not unprecedented phenomenon in church history touched off what may in perspective prove to be a movement of world-wide importance for Christianity. Pentecostalism spread rapidly through revivals in Texas and Los Angeles, developing in an exciting fashion the Holiness doctrine of the second blessing which became the baptism with the Spirit with signs following, the charismatic gift of tongues being the most unusual and, according to some Pentecostalist sects, an essential proof. It spread northwards to Canada, whence missionaries took it notably to South America where, today, it is the strongest Protestant group, its adherents numbering millions. The St Paul of Pentecostalism was T. B. Barratt, a Norwegian Methodist of English stock, who, catching it in America, carried it to Norway, Sweden, Germany, Denmark, Switzerland and Finland. England developed it through conferences arranged by an Anglican evangelical clergyman. France and Holland were slightly affected, but New Zealand, South Africa, the Congo, Nigeria, Indonesia, even Russia, received it with enthusiasm. Most surprising was its growth in Italy, whither emigrants returning from the United States carried it, and in Portugal. It is estimated that today there may be over a hundred thousand Italian Pentecostalists. The world Pentecostalist population may be ten to twelve million–so numerous and influential that it has been called a 'third force' after Catholicism and Protestantism.

In many respects Pentecostalism is a hotchpotch of other movements. Adult baptism by immersion comes from the Baptists, justification by faith from Lutherans, saving souls from the Salvation Army, sanctification from Methodism, the congregational election of ministers and elders from Presbyterianism, its eschatology from the Adventists, its organization from Congregationalism. Pentecostalists are Bible fundamentalists, mostly simple people with unsophisticated, anti-liturgical, free and, originally, undisciplined, noisy, emotional and joyful forms of worship. They are puritan in their modesty, self-sacrifices and abstinence from worldly pleasures, alcohol and tobacco.

Their theology consists of simple elements found in many Protestant communions. Man is a sinner needing a conversion experience of redemption through Christ followed by striving for sanctification. The Pentecostalist addition to this process is that every Christian must expectantly work for baptism by the Holy Spirit in 'waiting meetings'. His arrival is signalized by the appearance in the baptized believer of one or more of the gifts of the Spirit, usually an outburst of glossolalia. Some Pentecostalists distinguish between the *sign* of tongues, holding that Spirit baptism is always indicated by tongues, though this may be the only occasion on which the believer uses them; and the *gift* of tongues, which may be used regularly in worship.

The movement is particularly prone to schism and a book could be written on the sects within it. The Church of God, under A. J. Tomlinson, founded in 1906 and flourishing in Tennessee and North Carolina, fragmented into a number of others. Two among many negro Pentecostalist churches are the Church of God in Christ, formed in 1906, which includes a ritual of foot-washing; and the Apostolic Overcoming Holy Church of God, Alabama, founded in 1916. In 1918 Aimée Semple McPherson settled in Los Angeles, and there in 1923 she founded the International Church of the Foursquare Gospel, preaching Christ as Saviour, Baptizer, Physician and Coming King. She was a consummate showman, gaining as much publicity in the 1920s and 1930s as any Hollywood film star. She emulated their publicity methods by her vulgar yet vigorous campaign against local vice, and with her razzmatazz revival services and chorus of pulchritudinous angels. Six hundred Foursquare Churches existed in the United States in the mid-1950s. Mrs McPherson's British counterpart was Elim, with the same four planks in its theological platform, founded by the Welsh evangelist George Jeffreys.

By far the largest Pentecostalist church is the Assemblies of God, with branches in almost every country open to Christianity in the world. It has nearly half a million followers and more than seven thousand churches in the United States and is soberer than most Pentecostal communions, believing in gradual rather than instantaneous sanctification. Though allowing autonomy to individual chapels, and in spite of its fundamentalism and puritanism, its development of theological institutions for missionary work and its publishing enterprises are drawing it closer to general denominational patterns.

Of the fifty or more Pentecostalist sects in the United States a couple may be selected as typical of different tendencies. The Christian Catholic Apostolic Church in Zion, founded by J. A. Dowie, who built Zion City on Lake Michigan in 1910, is Fundamentalist, pre-Millennialist, completely Pentecostalist, emphasizing faith-healing, and worshipped at least, initially, with wild, enthusiastic spontaneity. It sent many missionaries to Africa, where the natives added African thaumaturgical practices to their already exuberant worship. The Church of the Nazarene, formed from the Los Angeles congregations of a former Methodist minister, Phineas F. Bresee, united in 1907 with the Association of American Pentecostal Churches, calling itself originally the Pentecostal Church of the Nazarene and resembling Methodism in its organization. The basis of union was holiness of heart and life and liberty in non-essential doctrines. It emphasized 'spirit-leading', experiences of glory, freedom of worship which should be joyous, but, shying at the Pentecostal emphasis on glossolalia, dropped the 'Pentecostal' from its title. It spread rapidly owing to its taking-in of independent missions and by evangelism in its American homeland and abroad.

In the British Isles another Pentecostal communion is the Apostolic Church, arising from a Welsh revival in 1904, with its headquarters in Wales and appealing especially to the Welsh and Scots. It has some 230 congregations and 10,000 members, with a Pentecostalist pattern of church life and a hierarchy of apostles, prophets, pastors, teachers, evangelists, elders, deacons and deaconesses, appointed by Holy Spirit guidance. It submits ecclesiastical, ethical and personal problems to Spirit guidance. It has adopted the principle of instantaneous sanctification, although it also allows gradual growth. The Church has had dramatic success in missionary work in Nigeria.

Not exactly Pentecostalist but of a similar family is the Dolley Pond Church of God with Signs Following. Taking literally Christ's promise, 'If they handle snakes they will come to no harm', and ignoring his injunction, 'Thou shalt not test the Lord thy God', the Dolley Pond worshippers include ritual snake-handling in their worship. Begun in 1909 in Tennessee by George Went Hensley, killed by snake-bite in 1955, the practice was introduced into a number of fundamentalist sects in Kentucky and, although now forbidden by law in Tennessee, Kentucky and Virginia, continues and has spread to North Carolina, Georgia, Alabama, Florida, West Virginia and California.

Other transatlantic sects include those arising out of the nineteenth century Holiness movement, such as the Canadian Holiness Church of the Nazarene, fundamentalist and ascetic. The Rosicruceans and Unity Truth preach 'reason' and promise 'success'. The Social Credit Party, founded by William Aberhart, besides claiming to be a panacea for all the economic ills of the 1930s depression, was associated with the Prophetic Bible Institute. In 1935 Aberhart became Premier of Alberta and in 1943 his protégé, E. C. Manning, reorganized the institute and succeeded Aberhart as premier. In 1946 the Fundamentalists in Alberta largely controlled the religious broadcasting of the province. Earlier, in 1937 The Great I Am sect had moved from Chicago, where it had begun in 1934, to Alberta. Its founder, Guy Ballard, claimed to be the recipient of revealed truths and preached a gospel of asceticism, vegetarianism and reincarnation.

A movement which made a great noise between the wars was the Oxford Group, later Moral Rearmament, preaching the four Absolutes – Absolute Unselfishness, Purity, Honesty and Love – and a system of group confession and 'sharing'. Founded by Frank N. D. Buchman (1878–1961), a Pennsylvanian, it aimed its message at the wealthy, the educated and those in high political, economic and social positions, including prominent Nazis, Fascists and similar 'catches'. It claimed imposing successes but failed to avert the Second World War, which it assuredly would have done if all its claims of changed lives had been true, and it was a suspect organization while hostilities lasted. It still exists but has little influence compared with its pre-war position. Orthodox Christians disliked it for its ethical over-emphasis and its naïve optimism as well as for its lack of depth and basic theology. More spiritual but of limited influence was George F. MacLeod's Iona Community which tried to give fresh spiritual insight to its many visitors from all denominations.

The twentieth century was marked by the rapid growth of some of the nineteenth-century sects. Between 1918 and 1955 the Mormons increased by 205 per cent, the Seventh Day Adventists by 220 per cent, the Assemblies of God by 436 per cent and the Jehovah's witnesses spectacularly, though they do not publish membership figures. Yet, to put the growth of sectarianism in its perspective, 80 per cent of American Christians belong to eight main denominational families, the remaining 20 per cent being divided among 238 communities large enough to be recorded.

Two European movements deserve a mention. The Bruderhof, founded by Eberhardt Arnold (1883–1935), one-time secretary of the German Christian Student movement, opened an informal colony at Sannerz in 1920. Spiritually related to the Hutterites, yet more idealistic and intellectual, they established Almbruderhof in Liechtenstein in the 1930s, but difficulties drove them to England where, in 1935, they established themselves in the Cotswolds. In 1940 most went to Paraguay, a small group remaining in England in a new colony in Shropshire.

F. L. Alexander Freytag broke with the Jehovah's witnesses in 1918 to form the Church of the Kingdom of God, later changed to the Friends of Man. He believed God intended man to overcome death by obeying God's universal law of altruism. Men made their own sufferings by departing from God's law of love. The time of the Advent was now come and those who obeyed God's law would find their lives lengthening until they conquered death. Two classes of believer existed, the band of 144,000 of the completely dedicated 'little Christs' and 'the Army of the Eternal' who would live according to God's law and populate the earth. Resurrection would occur when the law of altruism was obeyed. Freytag, the 'Ambassador of the Age', wrote a constitution for the Kingdom, including reafforestation to alter the world's climate, rejection of medicines, alcohol and tobacco, a vegetarian diet, the breathing of pure air, and character transformation through altruism. Upon Freytag's death in 1947, his sect divided on a question of leadership, not doctrine, into French and Swiss branches. The French branch passed from altruistic theory to action, becoming well known through its social relief, workshops and production and distribution of food. Like its parent body it spread its message through periodicals and house-to-house calls, gathering some fifteen thousand members in France and adherents in Austria, Germany and Belgium. Several thousands in Germany and Switzerland remained faithful to the Swiss branch.

Twentieth-century heresies also include the Aetherius Society, which believes that the Star of Bethlehem was a 'flying saucer' and Christ an extraterrestrial intelligence in a human body. Some members have millennial hopes, space-ships being vessels by which initiates will be saved. Another, New Thought, rejects damnation and eternal punishment in hell. It takes several forms, of which the most specifically Christian is the Unity School of Christianity, founded in Kansas City by Charles and Myrtle Fillmore.

Media religion

The fact that Fundamentalists at one time controlled Alberta province religious radio is an indication of the power of media religion. Nowhere has this been so much used and abused as in North America; for in England care has been taken to give the major denominations equality of opportunity, and European broadcasting systems are not open to the buying of time in the same way as American. A revivalist preacher or religious demagogue can be sponsored in the United States and thereby reach a public far wider than any in a church. His heresy, if heresy it is and harmful, can spread its poison in half an hour over an area bigger than would be covered by half a year of campaign meetings.

Charles E. Fuller was famous for his broadcasts in 1925, under the title 'The Old-Fashioned Revival Hour'; Harry Emerson Fosdick for the National Broadcasting Company's 'National Vespers'; and Oral Roberts, son of a Full Gospel preacher, an ultra-Fundamentalist cured through a Pentecostalist of a speech impediment, carried on a ministry of healing by prayer and laying-on of hands via the radio. The Worldwide Church of God, formerly the Radio Church of God, founded by Herbert Armstrong, broadcasts an essentially Millennialist message supported by a well-produced magazine, *Plain Truth*, often offered free on railway bookstalls. The Church concentrates on modern social and psychological problems.

Critics condemn much media religion for over-emphasis, one-sidedness and bad taste, and much of it could be proved heretical by a comparison of its teachings with those generally recognized as orthodox. That it has brought peace, conviction, help, perhaps even salvation, to many listening souls, is probable.

Messiahs

The *World Christian Handbook* mentions six thousand indigenous Christian movements in Africa alone, many of them Messianic and many anti-imperialist. But perhaps the best-known Messiah was the American negro, George Baker, born about 1880, who came to prominence by providing free meals for his followers in the 1930s depression and through the 1940s. Claiming to be God and known as Father Divine, he did this in his 'Heaven' (the Divine Peace Mission) which he opened in Harlem, New York, followed by other heavens elsewhere. How far this was an independent religious movement, how far a Christian heresy, it is difficult to say. Full members had to obey a rigorous ethical code: no tobacco, alcohol, gambling or sex even between spouses. The Bible was superseded by Father Divine's authority. True believers would not die, and Baker's own death in 1965 made no difference to his mostly negro followers, his wife carrying on his work and claiming that he was beside her directing the movement. The extravagance of Baker's claims was much derided, but he insisted on honesty, found jobs and provided food for the needy and, above all, gave hope and a sense of euphoria to his followers in desperate days.

In Africa Enoch Mgijima preached that negroes were a chosen people and founded his 'Israelites'. He refused to pay taxes and expected divine annihilation of Europeans. A conflict in 1921 at Bulhoek, South Africa, led to the deaths of 183 Israelites and the imprisonment of Mgijima. In 1950 Edward Lekganyane was acknowledged king by several thousand followers at Zion City, north Transvaal, claiming to be a thaumaturge who could destroy witches. The movement was widespread, its appeal deriving from its discipline and elaborate hierarchy. Among the Zulus, Shembe, a Messiah-thaumaturge, practically equated with Christ, founded the Nazareth Baptist Church. He promised protection against witchcraft (to which all illness was attributed) and wisely modelled his organization on Zulu tribal practices, combining this with taboos and injunctions drawn from the Old Testament. In the Congo Simon Kibangu, a Baptist, believed he had a divine commission to undertake a ministry of healing. Others imitated him. He was condemned to death but reprieved, and his movement faded for a time; but it revived in 1959 when its leaders proclaimed him to be the Messiah of Africans as Jesus had been of the whites, and that his teachings, including a national church, were those of Jesus himself.

Europe was not without her Messiahs. In the Tyrol Oskar Ernst Bernhardt founded the Gralsbewegung, claiming to be the new Son of God who had come to fulfil the mission unfinished by Christ and to bring God's final word to mankind. The movement continued in spite of his death in 1941. Louwrens van Voorthuisen, a Dutch fisherman, claimed that God had become incarnate in him. Christ had defeated Satan in the spirit; he would defeat him in the body. Only through him, who could not sin, be ill or die, could men come to God; coming they would be as Christ was on earth, true children of God. The world would end in the 1970s when Satan would be vanquished and believers attain deathless salvation. Van Voorthuisen died in 1968, but – as usual – his followers, undismayed, believe he lives on in them. In Provence, Georges Roux, a French postal inspector, after some time as a faith healer, announced that he was Christ, and gathered four or five thousand followers. These were first called Witnesses to the Returned Christ, later the Universal Christian Church. Salvation came from obedience to Roux's will. Churches of the sect were to be found at Cannes, Marseilles, Nîmes, Paris, Strasbourg and Toulon, and some adherents are to be found in Germany, Switzerland and Belgium.

Indigenous sects

These are often ephemeral but many have taken root. Rhodesia and neighbouring territories have the Watch Tower movement, derived from Jehovah's witnesses in the 1930s but anti-white, glossolalic and anarchistic. Also in Rhodesia is to be found the Alice movement, or Lumpa Church, led by Alice Lenshina Mulenga, who believed she had died four times, risen again, been called by Jesus to 'meet him at the river', been commissioned by him to attack witchcraft and polygamy and often talked to him. Uganda boasted the Malakites, 'The Church of the One Almighty God', which forbade recourse to doctors and rejected monogamy which, they said, is not found in the Bible. Since they refused smallpox vaccination the government took action against them on health grounds and the sect died out.

In Nigeria, during the First World War, there was an ex-Anglican evangelist who called himself Elijah II. He seems to have been a psychic sensitive, claiming 'second sight' and healing the sick. He forbade recourse to doctors, alcohol and idols, but was imprisoned for obtaining money under false pretences. Nigeria, with Ghana, Liberia and Sierra Leone, is also the home of the Church of the Lord, Aladura, founded by the Nigerian J. A. Ositelu. The Church has the organizational structure of a mission church adapted for a faith which is a syncreticism of Christianity and traditional African religion. It has something for everyone – a hierarchy of bishops, prophets and deacons; a Protestant evangelical hymnology; a Roman Catholic type liturgy; revelations, prophecies, miracles and guidance from God against evil and potentially harmful spirits.

In East London and Durban there are the Bhenguists. Founded by Nicholas Bhengu, they are a conversionist, Pentecostal sect, tolerating traditional ancestor cults and emphasizing healing and public confession. The sect protects countrymen coming into the cities for work against urban temptations, holding up ideals of thrift, honesty, cleanliness, prudence and industry and providing them with a community to set against the rootless existence of the town.

In Japan there is an indigenous sect called the Mukyokai-Shugi, important in that, unlike most native movements, it stems from the highly educated, not the humbler ranks of society. It is a churchless Christianity whose founder was committed to completing the Protestant Reformation which Luther had not taken far enough, by eliminating all organization except Bible study groups gathered about a teacher. He knew of the Quakers but rejected their doctrine of 'inner light' inspiration in favour of a Bible-centred faith.

A bird's-eye view of the centuries shows Christianity, itself originally a Jewish heresy and one sect among many in the ancient world, with little theology of its own, developing into a major religion. In a few centuries it outstrips its rivals, becoming the accepted faith in the Roman Empire. Parallel with this progress it evolves from its spiritual experience, and by the trial and error of dialectic, an orthodoxy expressed in the creeds that states certain allegedly historical facts and beliefs connected with them. Deviation from these can be clearly distinguished, and that is heresy. As the centuries pass, heresy also includes any questioning of or disagreement with the emerging authority of the Pope and the Church of which he becomes increasingly the head. So, at the Reformation, it is clear who represents orthodoxy and who are the heretics. But as the non-Roman churches become established like streams in a delta running alongside the main river, almost as wide as it and sometimes flowing faster, so heresy changes in nature. To Roman Catholics, heretics are still all Christians outside their own communion. To Protestants, heretics may be either those false to certain basic truths of Christianity or those who divide from their Protestant parent bodies on some doctrinal point, or those in differing bodies, Protestant or Catholic.

As the centuries pass heresy tends to disappear. Heretics are replaced by believers who are 'mistaken on certain points', 'do not have the full Gospel', 'follow Christ according to their lights but are not members of the true Church'. More knowledge leads to less dogmatism, at least among the wise, until the modern age is reached when full liberty of religious conscience is the ideal, at least among the western heirs of Christendom. Now there is no heresy, for no longer is there any certain orthodoxy or authority. The infallibility of Pope and councils do not bear the test of history. The rock of the Roman Church is being steadily eroded if it is not crumbling, much of its numerical strength being derived from members too frightened to let go of one certainty in an uncertain world or from others who, wearied of responsibility and decision, surrender these to an organization which claims to hold the keys. The

Bible, once the infallible authority for Protestants, has become a library of sixty-six books of varying dates and values, its every syllable examined textually, historically, scientifically, its shortcomings manifest, at best the subject of pendulum dialectic swinging now to radicalism in interpretation, now to conservatism. Psychology argues the subjectivity of the inner light and lists the neuroses which give rise to saintliness and the Beatific Vision.

Yet somehow the thin red line of Christianity holds. Somehow, in spite of knowledge that whittles away one former certainty after another, faith persists. Virgin Birth, miracles, resurrection and ascension may all go, yet Christ remains alive and continues to speak in the modern age and to men of nationalities of which the Jesus of first-century Nazareth did not even know the existence. Perhaps the orthodoxy that the centuries are shattering may be replaced by another, more embracing and closer to ultimate truth; perhaps the greatest heresy is the existence of any dogma at all. Mankind may be only at the beginning of the road to understanding, let alone certainty. Apposite are the words of William Temple, Archbishop of Canterbury during the Second World War, who, after listening to a discussion about the infant church, said, 'We are the infant church'. The true Nicaea of the Christian Church may be future millennia away.

Selected Bibliography
for Additional Reading

Atiya, A. S. *A History of Eastern Christianity* (Methuen, 1968)

Bainton, R. H. *Studies on the Reformation* (Hodder & Stoughton, 1963)

Baker, F. *John Wesley and the Church of England* (Epworth Press, 1970)

Barbour, H. *The Quakers in Puritan England* (Yale University Press; New Haven and London, 1964)

Bender, H. S. *Conrad Grebel, Founder of the Swiss Brethren* (Herald Press; Scottdale, Pa, 1931)

Bolam, C. G., Goring, J., Short, H. L. and Thomas, R. *The English Presbyterians* (Allen & Unwin, 1968)

Bouyer, L., trans by Littledale, A. V. *The Spirit and Forms of Protestantism* (Harvill Press, 1956)

Braithwaite, W. C. *The Beginnings of Quakerism* (CUP, 1955)

Brayshaw, A. N. *The Quakers* (Allen & Unwin, 1946)

Burrage, C. *The Early English Dissenters, 1550–1641* (CUP, 1912), 2 Vols

Butterworth, G. W. *Churches, Sects and Religious Parties* (SPCK, 1936)

Carrick Smith, K. L. *The Church and the Churches* (SCM, 1948)

Capp, B. S. *The Fifth Monarchy Men* (Faber & Faber, 1972)

Coad, F. R. *A History of the Brethren Movement* (Paternoster Press, 1968)

Danielou, J. and Marrou, H., trans by Cronin, V. *The First Six Hundred Years* (Darton, Longman & Todd, 1964)

Dillenberger, J. and Welch, C. *Protestant Christianity* (Charles Scribner's Sons; New York, 1954)

Donaldson, G. *The Scottish Reformation* (CUP, 1960)

Escott, H. *A History of Scottish Congregationalism* (Congregational Union of Scotland; Glasgow, 1960)

Fey, H. E. (ed). *The Ecumenical Advance* (SPCK, 1970), 2 Vols

Fortescue, A. *The Lesser Eastern Churches* (Catholic Truth Society, 1913)

——. *The Uniate Eastern Churches* (Burns Oates & Washbourne, 1923)

Gardner, P. *Modernism in the English Church* (Methuen, 1926)

Gay, J. D. *The Geography of Religion in England* (Duckworth, 1971)

Guitton, J., trans by Wieck, F. D. *Great Heresies and Church Councils* (Harvill Press, 1965)

Horsch, J. *The Hutterian Brethren, 1528–1931* (Herald Press; Scottdale, Pa, 1931)

Kidd, B. J. *Documents Illustrative of the Continental Reformation* (Clarendon Press, 1911)

Kot, S., trans by Wilbur, E. M. *Socinianism in Poland* (Starr King Press; Boston, USA, 1957)

Knappen, M. M. *Tudor Puritanism* (University of Chicago Press, 1939)

Lecler, J. *Toleration and the Reformation* (Association Press, New York, and Longmans, London, 1960), 2 Vols

Latourette, K. S. *A History of the Expansion of Christianity* (Eyre & Spottiswoode, 1938–47), 7 Vols

——. *A History of Christianity* (Eyre & Spottiswoode, 1954)

——. *Christianity in a Revolutionary Age* (Eyre & Spottiswoode, 1959–63), 5 Vols

McClachlan, H. J. *Socinianism in Seventeenth-Century England* (OUP, 1951)

Molland, E. *Christendom* (Mowbray, 1959)

Olmstead, C. E. *History of Religion in the United States* (Prentice-Hall; New Jersey, 1960)

Outler, A. C. *John Wesley* (OUP; New York, 1964)

Phillips, W. A. *History of the Church of Ireland* (OUP, 1933–4), 3 Vols

Plum, H. G. *Restoration Puritanism* (University of North Carolina Press, 1943)

Rilliet, J., trans by Knight, H. *Zwingli – Third Man of the Reformation* (Lutterworth Press, 1964)

Rouse, R., and Neill, S. C. *The Ecumenical Movement* (SPCK, 1954)

Russell, E. *The History of Quakerism* (Macmillan; New York, 1942)

Scott Pearson, A. F. *Thomas Cartwright and Elizabethan Puritanism, 1535–1603* (CUP, 1925)

Spinka, M. *John Hus at the Council of Constance* (Columbia University Press; New York and London, 1965)

Swihart, A. K. *Luther and the Lutheran Church, 1483–1960* (Peter Owen, 1961)

Summers, W. H. *Our Lollard Ancestors* (National Council of Evangelical Free Churches, Thomas Law, 1904)

Tisserant, E., adapted from the French by Hambye, E. R. *Eastern Christianity in India* (Longmans, Green & Co, 1957)

Todd, J. M. (ed). *Problems of Authority. A Symposium* (Helicon Press, Baltimore, and Darton, Longman & Todd, London, 1962)

Torbet, R. G. *A History of the Baptists* (The Carey Kingsgate Press, 1966)

van Rohr, J. *Profile of Protestantism* (Dickenson Publishing Co; California, 1969)

Verduin, L. *The Reformers and Their Stepchildren* (Paternoster Press, 1964)

Verheyden, A. L. E. *Anabaptism in Flanders, 1530–1650* (Herald Press; Scottdale, Pa, 1931)

Wigmore-Beddoes, D. G. *Yesterday's Radicals* (James Clarke & Co, 1971)

Wilbur, E. M. *A History of Unitarianism* (Harvard University Press and Humphrey Milford, 1945)

——. *Our Unitarian Heritage* (The Beacon Press; Boston, 1925)

Williams, G. H. *The Radical Reformation* (Weidenfeld & Nicolson, 1962)

Zeman, J. K. *The Anabaptists and Czech Brethren in Moravia, 1526–1628* (Mouton; The Hague and Paris, 1969)

Index

231

OXFORD

MORE OXFORD PAPERBACKS

Details of a selection of other books follow. A complete list of Oxford Paperbacks, including The World's Classics, Twentieth-Century Classics, OPUS, Past Masters, Oxford Authors, Oxford Shakespeare, and Oxford Paperback Reference, is available in the UK from the General Publicity Department, Oxford University Press (JN), Walton Street, Oxford OX2 6DP.

In the USA, complete lists are available from the Paperbacks Marketing Manager, Oxford University Press, 200 Madison Avenue, New York, NY 10016.

Oxford Paperbacks are available from all good bookshops. In case of difficulty, customers in the UK can order direct from Oxford University Press Bookshop, 116 High Street, Oxford, Freepost, OX1 4BR, enclosing full payment. Please add 10 per cent of published price for postage and packing.

DOCUMENTS OF THE CHRISTIAN CHURCH

Selected and Edited by Henry Bettenson

First published in 1943, this book won a world-wide reputation, so that 'Bettenson, *Documents*' is now referred to as a sourcebook in many important works. It is also fascinating reading, containing 'the hard facts of many disputed questions, the ammunition for controversy, the corrective to loose thinking and idle speech'. It is currently in a second edition, so that it now covers an additional twenty years of Christian history, from the earliest documents after the New Testament, down to the eve of the Second Vatican Council. It spans the periods of the Fathers and the Middle Ages, Roman Catholic and Protestant Churches, the Reformation, the Churches in Great Britain, and the beginning of the Ecumenical Movement, giving an indispensable background to history and current events.

'That invaluable Christian reference book.' *Church Times*.

'Covering the whole range of Christian history, it is especially valuable to the young Student.' *Church Quarterly Review*

'This source book can be used to make your own Do-it-yourself Church History. Here is varied material about which you can make up your own mind, with no partisan scholar coming in between.' *Methodist Magazine*

JUDAISM

Nicholas de Lange

Among the religions of the western world Judaism is the oldest-established and in many ways the most familiar, yet it is a religion about which there are many misconceptions. This book aims to set the record straight, presenting contemporary Judaism in a way accessible to non-Jewish readers.

AN INTRODUCTION TO THE PHILOSOPHY OF RELIGION

Brian Davies

Does rational inquiry show religious doctrines to be false, incoherent, or meaningless? Are there logical arguments for thinking that God exists or does not exist? And what, in any case, does 'God' mean? Does it make sense to postulate a good God, given the reality of evil? Does the idea of 'miracles' have any meaning? Can there be a rational basis for ethics which takes no account of God? Is the notion of human survival after death coherent?

This book is written for all who have been puzzled by these and similar problems, not just for students and professional philosophers. None of the questions is new, and Brian Davies examines critically the way they have been treated in the past by such philosophers as Anselm, Aquinas, Descartes, Leibniz, Hume, and Kant, as well as looking at the work of a number of modern thinkers.

An OPUS book

IN THE VATICAN

Peter Hebblethwaite

The administration of the Vatican is a highly complex affair, and the men who run it are talented, exceptional, and often enigmatic people. In this book, Peter Hebblethwaite has used his skills and experience of everything papal to reveal the inner workings of the Vatican and the personalities of those (including the present Pope) who help to run it.

'The book is a brilliant study of the Church's administration . . . a fascinating evaluation of the present papacy.' Peter Nicholas in *The Times*

CHRISTIANITY IN THE WEST 1400–1700

John Bossy

It was impatience with conventional histories of the Reformation which led Professor Bossy to write this book. His aim is to improve our understanding of what happened to Western Christianity at the time of the Reformation by concentrating on Christianity as a way of life, not just on the institution of the Church. He also renounces the use of the term 'Reformation' and its associated values, and, contrary to views now widely held, assumes that the population of the West consisted of Christians throughout the centuries in question, and that the social history of Europe and the history of Christianity were in this period substantially the same thing.

An OPUS book

THE CONCISE OXFORD DICTIONARY OF THE CHRISTIAN CHURCH

Edited by E. A. Livingstone

This is the abridged version of the second edition of *The Oxford Dictionary of the Christian Church*. It makes available for the general reader the vast majority of the entries in the parent volume. The range of the *Concise Dictionary* is considerable. It includes the major Christian feasts and denominations, historical accounts of the lives of the saints, résumés of Patristic writings, and histories of heretical sects. It also outlines the opinions of major theologians and moral philosophers, and explores many related subjects.

Oxford Paperback Reference